Points of Departure

Points of Departure

International Writers on Writing and Politics

Interviews by David Montenegro

with

Adrienne Rich

Bapsi Sidhwa

Carolyn Forché

Derek Walcott

Isabel Allende

Joseph Brodsky

Linda Ty-Casper

Seamus Heaney

Stanislaw Baranczak

Yehuda Amichai

with selections from their work

THE UNIVERSITY OF MICHIGAN PRESS

Ann Arbor

Copyright © by the University of Michigan 1991
All rights reserved
Published in the United States of America by
The University of Michigan Press
Manufactured in the United States of America

1994 1993 1992 1991 4 3 2 1

Library of Congress Cataloging-in-Publication Data

Montenegro, David, 1950–
    Points of departure : international writers on writing and
politics / interviews by David Montenegro : with Adrienne Rich . . .
[et al.] : with selections from their work.
        p.   cm.
    ISBN 0-472-09741-8 (cloth : alk. paper). — ISBN 0-472-06471-1
(pbk. : alk. paper)
    1. Authors—20th century—Interviews. 2. Politics and literature.
3. Literature—Censorship. I. Rich, Adrienne Cecile. II. Title.
PN452.M57 1991
809′.93358—dc20   91-32434
                                                              CIP

For my mother and father and for Mimi

Acknowledgments

I am grateful to many people for their help, above all my wife, writer M. E. Hirsh, who brought many of these issues home through her work, and whose humor, insight, and inspiration were crucial to the completion of this book.

Many thanks to David Bonanno at the *American Poetry Review,* Jane Uscilka at *Partisan Review,* and Carole Chanler for assisting the prior publication of several of the interviews; to Patricia King at the Schlesinger Library at Radcliffe; to Richard Lourie, Donald Hall, John C. Hirsh, and Prita Shalizi for thoughtful referrals; to Jamie Fenwick for his hospitality in New York; and to LeAnn Fields, my editor at the University of Michigan Press, for her careful shepherding of myriad elements.

All of the writers who took part in this series gave graciously and generously of their work and time to see it through. My deepest thanks to each of them. I am especially indebted to the encouragement of Stanislaw Baranczak and Adrienne Rich.

The kind spirits of Margaret Kelly Hirsh, Nora and Robert Rosenbaum, Ray and Caroline LeDuc, Margo Kelly, Stewart Wooster, Rosemary Blanchard, John McLean, Dore Gardner, Michael Siff, Garrett Rosenblatt, and Matthew Keamsdog sustained me throughout.

My thanks ever to my parents, Enrique and Sara Montenegro. My late grandfather, Ernesto Montenegro, a Chilean journalist and essayist, must also bear some responsibility for this work. Finally, salutations to my sister Rachael Montenegro, for a battle fought with great courage.

Grateful acknowledgment is given to the following periodicals for permission to reprint previously published interviews: *Partisan Review,* for "An Interview with Joseph Brodsky" (Fall 1987) and "An Interview with Derek Walcott" (Spring 1990); the *American Poetry Review* for "Yehuda Amichai: An Interview" (November/December 1987), "Stanislaw Baranczak: An Interview" (September/October 1986), "Carolyn Forché: An Interview" (November/December 1988), and "Adrienne Rich: An Interview" (January/February 1991); and the *Massachusetts Review,* for "Bapsi Sidhwa: An Interview" reprinted from the *Massachusetts Review* (Winter 1990), © 1991 The Massachusetts Review, Inc.

Grateful acknowledgment is made to the following authors and publishers for permission to reprint materials in this book:

Adrienne Rich. "North American Time" is reprinted from *Your Native Land, Your Life, Poems by Adrienne Rich,* by permission of the author and W. W. Norton & Company, Inc. Copyright © 1986 by Adrienne Rich. "Divisions of Labor" is reprinted from *Time's Power, Poems 1985–1988* by permission of the author and W. W. Norton & Company, Inc. Copyright © 1989 by Adrienne Rich.

Bapsi Sidhwa. Chapter 1 of *The Crow Eaters* by Bapsi Sidhwa, first published in Great Britain in 1980. Copyright © 1978 by Bapsi Sidhwa and Jonathan Cape Ltd. Reprinted by permission of the author and Peters, Fraser, & Dunlop.

Carolyn Forché. "The Colonel" and "Return" (pp. 75–79) are reprinted from *The Country Between Us.* Copyright © 1980 by Carolyn Forché and © 1981 by Carolyn Forché and Jonathan Cape Ltd. Reprinted by permission of the author, HarperCollins Publishers, and Jonathan Cape Ltd.

Derek Walcott. "North and South" is reprinted from *The Collected Poems, 1948–1984* and *The Fortunate Traveller.* "Midsummer XXIII" is reprinted from *The Collected Poems, 1948–1984* and *Midsummer.* Copyright © 1981, 1984, 1986 by Derek Walcott. Reprinted by permission of the author; Farrar, Straus, & Giroux, Inc.; and Faber and Faber Ltd.

Isabel Allende. Excerpt from *The House of the Spirits* by Isabel Allende, translated by Magda Bogin. Translation Copyright © 1985 by Alfred Knopf, Inc. Reprinted by permission of the publisher.

Joseph Brodsky. "Odysseus to Telemachus" and "Plato Elaborated" are reprinted from *A Part of Speech* by Joseph Brodsky. Translations by George L. Kline. Translation copyright © 1980 by Farrar, Straus, & Giroux, Inc. Published in Great Britain by Oxford University Press. Copyright © 1980 by Joseph Brodsky. Reprinted by permission of the author; Farrar, Straus, & Giroux; and Oxford University Press.

Linda Ty-Casper. Chapter 1 of *Awaiting Trespass* by Linda Ty-Casper. Copyright © by Linda Ty-Casper and Readers International, Inc., 1985. Reprinted by permission of the author and Readers International, Inc.

Seamus Heaney. "The Ministry of Fear" and "A Constable Calls" are reprinted from *Poems 1965–1975* and from *North.* Copyright © 1975, 1980, 1985 by Seamus Heaney. Reprinted by permission of Farrar, Straus, & Giroux, Inc., and Faber and Faber Ltd.

Stanislaw Baranczak. "Some Day, Years from Now," "A Second Nature," and "After Gloria Was Gone," are reprinted from *Selected Poems: The Weight of the Body.* Copyright © 1989 by Stanislaw Baranczak. Reprinted by permission of the author and TriQuarterly Books.

Contents

Introduction   1

Interviews with

  Adrienne Rich   5
    North American Time   21   •   Divisions of Labor   25

  Bapsi Sidhwa   26
    From *The Crow Eaters*   51

  Carolyn Forché   62
    The Colonel   75   •   Return   76

  Derek Walcott   80
    Midsummer XXIII   105   •   North and South   105

  Isabel Allende   110
    From *The House of the Spirits*   127

  Joseph Brodsky   133
    Odysseus to Telemachus   145   •   Plato Elaborated   146

  Linda Ty-Casper   149
    From *Awaiting Trespass*   171

  Seamus Heaney   180
    From Singing School
      The Ministry of Fear   195   •   A Constable Calls   196

  Stanislaw Baranczak   198
    Some Day, Years from Now   213   •   A Second Nature   213
    •   After Gloria Was Gone   214

  Yehuda Amichai   216
    The Diameter of the Bomb   230   •   *From* Seven Laments for the
    War-Dead   230   •   Inside the Apple   232

Epilogue   233

Introduction

On December 29, 1989, playwright Vaclav Havel—who, not many months earlier, had been imprisoned by the Communist government as a political dissenter—was elected president of Czechoslovakia. This seemingly meteoric rise of a writer from political imprisonment to an *official* position of political power was of course not a simple matter. It involved as much Havel's long activism and his incisive examination of the mechanics of power and politics in his essays and plays as it did the influence of Mikhail Gorbachev's policies of *glasnost* and *perestroika*.

That a country long ruled by a totalitarian regime had suddenly found its way to democracy and, moreover, that its citizens should elect a writer as their first representative certainly marked a dramatic shift in world events. However, as time had earlier shown in the Philippines and the USSR, such welcome change can be accompanied by unforeseen complexity and ambiguous aftershocks.

These interviews with ten international writers on the relationship of writing to politics took place from 1985 to 1989, years that saw the development of many conflicting undercurrents, leading to what has been called a new world order. I chose these writers in particular for their ability to treat certain difficult political issues in their work without sacrificing the richness and subtlety of their art. Further, each has in some way influenced the political climate in his or her country. The conversations were planned as a collection with the writers and were woven together around issues of censorship and political oppression, whether from the right or the left.

In November, 1990, I asked each writer to reflect on some aspect of the political upheavals that had taken place since our interview. The striking element in each was not a sense of relief, as might be expected with the fall of totalitarian regimes, but in fact the opposite—an increase in critical attention paid to the intricacies of language and power and to the interplay, often subtly complex, between new freedom of expression in some areas and a corresponding degree of oppression developing in other areas where attention is no less warranted. These writers seemed to be observing the spread of democracy and the end of the cold war with caution, pointing out that oppression, exclusion, and political violence take many forms.

As the 1980s came to an end and the 1990s began, a case in point happened close to home. Shortly after Havel was elected, he addressed the U.S. Congress, where elected officials applauded his steadfast courage and integrity in facing down Soviet oppression. Ironically, among his audience were many who recently had cast votes that eventually would lead to a requirement that artists selected for National Endowment for the Arts grants sign an oath restricting the content of their work. Democratically legislated censorship arrived on our doorstep.

If the political landscape has grown both more open and more ambiguous, the problems of the writer's engagement with meaning—ultimately political—remain the same. How do writers, immersed in the life of their countries, avoid the artistic dangers of assuming a public stance in their work? How do they keep the spontaneity of the imagination free of the manipulations of political intention? What is the responsibility of the writer and literature to other people's lives, to political violence, dictatorship, silence, censorship, to the wilderness of democracy?

Paradoxically, these conversations begin with the subject of silence and absence. In the first interview Adrienne Rich says, "... how little the conditions of our *actual* lives are reported or represented—what's left out as well as what is represented.... I think that there is a way in which that self-alerting process—'what is missing here? How am I using this?'—becomes a part of the creative process." This need to discover what is being left out and why it is left out, and to begin the work of inclusion, is expressed by every writer in this series. Essentially, it is a personal need to uncover the true contexts and the histories of words as they are being used and, consequently, of cultures and peoples who, for whatever reason, have been left or kept out of both the dominant cultural life and political life of a country.

For these writers to describe the world faithfully, then, requires an awareness of the history and politics of what is being said and of how it is being said. As Derek Walcott suggests here, not only words and issues such as *justice* or *socialism* but even more common, household words such as *wheat* or *sugar* are intimately related to the political structures within which they are spoken. Writers in their search for the right word cannot avoid a parallel struggle for precise observation of their languages' impact on people's lives, and of lives, past and present, on language.

And yet the sense of responsibility to speak out is tempered with caution, even skepticism. There is a wariness evident in all of these writers when it comes to engineering a particular artistic response and, consequently, a resistance to assuming the role of public spokesperson. Indeed, it is not the rigors of a political program but the lyric instinct and spontaneity of their art that guide these writers from image to provocative insight. Sheer wordplay, humor, delight in language and metaphor break boundaries of sound and meaning, of history and personal perception, of norms and the assumptions that lie behind them—sometimes in ways unforeseen by the writers themselves. A string of sounds drawn from what Seamus Heaney calls "the evolutionary chain of human ear-knowledge" sometimes leads back to where the social fabric is torn. And such forbidden play cannot be legislated. In fact, each writer seems to hold to only one cardinal rule: that it is the spontaneous and unforced in art that is the genuine, though meditation and intuition may go hand in hand as the poem or story evolves.

Still, for each of them, sometimes despite outright resistance to it, a sense of social responsibility is a constant point of departure and point of return. Yes, the poem will be written on its own terms, the metaphor will be chosen according to the needs of the imagination and the artistic moment, but these must be informed by a knowledge of the world and of people that is *not* metaphorical (as Adrienne Rich suggests here), a knowledge that is a vital part of the imagination itself.

In many ways it is disturbing that the question of the relationship of writing to politics should be asked at all. The implied separation or dissociation of the two perhaps indicates a fractured sense of the role of language in society and leads to an image of the writer as alienated, frivolous, or simply indifferent. To believe that somehow words can operate outside the realm of contention and responsibility is simply to misunderstand the nature of language, the social contract weaving the conflicting tensions of a society together on a daily basis. The question would perhaps more accurately be posed: What is the relationship between literature and *silence?* What makes a particular spoken or written work of art essentially silent when a living language inevitably leads to questions that need to be asked or reflections that are due to be made in order for a community to voice its deepest concerns through art?

If there is any common thread in these interviews, it is one of paradox. Perhaps most central to a discussion of the relationship of literature to politics is the one with which Stanislaw Baranczak closes his interview. He points to the essential relationship between the individual voice and society:

And the miraculous thing about poetry is that, by revealing your individuality, it binds you together with other people. By making you individual, it makes you social at the same time. The reverse paradox is that all the automatized ways of behavior in society make you feel isolated, as a matter of fact, because you can't have a true contact with other people. You are more and more enclosed within your shell, so to speak. You can't find any appropriate words to express your emotions, to understand other people's emotions, et cetera. And poetry, again by making you utterly individual, helps restore those possibilities of communication within you and helps to restore some common language—but in a much more profound sense than the language of everyday life—a common language that is at the same time spontaneous, true, and authentic.

To prepare for each interview I spent several months reading the writer's work within political and literary contexts. The conversations, which lasted about two hours, were tape-recorded, transcribed, and edited. For the most part, my editing consisted of deleting asides and repetitions and merging related sections.

I then sent the manuscript to the writer for corrections and clarifications. The revisions made were always for the sake of greater clarity. As mentioned, in late 1990 I asked as many of the writers as possible (several were out of the country) to reexamine some aspect of the material they had discussed. These comments are in most cases incorporated in the preface to the interview.

Any collection of this kind is of necessity limited. Time and geography prevented me from speaking with many writers whose work should be included in any discussion of the relationship between writing and politics. Further, the censorship that has long been a factor in some of the countries discussed in this book makes it all the more imperative that other writers be suggested here for the reader's further exploration. In the epilogue I have provided a brief list of other writers who have eloquently addressed the role of the writer in relation to politics.

Adrienne Rich

Adrienne Rich was born in Baltimore, Maryland, in 1929, to middle-class parents with Jewish and Protestant roots in the South. She graduated from Radcliffe College in 1951, when her first book was selected by W. H. Auden for the Yale Series of Younger Poets. She was married for seventeen years and has three sons. She has taught basic writing, poetry, and women's studies at a variety of universities. She has been politically active since the movements of the 1960s and in the early 1970s became increasingly indentified with the women's liberation movement and the movement for lesbian and gay liberation. She was co-editor of the lesbian-feminist cultural journal *Sinister Wisdom* in the early 1980s and is a founding editor of *Bridges: A Journal for Jewish Feminists and Our Friends,* which attempts to connect art, identity, and progressive activism. She lives in California.

She has published numerous books of poetry, including *A Change of World* (1951), *The Diamond Cutters* (1955), *Snapshots of a Daughter-in-Law* (1963), *Necessities of Life* (1966), *Leaflets* (1969), *The Will to Change* (1971), *Diving into the Wreck* (1973), *Poems Selected and New, 1950–1974* (1975), *The Dream of a Common Language* (1978), *A Wild Patience Has Taken Me This Far* (1981), *The Fact of a Doorframe: Poems Selected and New 1950–1984* (1984), *Your Native Land, Your Life* (1986), and *Time's Power* (1989). Her most recent collection is *An Atlas of the Difficult World* (1991). Her works of prose include *Of Woman Born: Motherhood as Experience and Institution* (1976; 10th anniversary ed., 1986), *On Lies, Secrets and Silence: Selected Prose 1966–1978* (1979), and *Blood, Bread and Poetry: Selected Prose 1979–1985* (1986).

Our interview took place in May, 1987, in Cambridge, Massachusetts. As this book went to press in late November, 1990, I asked if she might compare the growing censorship debate in the United States with the spread of democracy overseas. She wrote the following.

Since you and I spoke in 1987, the contours of the map have buckled and slid to a degree we couldn't then have imagined. And yet what we've seen is not the beginnings of a new world but the acceleration of the collapse of the old. Now we are supposed to be in the post–Cold War era, with the victory of democracy and the death of socialism. Yet as I write this, in

November 1990, the ground is being laid for literal war in the Middle East, to be fought by the children of the U.S. underclass, whose hope of education and job training lay in joining the "peacetime" military. Meanwhile we're shown the brutal underside of that false socialism in which Eastern Europe was stagnating, culturally and economically. But no word of the brutal underside of capitalism here, that has *always* required an underclass—slaves, disenfranchised African Americans, Irish, Chinese, immigrants fleeing starvation and tyranny in Europe—women always the unpaid and underpaid—to create the wealth of the promised land. The literature that speaks to this, or that insists there are other ways of existing on this earth, has been treated as axegrinding, as relevant only to "special interests," as artistically suspect.

When I read articles on censorship, the Helms amendment, the attempts to abrogate or draw limits on content for NEA [National Endowment for the Arts] grants, I think, yes, but this is only a more overt and visible kind of censorship. There's been a censorship of art practiced under capitalism which works through the means of distribution, rather than through book banning and the imprisonment of writers. It's made difficult, unless you are already aware and motivated, to find certain ideas, read certain kinds of books, be exposed to certain kinds of experience. Feminist critics have written exhaustively of this as it has pertained to women's writing. But it applies to all true expressions of minority experience, of working-class experience, of lesbian and gay experience. By "true" I don't mean monolithic, or that there's some "correct" way in which literature should represent us. But I do mean that our lives should and shall not be trivialized, caricatured, held cheap, or erased. A system that holds our lives expendable in other ways will not foster and abet an art that holds our lives to be precious and significant.

This is the work I see for us now: to insist in our art on the depth and complexity of our lives, to keep on creating the account of our lives, in poems and stories and scripts and essays and memoirs that are as rich and strange as we are ourselves. Never to bend toward or consent to be rewarded for trivializing ourselves, our people, or each other. (Copyright ©1990 by Adrienne Rich)

David Montenegro: Would you prefer to start with language or politics?
Adrienne Rich: We'll get to both, I'm sure; so start wherever you like.
DM: It seems language can be a means of containment—loaded as it is with tradition—or it can be a means of liberation, if used as a probe. How do you deal with the double edge of language? What are your means of *using* language, without being used *by* language?
Rich: Well, I feel one of the underlying themes of my poetry is that tension between

the possibilities in language for mere containment and the possibilities for expansion, for liberation. But there is also the fact that ultimately language alone cannot liberate us. As I said in "Cartographies of Silence," language cannot do everything. There really are times when, as a poet, I feel I would simply like to be able to create something like a monumental head, some kind of great unitary visual image that would possess its own force and power, and stop all this struggle with words and meanings.

I've written a great deal about that whole issue of dead language, the oppressor's language, the need to try to find a new language, a common language, if you will. It's the question of associations with words and of the history of words, and how they come down to us and how we go on with them. But I'm beginning to think and talk a lot more again about that which goes along with language and poetry—which is music, the vibration of a voice. I see that intonation, that vocal quality as something that *is* very personal, out of the self, and then combines with the many traditions, the many histories that we come out of, are exposed to.

Let me give you an example. I went into a bookstore when I was in New York—I had been for some weeks thinking about a way of starting to write poetry again—I had been writing it less over the past few months. I was starting to write again and feeling the necessity for some new kind of political voice, for myself, but also to keep the work going on and to keep it fresh. I saw an anthology of Italian poetry since World War Two, and I pulled it out. This book literally opened for me to some poems by Pier Pasolini, the great filmmaker. I hadn't know he was a poet at all. One of them was a long meditation on the ashes of Gramsci, the Italian revolutionary. And it's a very intimate voice, very personal. He's using terza rima, which is, of course, laden with the history of Italian poetry, Dante in particular. So he's drawing on that tradition, yet the poem has this curiously intimate, grieving, contemporary quality. And I felt as if I was drawn to pick up this book and open it in this way, to find an example of what I was searching for—an intonation, a quality of speech. It's deeply personal, and yet it *is* public.

DM: Since you mentioned Pasolini, poet and filmmaker, how is this quality of speech related to imagery? Are there ties between the sound of a voice and the use of an image?

Rich: I think visual images are one of the great sources for refreshment. And the most effective ones come back to something that's very personal and ordinary perhaps, just the glass of water you're looking at or what have you, not necessarily images that will be exotic or arresting.

DM: Not sensational.

Rich: No. And that was something those early postwar Italian films did so wonderfully—just took nitty-gritty visual facts of everyday life and played off them.

DM: In the notes to *The Fact of a Doorframe,* you mentioned something about your use of metaphor in your poem "The Diamond Cutters," that after thirty years you were unsure you had taken responsibility when you had used the metaphor of diamond cutting, that you had not taken into account, had not known at the time the actual circumstances of South African diamond miners' lives. Choosing a metaphor, then, has a political responsibility attached to it?

Rich: Yes, to be as aware as possible of the history and politics of the image or metaphor we're using. But another problem in that poem was that I was going so far afield to get that image. It was *not* something in my own experience; I had this imaginary diamond cutter and these imaginary diamond miners, and some knowledge, some sense of the fact that it was indeed a matter of travail.

DM: Travail of craft rather than . . .

Rich: Well, I was equating the travail of craft with a very different kind of labor—virtual enslavement, peonage.

DM: When you choose a metaphor now, do you examine it right away in those political terms, or do you live with it and see what emerges after a time before accepting or rejecting it? In other words, do you have a sensor or countersensor going while you're writing now?

Rich: Well, I think you have a sensor going if you're—how shall I put it?—in a position of dissent in this country. You need a consciousness alerted about what images you yourself are receiving from outside, what the media are representing, what mainstream art is representing. A lot of critical antennae develop as you become aware of the amount of disinformation that's being purveyed, how little the conditions of our *actual* lives are reported or represented—what's left out as well as what is represented. And I think these sensors inevitably also refer to what you yourself are creating. You can't live in a constant state of *checking* everything as it swims to the surface of consciousness. But I think that there is a way in which that self-alerting process—"what is missing here? How am I using this?"—becomes a part of the creative process. Then there's also the question of how what you write gets used, which I try to talk about in "North American Time."

DM: You say there that what we write is sometimes used against us and is out of our control.

Rich: Yes. There really isn't any way to control how it's used. And I think it's probably a waste of energy to try.

DM: It seems that, instead, your impulse is to try to enlarge your awareness of what's happening in the world, your sense of accountability.

Rich: It feels to me that I need to know more than I ever did in order to be a poet, that I need to be conscious of what is happening on this planet in ways that I never used to think about. And it's not that that takes the place of the work of the imagination, but that each of us has an imagination that has itself been created by a set of circumtances, some very nourishing, some very negative—the lacunae, the cartoon imagery.

DM: You mentioned earlier a quality of speech that's both personal and public. Do you see poetry as still being part of an oral tradition and as having some responsibility for warding off public amnesia?

Rich: Well, I feel as though poetry has never really ceased being an oral art. It just hasn't been treated as one by critics and in academe and very often by reviewers and *readers.* The idea of the *text* on the page has become such an obsession, and yet it seems to me that, as long as I've been a conscious, adult poet, there have been poetry movements that placed a great deal of importance on the reading aloud of poetry, the reciting of poetry. Most of the poets I knew when I was younger— even though they themselves might have thought of their work as very textual and confined to the page—*loved* to recite poetry, people knew reams of poetry by heart. Then later, in the 1960s, the public reading or recitation of poetry became a natural part of political movements—the black and antiwar movements, the women's movement, the lesbian and gay movements. And that still continues. Poetry as words spoken and heard in the community.

DM: In your essay "Toward a More Feminist Criticism"* you suggested you were uneasy about movements that rely too heavily on the word at the expense of action. Again, is this part of your mixed feelings about the operation of language?

Rich: I guess I was talking about how, specifically in the women's movement, writers have so often been seen and cited as spokespeople and as leaders. My feeling is that it is the *activists* who move the rest of us. You don't make a political movement simply out of words. I'm thinking about grassroots women's organizations, activists who have sat through hundreds of interviews with battered or raped women, helping to empower them, and who have a knowledge about these things which is not metaphorical. Of course there are many activist-writers, activist-publishers.

DM: The necessity of ending the general erasure of women's history and of repairing the damage done is a principal focus of your work. Is a transformation occurring as women reclaim their history? Are women now more empowered by having a broad historical base from which to move forward?

Rich: Some. I see it happening in women's studies programs in universities, in community colleges. Something happens for women who take those courses, who can avail themselves of them. There is even some revision of the curriculum generally,

---

*See *Blood, Bread, and Poetry,* p. 90.

even in some high schools. Of course, the ignorance is damaging both to women and to men. Ignorance of the history and experience of more than half the human species. And therefore the history of the entire species distorted.

But outside the sphere of the kind of education where you would expect to find a certain liberal stance toward feminism, the issue becomes *what* women have any education available to them *at all*. Thinking on a global level, how early do women leave school, if they've gone to school at all? The illiteracy rate among women overall is rapidly increasing. And so it's not just a question of, do we as women know our history, but do we know how to *read*, how to write? Do we know that there is such a thing as history, that we can be part of it, makers of it? I don't mean that a sense of history necessarily goes along only with literacy because obviously it doesn't. Women have an oral historical tradition in many cultures, but the disempowerment of women overall, I think, limits very much what those of us who are literate and educated can expect in the way of our history liberating us. It's important; I've argued for it passionately, but I also see the limits of what can be done in an educational system that in itself is so class bound, so racist, so restrictive.

DM: Would this include women's studies programs themselves? Do they create antagonism between black studies and women's studies?

Rich: Racism in the academy does, and sexism in the academy. Black studies programs have been and can be very sexist; women's studies programs have been and can be very racist. The antagonisms are not peculiar to those programs but are embedded in the whole structure of the society where we live. We don't shed racism or sexism because we're in a liberation movement unless we struggle hard to try to create bridges, to find out where our common base is, to become educated in each other's realities, to search for and document the mistakes of the past so we can stop making them. I'm thinking particularly of the history of the nineteenth-century white suffrage movement, the early North American feminist movement, its visions, and its racist stances, despite its roots in the abolitionist movement.

DM: How did the civil rights movement affect you, your awareness of the women's movement as it was developing, your work as a writer, the growth of your voice as a woman and a poet?

Rich: Well, you have to understand that I grew up in a social and familial world in which there was a great deal of splitting. I've written an essay called "Split at the Root" which actually speaks about my own family roots, Jewish and Gentile. But it was also a world split by segregation. Baltimore in the 1930s and 1940s was a deeply segregated city. There weren't back-of-the-bus rules, but black people did not shop in the same department stores as white people, there was the interracial eating taboo, and so on. A child grows up acutely aware of that kind of thing, even if it's never talked about, and of course there was a great deal of pressure not to talk about it. It was a given. And it was a given that, needless to say, white people were extremely tense about. But we learned not to ask questions about it or to discuss it. We did not go to school with black children. The black people I grew up knowing all worked for white people as domestic workers.

So that left a profound impact, in the sense that it was a situation which, I think from a very young age, I felt was so—*uncomfortable* is hardly the word— almost intolerable. There was so much that wasn't explained; there were codes of behavior that you couldn't question but that you couldn't figure out. They didn't seem to make any sense. And there was this general attitude that, because of being black, people somehow deserved and needed less in the world. But there was also a great deal of talk about how far black people had come. Things were said like: "Since the Civil War these people have come a long way," and so on. So that was all very confusing.

When the civil rights movement came along in the late 1950s, early 1960s, and I began to hear black voices describing and analyzing what were the concrete issues for black people—like segregation, like racism—it came to me as a great relief. It was like finding a language for something that I'd needed a language for all along. That was the first place where I heard a language to name oppression. And it was an enormous relief, even as it threw up a lot of questions for me as to where *I* stood with all this. Well, I felt I understood exactly why black people had to do what they were doing. It felt like a completely intuitive knowledge, because I was still politically very ignorant. And that movement, as it grew and became a movement around the country, and as it went through changes and the Black Power movement separated out of it and many white activists became involved in the antiwar movement and various groups against imperialism—groups like SDS— all of that continued to make a great deal of sense to me.

I think that all of that early splitting and fragmentation has made me hungry for connections to be made. Where connections are being made always feels to me like the point of intensest life. So, there was no way that all of that wasn't going to affect me as a poet because the point of intensest life is where I write poetry.

At the same time, I was thinking a lot about something that wasn't being talked about at the time very much. I was thinking about where sexuality belonged in all this. What *is* the connection between Vietnam and the lovers' bed? If this insane violence is being waged against a very small country by this large and powerful country in which I live, what does that have to do with sexuality and with what's going on between men and women, which I felt also as a struggle even then? I was married. I was trying to define myself in a number of ways. I couldn't fit into the . . . I couldn't find a model for the way I wanted to be, either in a relationship with a man or as a woman in the world. So when the women's movement began to crystallize from the Left and the civil rights movement, that was another and certainly one of the most powerful connections for me.

DM: Nineteen sixty-eight seems to have been a very important year for you. You wrote a lot of poetry and your essays began to be less literary, more political. Many things happened that year: the Tet offensive, the assasinations of Martin Luther King and Robert Kennedy, student strikes at Berkeley, at Columbia, in Belfast, Prague, Warsaw . . .

Rich: It was also the year of my father's death. He had been sick a long time, really not present. That loss, of an extremely adversarial relationship, had been happening for some time. I suppose, knowing that there was a real end gave me some sense of relief—as if then I could begin to put it all in order? But it took much longer than I thought it would.

DM: Are you still continuing a conversation with him, in a sense?

Rich: Yes.

DM: Has anything been resolved or has your relationship become more complex?

Rich: I see him more and more as a person. You know, you see your parents first of all as these great looming figures who have no past, no context. They're just *there* and over and against you. Or they're *not* there, which is another kind of looming presence—looming absence. But I've been thinking about my father more and more in the context of the social and political world that he grew up in, about the things that brought him to where he was when I knew him, especially the meaning of his Jewishness. He had been, for me, such an ambiguous figure, so tremendously rewarding, on the one hand, and also such an obstacle. Now, it's much more that there was this person who had his own history and his own family background and parents who had a certain life themselves and who came from certain kinds of families, that they were Jews in the South in a particular period. I think about him in that field much more than I ever used to be able to.

DM: And your mother—she was a pianist and composer?

Rich: Well, she still is a pianist at eighty-eight. She has her piano—which she's had from the age of fifteen—in her apartment, and she still plays extremely well.

DM: How do you feel about her not having been able to pursue music as a career, perhaps for family reasons? Is that an issue?

Rich: Oh, I think it was a tremendous issue. And very complex. I think, given her context, that she made a choice not to become a professional woman pianist in that musical world that involved the depreciation of women, sexual harassment, which she experienced.

She was fascinated by my father. He had a very powerful personality. I think that she felt that her life would always be interesting with him and also that she had no models for living in the world on her own. I think she would have had to come out of a different background and had a different character and personality to be able to make that decision. Her family were southern people who'd had land but, after the Civil War, little money. My grandmother went to a convent school, which was the best education she could get at that time. My grandfather was a tobacco salesman. I doubt that he'd been to college. There was a lot of struggle for education in that family, but there was not a tradition of women being independent or creative in any public way. Although my grandmother, I think, would have been a writer if she'd herself come out of another time and place. She did write. She loved books. She desperately wanted education, and she wanted her children to have education.

But I think that, for me, there was always this question: Is that what happens? You pursue an art, win prizes and scholarships, and then, when you marry, you stop doing it except in the privacy of your living room? That was what I saw, growing up.

DM: My mother is a pianist also. She must have gone through a similar conflict between family and music.

Rich: She gave it up?

DM: As a performer, for the most part, yes. She had five children, though she still plays piano with a chamber music trio. And she has taught and enjoyed teaching for many years. Still, it must have been a difficult choice to make.

Rich: Choice is a very loaded word. Choice depends a lot on what you know is possible. There *do* have to be choices indicated. Some people actually seem to invent their choices, but I think that more often we learn about a possibility and think: *I* could do that, or, I don't want to do that, I don't want to be like that.

DM: Do you think there has been a regression during the past ten years from the progress made by the women's movement? Has its momentum slowed, and, if so, will the movement pick up its pace again to what it was in the 1970s? Is there now a sense of exhaustion?

Rich: Well, it very much depends on how you look at the contours of the landscape. An astonishing number of feminist institutions were founded in the 1970s. And a lot of movement was going on within existing institutions like universities. But the kind of political retrenchment that began, I think, before Reagan was elected, and in fact led up to his election, inevitably was accompanied by the reassertion of old conservative values about women, and about sexuality. And those attitudes have come down hard.

I think that a couple of things have happened. One is that the economy worsened so much and so fast. And where there used to be bits of funding about here and there—CETA [Comprehensive Employment and Training Act] grants, let's

say, which could be used to pay someone for a part-time job in a feminist institution—that money disappears. Suddenly there are no grants, or everybody's competing for them because there are no other sources. Women are jobless or working
several poorly paid jobs to survive. So there's a scarcity of resources that were still
around at the end of the 1960s, just in view of the fact that the economy was still
grinding on. And everything that we do at this point, it seems to me, is done
with a great deal more effort because those resources are depleted, those *human*
energies are spread thinner. People have to put bread on the table, and they're
trying to do political work as well.

Then there's the fact that the conservatives have been making a lot of work
for us with their legislative proposals and their political campaigns. We have found
ourselves fighting back at a level that we were not having to fight on in the 1970s.
We've found ourselves thrown back on old ground again, not able to push forward
as much as one would have hoped.

At the same time, though this is all absorbing a tremendous amount of energy,
I think the energy is there. Some people are tired and burnt-out, but I see new
women—and men—coming along all the time. And that is very refreshing and
very inspiring. It's not as though the same people who were there in the early
1970s still have to be doing it all now. The cast of characters has grown; some
have left, some have taken time out and returned, others have come in, many with
new understandings, with new contributions.

One of the things that has been growing in the women's movement in this
country—and, again, in a society like this it can't, it doesn't, happen easily, and
it doesn't happen overnight—is the consciousness that we aren't a homogeneous
movement, that we are a multiethnic movement, that women's experiences across
the board are different, even though we share common female experiences. There's
been tremendous enrichment through those understandings and through the visi-
bility, the leadership, of women of color and the work of Jewish feminists; that
has certainly been part of the last few years.

In fall 1986 the *New York Times* published yet another article about the young
white woman of thirty-eight who is an attorney and feels the biological clock is
ticking. And the last paragraph began: "At a time when the women's movement
is virtually invisible . . . " I brought that article to my class in feminist theory. I
also brought in an armful of publications that had been lying around my house,
from all over the world, from the global women's movement. And I said: "All
right: here's this pile of papers, journals, newsletters, pamphlets. It's concrete, it's
here, it's visible. And here you have a statement that the women's movement is
virtually invisible. Now *to whom* is it invisible? And why? And who is saying that
it is invisible? And who benefits if it is?"

An enormous amount is happening globally—different kinds of struggle in different countries, in different societies. When you look at South Africa, there's enormous leadership by women. Black women in South Africa are maintaining and creating a structure. In that violence-ridden society, in the midst of revolution, they are creating childcare centers and soup kitchens, planting gardens, keeping things going on that human level. That's not just women doing the service work of the world; those women are also leaders of their communities. We could talk about feminism in the Philippines, in India, in Latin America, in the Caribbean, not a monolithic global movement but many movements, all over the world, contending within and against many different cultures. The United States movement is only a small part of the picture.

DM: As with language in general, your relationship to abstractions, it seems, is a mixed one. What are the dangers of abstractions, whether in poetry—where the risks of their use are fairly clear—or in prose? For example, the "feminization" of poverty, which, in a way, does not reflect at all the realities of a single woman with five children living in an apartment she can't afford where there is lead paint on the ceiling.

Rich: Well, these phrases become a kind of shorthand, a kind of code: "You know what I mean, and I know what you mean when we say this." And we may ourselves lose the truth behind it, the concreteness behind it, besides not being able to communicate that to someone else. All movements have a tendency to in-group language, and that language can become abstract, a language of stereotype. And yet, it's a powerful thing to talk about your concrete experience in its unique details and then begin to abstract from it. That was really what happened in those early consciousness-raising groups.

DM: To generalize and connect?

Rich: Yes. There has to be abstraction, but we have to keep coming back to the concrete again.

DM: Looking at the evolution of your work, do you see a relationship between the poetry and the prose, and, if so, what do you feel is the connection?

Rich: Well, I first started writing prose about poetry. The first prose I wrote for publication were some book reviews for *Poetry.* I reviewed *The Collected Poetry of D. H. Lawrence,* some anthologies. That was way back—in the early 1960s, I think. And then I was asked by the Harvard University Press to write the foreword to an edition of Anne Bradstreet. But I didn't think of myself as an essayist, and I didn't pursue writing prose on my own, except in my journals. I guess that it was finally involvement in politics that got me writing prose more, as a part of my life, as a regular part of my writing. And very often it was because somebody asked me to speak or asked for an essay.

So, I feel as if, in some ways, the prose has always been initiated from an exterior point, but it wasn't an exterior point that was irrelevant to what was happening in me, in my life, or even in my poetry. I was writing poems out of a lot of the same experiences that I discussed in the essay "When We Dead Awaken," and I have a poem with the same title. Certainly a lot of my other essays have points of intersection with poems, probably none so much as "Split at the Root" with "Sources"—which I was writing at about the same time. I was having a lot of difficulty with the poem, and then I wrote the essay, and came back to the poem feeling very freed because I'd worked out a great deal in the essay, and then didn't have to spell it out in the poem at all.

DM: In the poem it was concentrated?

Rich: Yes.

DM: And, in a sense, resolved?

Rich: If such things ever are.

DM: In "Sources" you use prose also.

Rich: Well, I've used blocks of prose in poems for some time, actually.

DM: Since the late 1960s?

Rich: Yes.

DM: In one poem written at that time, "The Burning of Paper Instead of Children," you use prose, including a passage in so-called poor grammar, black English. Was this written during your years as a teacher at City College in New York?

Rich: Yes.

DM: At the end of that poem you say: "A language is a map of our failures."

Rich: Well, that was a very specific reference. I was teaching writing in the SEEK program at City College then,* and there was, of course, as in all schools, this terrible thing that hung over you—the threat of failure. I mean, that the *student* would fail. Those students were *expected* to fail, they were *intended* to fail, and the SEEK program was trying to show that, no, they don't have to fail. And we teachers used to talk a lot about who fails—the teacher or the student—when you have a classroom situation that is rigged entirely against the student, or in which the teacher is too ignorant to teach. Not ignorant of grammar but ignorant of the students, ignorant of their cultures. So I was thinking very much about *our* failures, the map of *our* failures—we who consider ourselves so possessed of language, so articulate.

DM: The privilege . . .

Rich: To speak so people will listen to you.

DM: In your essay "When We Dead Awaken," published in 1971, you looked back over the span of your work and picked out "Aunt Jennifer's Tigers," "Orion,"

---

*See her essay "Teaching Language in Open Admissions" in *On Lies, Secrets, and Silence.*

and "Planetarium" to show turning points in your poetry. That was sixteen years ago. What poems would you now add to that list, as landmarks of your development?
Rich: Well, after "Planetarium": "The Burning of Paper Instead of Children," "I Dream I'm the Death of Orpheus," "When We Dead Awaken," "The Phenomenology of Anger," "Diving into the Wreck," "Twenty-One Love Poems," "Natural Resources," "A Woman Dead in Her Forties," and "For Ethel Rosenberg."

"For Ethel Rosenberg" was a very important poem for me to write. It was like touching the tip of an iceberg. I'm still struggling with a lot of that stuff. When I wrote the poem, I wrote it as best I could, but there's so much more.

Other poems would be: "Frame," "Grandmothers," "In the Wake of Home," "North American Time," "Sources," "Yom Kippur, 1984." I guess I'm thinking about poems that were the result of very long struggles to understand what I was writing, why I needed to be writing this at all, and to make it happen—poems that reflect to me some kind of watershed, perhaps.

DM: In the span of your work, one thing that's striking is that, at a certain point, you seem to have had to destroy language, or maybe only structure, or maybe only logic in poems—for example, "Shooting Script," where you do not keep to a logical progression, as you did earlier in poems like "Orion" or "The Trees," where the metaphor is developed in a very clear and traditional way. It seems that, in the late 1960s, you broke the language down, you *let* it break down. And then you dove into the wreck—to use your title—and came out the other side with *The Dream of a Common Language.* In this book, it seems, the language is fulfilled. It's wearing its own skin, in a sense. Do you feel that you had to go through that period of destruction of traditional order to go on with your work?

Rich: Well, I certainly had to find an equivalent for the kinds of fragmentation I was feeling, and confusion. One thing that was very helpful to me was working on the translations from the Urdu poet Mirzah Ghalib, which led me to write original *ghazals.* There, I found a structure that allowed for a highly associative field of images. And once I saw how that worked, I felt instinctively, this is exactly what I need, there is no traditional Western order that I have found that will contain all these materials.

And another thing was that, in the 1960s, I was going to the movies more than I ever have in my life and seeing a vast number of filmic images. I was very much struck by Godard's use of language and image in films. I think I've probably overreferred to him in some of the poems of that era. But that was very helpful to me too. It suggested a way of making images work. So, yes, I feel like that period was essential.

DM: It released certain energies that otherwise would not have been able to express themselves?

Rich: Well, the absolute content of my life. And my times, in so far as I knew them.

DM: One other question about form. In your early poems, you use a very strict meter—for example, in "Storm Warnings." Here you have the storm contained within a very tight capsule. What *new* forms—whether it has to do with freeing a personal voice or freeing a woman's tone of voice—are necessary? Does traditional metric—iambic pentameter or whatever—imply a frame of mind? Does it limit content?

Rich: Of course, there's been a lot of argument about that, back and forth, in American poetry for the last many decades since the beginning of the twentieth century, and I was, to a certain extent, involved in that kind of debate in the 1950s, when there was considered to be a tremendous divergence between the so-called Beats and the academics. I never really felt I was part of either group. I had started to write in open forms in the 1950s, and I felt I would never go back to writing the kind of formal poems that were in *The Diamond Cutters* or in *A Change of World*. Experience itself had become too much for that.

At the same time, I did not want to "smash the iamb." It seemed to me that iambic pentameter was still a useful line, a line that could also be very elastic, as poets like Wyatt and Hopkins had long before shown. And it has a kind of organic relation to the way Anglo-American is accented, Anglo-American speech patterns. And so I never wanted to get rid of it.

So, at the time I started writing, that was already set up as a problem. If you were going to be writing a truly new poetry, could you use the old forms? It's a question that is being asked now in a feminist context—for instance, in the work of the feminist language poets, a group primarily located on the West Coast. Susan Howe (who wrote a quite provocative book on Emily Dickinson), Kathleen Fraser, Frances Jaffer, and Rachel DuPlessis have a journal called *How(ever),** which publishes what has always been labeled experimental poetry, in the sense of under-cutting traditional syntax, emphasizing typography as part of the statement of the poem, using more open field arrangements on the page.

I have a real question about it though because it feels to me like experimental poetry from the early 1920s, or of Black Mountain. It does not feel particularly experimental now. The fact that women are doing it is interesting, but women were doing that kind of thing in the 1920s also—Mina Loy, for example; Gertrude Stein obviously. I guess what I'm searching for always is a way of staying linked to the past, pulling out of it whatever you can use, and continuing to move on. And I'm not sure that a new textual form creates—it certainly *doesn't* create—a

---

**How(ever)* is not being published at this time.

new consciousness. It can equally well be said that a new consciousness, a radically divergent one, doesn't necessarily create a new form either. I hate that form/content bifurcation, but sometimes it has to be used, for an attitude, a stance, a positioning of the poet.

I'm trying to think of some examples of the kind of thing I'm talking about. There's a poem by Derek Walcott in his sequence called *Midsummer* [XXIII] which is, in a sense, an expanded sonnet sequence—sprung sonnets, or whatever. He's witnessing a confrontation between skinheads and blacks in London. He himself is located in Britain working in the English theater, a token West Indian in a racist society. The poem moves very rapidly; it's got a strong iambic pentameter base, as they all do, and images fold and collapse into each other very fast. And it ends with this incredible reference to "an empire / that began with Caedmon's raceless dew, and is ending / in the alleys of Brixton, burning like Turner's ships."

It gives me a great rush, and I think I know why. It's because he is pulling on this contemporary, immediate, and historically powerful image of the riots in Brixton, as a West Indian, with everything that lies behind that—the British colonization of his own country, his own internal colonization. And here is the mother country, and now not only he, but that history, is coming back "home." Then he draws on Caedmon and Shakespeare and Turner. And underlying the whole is the pulling together of a consciousness split by colonization and diaspora, through an integrative kind of anger. And it seems to me that that's genuinely *new*. Nobody had done just that, in poetry, until the West Indians did it. It's a fusion of old form and old consciousness with new form and new consciousness that is explosive.

DM: Even visually—by bringing in Turner's paintings.

Rich: Yes. It's the poem that begins with an extraordinary visual image of trees moving in the wind, a tremendous sense of unrest and the storm in the trees. It's a wonderful poem.

DM: And it doesn't matter whether it's in iambic pentameter or not?

Rich: It *does* matter, especially when he refers to Shakespeare's sonnets.

DM: Poetry is a relationship to language, and language, for a poet, is often an almost physical, sensuous thing. If now women's experience, including lesbianism, is finding a voice, doesn't this or shouldn't this change the sound or feel of language? "Twenty-One Love Poems," for example, expresses a different sensibility and in a changed language.

Rich: Well, a lot of those poems are about looking at sexual passion and, instead of saying: "yes, love is like this," it's saying "no, love is not like this." This is something different, a female and lesbian sensuality and sensibility that has not been in poetry before. One of the most sensual and sensuous women poets I can think of is Audre Lorde. She *thinks* in images that are most certainly lesbian. But also images from Afro-Caribbean culture and from African mythology and experience. And that's a very powerful combination. Because that also has not been available in most poetry in English.

DM: Just a few more questions. Costs—in a word. So much of your work has been a struggle to speak honestly and openly, whether about poetry itself or about social issues, about racism, about lesbianism. What are the costs of doing so, as a poet, as a person?

Rich: What would be the cost of *not* doing it? I feel as though it's for my survival, first and foremost. This is how I cope; this is how I survive. I have learned from my peers that this way of creating can be a way of surviving. I didn't invent that.

DM: You do head for the breaks in the fabric. There's an instinct in your poetry for that spot where the seam's coming apart. Your language goes where the danger is. Do you know why?

Rich: For a very long time, poems were a way of talking about what I couldn't talk about any other way. And why is it that you're not able to talk about certain things? It's because they are the points of danger; you feel that in the social fabric, you feel you are forbidden to raise this question, or—if you're a child—to ask this question. That is the threatening place, and of course it becomes a place of great fascination too. I was equipped from a very young age to use language in this way because of how I was brought up, and by whom, and the fact that poetry was available to me as a choice, when it might not have been for another seven or ten years if I'd been another child.

If I had become my mother's student—and she did teach me piano from a very young age—if I had really become her student, become a musician, I would have been, I suppose, fulfilling my creative and expressive needs. But it wouldn't have been through language, and language is this medium that we hand back and forth between us in all human relationships all the time; it doesn't really have a privileged place. It's this coinage in which we keep trying to get ahold of each other or make ourselves clear. So, the fact that poetry was available to me for that is very important. I think the fact that it was poetry rather than, say, fiction or some other kind of prose was important because I learned while very young that you could be fairly encoded in poems and get away with it. Then I began to want to do away with the encoding or to break the given codes and maybe find another code. But it was a place of a certain degree of control in which to explore things before acting, perhaps, in which to start testing the waters.

DM: Then your certainty in language came to be matched by an uncertainty in vision? You had to keep testing, back and forth?

Rich: Oh, tremendous uncertainty, yes.

DM: Is there some feeling of dissatisfaction when you've finished a poem, particularly a poem where you have resolved or clarified certain issues or made some connections? Do you have the sense that you have to push forward, to move the next step, as if the most recent poem were not enough? Do you ever feel you have actually falsified the experience?

Rich: Experience is always larger than language. And there's always the next poem, yes. Not necessarily because I feel I've falsified something, but because I wrote it as I knew it then, and I'm going to know it differently in six months. Or I'm going to know something else. Or I'm going to *need* to know something else, and the only way I can get to it is by writing that poem.

DM: By choice you would write a poem then, if you were dealing with certain unnameable sensations or experiences? It would be poetry rather than prose that you would go to?

Rich: Increasingly, I feel as if right now I don't want to write any prose, except necessary workmanlike statements. I'll write an ad hoc political manifesto or statement, but, for the kind of exploration we've been talking about, I need to be working in poetry more. I feel there are a lot of places that I still need to go— I'm just getting the outlines of certain things.

North American Time

I
When my dreams showed signs
of becoming
politically correct
no unruly images
escaping beyond borders
when walking in the street I found my
themes cut out for me
knew what I would not report
for fear of enemies' usage
then I began to wonder

II
Everything we write
will be used against us
or against those we love.
These are the terms,
take them or leave them.
Poetry never stood a chance

of standing outside history.
One line typed twenty years ago
can be blazed on a wall in spraypaint
to glorify art as detachment
or torture of those we
did not love but also
did not want to kill

We move   but our words stand
become responsible
for more than we intended

and this is verbal privilege

III
Try sitting at a typewriter
one calm summer evening
at a table by a window
in the country, try pretending
your time does not exist
that you are simply you
that the imagination simply strays
like a great moth, unintentional
try telling yourself
you are not accountable
to the life of your tribe
the breath of your planet

IV
It doesn't matter what you think.
Words are found responsible
all you can do is choose them
or choose
to remain silent.   Or, you never had a choice,
which is why the words that do stand
are responsible

and this is verbal privilege

V
Suppose you want to write
of a woman braiding

another woman's hair—
straight down, or with beads and shells
in three-strand plaits or corn-rows—
you had better know the thickness
the length   the pattern
why she decides to braid her hair
how it is done to her
what country it happens in
what else happens in that country

You have to know these things

VI
Poet, sister: words—
whether we like it or not—
stand in a time of their own.
No use protesting   *I wrote that*
before Kollontai was exiled
Rosa Luxembourg, Malcolm,
Anna Mae Aquash, murdered,
before Treblinka, Birkenau,
Hiroshima, before Sharpeville,
Biafra, Bangla Desh, Boston,
Atlanta, Soweto, Beirut, Assam
—those faces, names of places
sheared from the almanac
of North American time

VII
I am thinking this in a country
where words are stolen out of mouths
as bread is stolen out of mouths
where poets don't go to jail
for being poets, but for being
dark-skinned, female, poor.
I am writing this in a time
when anything we write
can be used against those we love
where the context is never given
though we try to explain, over and over

For the sake of poetry at least
I need to know these things

VIII

Sometimes, gliding at night
in a plane over New York City
I have felt like some messenger
called to enter, called to engage
this field of light and darkness.
A grandiose idea, born of flying.
But underneath the grandiose idea
is the thought that what I must engage
after the plane has raged onto the tarmac
after climbing my old stairs, sitting down
at my old window
is meant to break my heart and reduce me to silence.

IX

In North America time stumbles on
without moving, only releasing
a certain North American pain.
Julia de Burgos wrote:
That my grandfather was a slave
is my grief; had he been a master
that would have been my shame.
A poet's words, hung over a door
in North America, in the year
nineteen-eighty-three.
The almost-full moon rises
timelessly speaking of change
out of the Bronx, the Harlem River
the drowned towns of the Quabbin
the pilfered burial mounds
the toxic swamps, the testing-grounds

and I start to speak again.

1983

Divisions of Labor

The revolutions wheel, compromise, utter their statements:
a new magazine appears, mastheaded with old names,
an old magazine polishes up its act
with deconstructions of the prose of Malcolm X
The women in the back rows of politics
are still licking thread to slip in the needle's
eye, trading bones for plastic, splitting pods
for necklaces to sell to the cruise-ships
producing immaculate First Communion dresses
with flatiron and irresolute hot water
still fitting the microscopic golden wires
into the silicon chips
still teaching, watching the children
quenched in the crossfire alleys, the flashflood gullies
the kerosene flashfires
—the women whose labor remakes the world
each and every morning
                                I have seen a woman sitting
between the stove and the stars
her fingers singed from snuffing out the candles
of pure theory Finger and thumb: both scorched:
I have felt that sacred wax blister my hand

1988

Bapsi Sidhwa

Bapsi Sidhwa belongs to the tiny Zoroastrian (Parsi) community of Pakistan. She was born in Karachi in 1939 and was brought up and educated in Lahore. Married, with three children, she now divides her time between Pakistan and the United States, where she has taught at Columbia University and the University of Houston. She is an active social worker among Asian women and in 1975 represented Pakistan at the Asian Women's Congress.

Sidhwa has published short stories and three novels, *The Bride* (1983), *The Crow Eaters* (1982), and *Ice-Candy-Man* (1988). She was a Bunting Fellow at Radcliffe/Harvard in 1986–87, and was awarded a National Endowment for the Arts grant in 1987. She received the Pakistan Academy's National Award in 1985 and received the Sitara-I-Imtiaz, a national honor, in March, 1991, in Pakistan.

This interview originally took place in March, 1988, in Cambridge, Massachusetts. Because of the Salman Rushdie affair and radical changes that occurred in Pakistan in the interim, and because Sidhwa again visited Boston, a second interview followed in March, 1989. The later questions appear first in the interview.

At the time of our first conversation General Zia-ul-Haq had ruled Pakistan for over ten years—since a bloodless coup and the imposition of martial law in 1977, followed by his government's execution of Prime Minister Zulfikar Ali Bhutto.

Before the second interview, one year later, General Zia had died suddenly in a plane crash, democratic elections had been held, and Benazir Bhutto had been ushered into power, the first woman head of state in a Muslim country. In February the Ayatollah Khomeini had pronounced a death sentence on Pakistani writer Salman Rushdie for alleged blasphemy against Islam in his novel *The Satanic Verses*. Rushdie went into hiding in Great Britain.

In late 1990 Sidhwa observed the collapse of Bhutto's government from her home in Lahore and commented on the situation there.

Benazir Bhutto's government in Pakistan was dismissed on October 6, 1990, on charges of corruption, nepotism, and incompetence by President Ghulam Ishaq Khan, in what Bhutto termed "A Constitutional Coup." The controversial eighth amendment to the constitution, introduced by the late General Zia's government, allows for this.

It has been Pakistan's misfortune to be ruled by a succession of corrupt individuals and governments—military or otherwise—but the escalation in the scale of corruption during Bhutto's regime has been shocking. Perhaps more was expected of her. Perhaps the press, free under democracy, reported the corruption that military regimes were able to conceal through censorship. Many Pakistanis feel that the clamor for accountability is directed solely against Bhutto's family and her supporters in the People's party, while some members of the opposition, reputed to have amassed vast fortunes, are let off scot-free.

As a woman and a writer, I am all too aware of the vengeful force of the chauvinism directed against successful Pakistani women. It certainly has played its part in undermining Benazir Bhutto's capacity to govern, although it has not been the major reason for the failure of her government.

Bhutto has disillusioned many Pakistanis, particularly the women. They feel she had it within her capacity to take a stand on the unfair laws oppressing them when she was newly elected—after all, she won on a huge mandate from the women—but, busy with other priorities, she did not appear even to consider women's issues. By the time she got around to mentioning the laws victimizing women, just before she was dismissed, her popularity was at its lowest, and it was too late. On the whole Bhutto's tenure is seen as incompetent and weak. Her government has not been able to control the contending forces in the country—specially in Sind—where political murder, kidnapping, extortion, and crime have terrorized the cities and villages.

The elections of October 24, in which the combined nine-party opposition alliance won hands down, reflect this disillusion. How long the tenuous alliance will last is another matter.

But given Bhutto's formidable destiny—which has swung her from a life of privilege to the humiliations of imprisonment and exile, and then again to the giddy heights of power as Pakistan's prime minister—one suspects, and hopes, her role in Pakistani politics will continue. She has been reelected from her constituency and should prove to be a power in the opposition.

March 24, 1989

David Montenegro: Could we begin by talking about how the sudden death of Zia and the subsequent election of Benazir Bhutto will affect the course of political life in Pakistan?

Bapsi Sidhwa: Well, when Zia suddenly dismissed the then existing parliament (elected on a nonparty basis), he promised to hold elections on the nineteenth of November. This date was supposed to coincide with Benazir Bhutto's delivery of her child and would put her out of circulation at a crucial time in her campaign. She surprised everyone by producing her baby a full month earlier, in October. The real date she was due was one of the better kept secrets in Pakistani politics. Only Benazir and the doctors knew the real date. I think this is fascinating—unprecedented. Here is a young woman standing for elections, and never before in the world of democratic politics has something like this been featured—that is, events being influenced by when a baby is due. Women entering politics adds a new dimension certainly.

Of course, very few people think Benazir Bhutto would have been elected had not Zia died when he did. He would certainly have created some excuse to outlaw the People's party or by some means seen to it that she would not be elected.

The elections went off very smoothly. We had hundreds of people from the foreign press waiting in Pakistan; everybody was expecting a bloodbath. But fortunately none materialized. I think Benazir knew her limits. Suddenly she really had this opportunity of being elected, so she and her party played it very cool. They didn't want to give anyone an excuse to rush in at this point and enforce martial law again and in any way disturb the election process.

DM: How do you see her presence as prime minister affecting women's rights in Pakistan and the Muslim world in general?

Sidhwa: Well, the opposition certainly made a lot of noise that they didn't want a woman head of state, but the majority in the country wanted her. The elections were fair and yet not totally fair, because we had the system of ID [identification] cards. It was declared that only those who had ID cards could vote, and not everybody had an ID card. Now the chief minister at that time—Punjab's chief minister and her main opponent—was in a position to issue ID cards, and he did apparently do so only to his party followers, by the thousands. And this was Benazir Bhutto's party's complaint—that they were not getting the ID cards to vote with. I think that has influenced the figures that came out in the Punjab during the elections because the chief minister *did* win there. And one feels that if the elections had been on just the adult franchise basis, Benazir would have had a much bigger triumph.

As for women's rights, of course there was jubilation among the women. Well, not only among the women—who probably had the most to gain by it— but also among the vast majority of poor people. They were jubilant because her father had championed their cause. Benazir Bhutto got elected mainly on account of her father's memory. Otherwise, she had no real political standing. She did develop a bit of support on her own, but the basis was her father's.

Now, when she was appointed prime minister after the election, the opposition made a few noises, but one knew they wouldn't prevail. The very strange thing was that, when they had to give her a vote of confidence in the national assembly, a lady from the opposition cast a vote for her, saying: I just want to show my support for the idea of a woman head of state in Pakistan. After casting her vote she crossed over to the opposition seats.

Many women hoped that she would now be in a position to repeal the Hudood Ordinance and the Sharia laws. These Islamic laws are interpreted harshly where they concern women. The women of Pakistan, because of their strong opposition to these laws, have developed a power base over the last few years. Pakistanis have become accustomed to seeing them out on the streets protesting. In fact, people have had the most hope for change from women because they have been the most vocal on several issues. I think part of Benazir Bhutto's success in the elections is based on this phenomenon of women in Pakistan suddenly coming to the forefront and fighting the battles. The protesting women assumed leadership roles, and their acceptance by people created the climate of acceptance for Bhutto. Otherwise, it might have been too sudden for a country that was being dragged toward fundamentalism by a handful of people to accept a woman head of state.

While I was in Pakistan, there were rumors of a sort of maneuvering going on, that we will accede these points, let's say, in one of the provinces somewhere, and the bargaining chip we want is that we should be able to do away—I'm talking for the P.P.P. [Pakistan People's Party], Benazir Bhutto's party—with the Sharia laws. It would take time, but she was on the path. Everybody was feeling encouraged.

But, as things stand today, the timing of Rushdie's *Satanic Verses* couldn't have been worse for Pakistan. Suddenly the fundamentalists are able to say: Look what the West is doing to us. Because of this book the West is making very angry noises at the Islamic world. We have to fight this demon that is attacking our faith. And, of course, such people can manipulate religious sentiments. At this point I think Benazir *dare not* bring the Sharia laws issue forward. Her hands have been tied for this issue. It would shake her government if she did. The fundamentalists were losing support, but they are now organized again around the fury over Rushdie's book.

DM: Would you describe the role of the book in Islam?

Sidhwa: In Islam the word *book* means more than it means in the West. Perhaps all over the East it means more. For example, the Muslims call the Jews and the

Christians "those of the book." The printed word in Third World countries is still rather dear. No one puts their feet on a book; a book is seldom destroyed. And all this gives the printed word and a book more power than it has in the West. In the West one is so used to reading profanity in books, but the same thing in an Islamic country or a Third World country has a different connotation. Anything written down there is so much more powerful. After all, the faith of the Muslims is based on the Book, on the Koran, which is God's word.

DM: Do you think Ayatollah Khomeini, in making an issue of Rushdie's book, partly hoped to destabilize Bhutto's government?

Sidhwa: No, I believe the situation was quite different. I heard that the moderates in Iran did not want the ayatollah even to know about this furor over Rushdie's work. But after the deaths in Pakistan and India the news could *not* be kept from him. It was on TV. When he asked what was happening, they had to tell him. Then inevitably, you know, somebody asked him: What is the punishment for this? So he pronounced the death sentence. And, I think, if it hadn't gone to this extreme, if the ayatollah had not gotten into the picture, things would have been different. It's a pity because in Iran the moderates were looking to the West for help to rebuild their shattered economy. And they were changing this absolutism. They are also in a bind.

I was in Pakistan during Benazir's election and, of course, the Rushdie trouble had started sometime in September. Many of Rushdie's fans had read the book. He was one of the very few Muslims who'd really made it big in the West, and many Pakistanis identified with his success, and they admired him for it. But now they felt they were betrayed. They couldn't see *why* he had done this, why he had mocked their religion. They felt that, as it is, they were being stereotyped in the Western press, and Rushdie, in fanning the flames, was encouraging the stereotyping of the Muslims as fanatical. Again, a negative image was being projected.

DM: Fanning the flames? In what way did he do this?

Sidhwa: Well, Rushdie—and I believe he said this in an interview—expected this confrontation to take place. I think, like many writers, he wanted some incident to make his sales grow. When the book was first banned in India, Rushdie dashed off letters to newspapers and magazines there to create a greater controversy. And I think he was at first very pleased with all the media attention. He said that if he'd known this was to be the reaction he would have written even more provocatively. But I don't think he was at all prepared for the ayatollah jumping in as he did with the death sentence. The situation was exploited by everybody. I mean, the book and Rushdie are sort of in the background now, and only the mistrust between the West and the Islamic East prevails.

DM: What effect do you think the death threat, which crosses international boundaries, will have on free expression worldwide? Do you think it will have a chilling effect on writers?

Sidhwa: I don't think so. I think it's had an absolutely warming effect on writers. They're so enamored of the thought that a writer has been able to create such a stir all over the world. I think the feeling among some people is that the First Amendment in America is also being waved about a little opportunely. I think people in the writing business *do* know there is censorship here as well. It is much more subtle and much more effective. A book that is not wanted or an author who is not wanted is not *published*, which leaves no recourse to the author. At least in Pakistan or India a book is banned. That leaves some authors—like Rushdie— the recourse to protest and to make a worldwide noise. So I don't think this is going to have a chilling effect on Western writers. Except maybe it will bring all this out into the open—that this very self-righteous tone is a little hypocritical.

DM: Do you think reviewers here also exercise a degree of censorship in their choice of whom to review, and editors as well, in their choice of reviewers?

Sidhwa: Yes, of course. In fact, I have had personal experience with what these people can do.

DM: There is also the painful fact that people in Pakistan and India were killed because of the book or, perhaps, not the book itself but the political furor. How do you feel about that equation where there is loss of life and there is literature and there is also politics?

Sidhwa: It's very sad. I believe twenty-three people have died. Rushdie is an extremely powerful man. If he were not so powerful, there wouldn't have been such a big hue and cry over his book in such terms as Britain withdrawing its relations with Iran, and the whole world going topsy-turvy—everybody ready to bomb Iran for Rushdie's sake.

March 26, 1988

DM: The partition of India and Pakistan appears in some form in all three of your books. You were nine years old at the time. What are your memories of Partition?

Sidhwa: Well, the main memory is of hearing mobs chanting slogans from a distance. It was a constant throb in the air and very threatening. Then I saw a lot of fires, it was almost like blood was in the sky, you know. And I saw a few dead bodies on my Warris Road. In fact, that's figured in two of the novels. I was actually walking to my private tutor, and there was this gunnysack lying by the roadside. The gardener, who was with me, just kicked the gunnysack, and a body spilled out, a dead body of a very good-looking man. There was a bloodless but big wound on the side of his waist, almost as if it trimmed the waist. And I felt more of a sadness than horror. It seemed so futile—even at that time when I wasn't really conscious of death—the waste of life.

DM: And did your family feel the pressures of what was happening?

Sidhwa: Apparently. I didn't feel the pressures myself, but my parents were tense; they were up much later than usual whispering and working all the time. And there were a lot of visits from aunts and uncles. Subsequently, I learned that some of my aunts and uncles from Bombay had advised my parents to get away from Lahore, but they chose to stay in Lahore.

DM: Did the fact that your family was Parsi rather than Muslim or Hindu make a difference in how you were affected?

Sidhwa: Yes, it certainly made a big difference, because Parsis, though involved in the independence struggle, were not with any one side during the partition. Like the Christians. And, as such, they weren't harmed by any party. In any case, they were such a tiny minority that they had no clout this way or that.

In *Ice-Candy-Man* it was very useful to use the voice of a Parsi child narrator, because it does bring about an objectivity there. Your own emotions are not so . . . or at least your participation in events is not so involved. You are more free to record them, not being an actor immediately involved.

DM: So an outsider sometimes sees more clearly?

Sidhwa: A child's point of view, certainly; I thought that would give more clarity to the book. When you put yourself into the persona of a child, in a way you remove all those blurred images—other people's opinions, expectations about what life is teaching you and the stereotypes that come in. Everything is a little fresher and refreshing, I think, from a child's point of view—more direct.

DM: In *Ice-Candy-Man* Lenny is very candid. At one point, however, she finds that her honesty has harmed someone close to her, has betrayed her nurse, Ayah. Then she thinks to herself, "My truth-infected tongue." At another point she also asks herself, "A life sentence? Condemned to honesty?"

Sidhwa: Well, I'm doing two things here. I'm establishing a sort of truthful witness, whom the reader can believe. At the same time Lenny is growing up—learning, experiencing, and coming to her own conclusions—one of them, that truth, truth, nothing but the truth can lead to a lot of harm, too. And in understanding the nature of truth, its many guises, she gradually sheds her innocence and understands the nature of men.

DM: In contrast, there is the lead character of *The Crow Eaters,* Freddy, who in the hilarious opening scene tells his children, "The sweetest thing in the world is your *need* . . . Need makes a flatterer of a bully and persuades a cruel man to kindness. Call it circumstances—call it self-interest—call it what you will, it still remains your need. All the good in this world comes from serving your own ends."

Sidhwa: Well, for all his apparent guile and unconventional thinking, he is a thoroughly moral man. He's very close to my ideal of what a man should be. He is smart enough to inhabit this world and protect his family, friends, and community and realistic enough not to search after ideals that would make him ineffectual and cause problems in this world. He's not an evil man; in fact, he sticks very close to the tenets of his faith, Zoroastrianism. Whatever his motives or reasoning, he ends up doing good to the people he knows. He's an active force for the good in this world.

DM: He uses his gains to benefit other people?

Sidhwa: That's right. No matter how suspect his motives, you know, he ends up doing more good than a do-gooder might in the end.

DM: The Crow Eaters really portrayed the Parsi community—a secretive community—for the first time in literature. When the book was published, did you have any difficulties within the community in Lahore?

Sidhwa: Yes, very dramatic difficulties. The book launch took place at an international hotel in Lahore, and, since there are not so many books written in English launched, it was quite a function, with a lot of writers and eminent people reading out papers on the book and all that sort of thing. And there was a bomb threat, which subsequently I realized was from a Parsi who felt very strongly about the book. It took me some time to realize what turmoil the book had created within the community. They thought I was revealing secrets that I had no business giving out. The Parsis are a popular minority and flourish partly because of their image as a noble and charitable people. And they felt I was damaging the image. But this is a typical reaction, I think, for anybody who breaks new ground in a community like this. They felt threatened by it, although it was written out of great affection.

DM: Was there anything in particular that they objected to most?

Sidhwa: The choice of title was unfortunate. I mean, just straight away, without reading the book, they said, we will never read a book with a name like this. They misunderstood the title. It just means a chatterbox. In a lot of our dialects— in Punjabi, Urdu, Gujarati—they say, "Have you eaten a crow that you're talking so much?" They linked the title to the system we have for the disposal of the dead in the tower of silence, where dead bodies are placed in walled enclosures that are open to the sky. And the birds of prey eat the body. They thought I was capitalizing on this sensitive aspect of a Zoroastrian custom, making fun of it, which was not so. Not in the title, at least.

DM: Was part of the problem the fact that the book was written in English?

Sidhwa: No, not at all.

DM: In each of your books people appear in flight—most dramatically, Zaitoon's flight from her husband in *The Bride* and, in *Ice-Candy-Man,* Ranna's story of his flight from the Sikhs. Why so much fleeing?

Sidhwa: I've never thought of it quite that way. It's interesting that you should see a connection there. Perhaps it has something to do with my personality. I always want to be somewhere I am not at that moment. Maybe I do want to flee situations, so I visualize people as wanting to get out of situations and flee.

And then, of course, there is the dramatic element, the tension in a flight and a chase and the effort to survive. As a novelist, you always like to link yourself with something dramatic. I think that's why you see the theme of Partition played out so often in my novels.

DM: Zaitoon's flight in *The Bride* is striking. But the fact is the woman you based the story on actually didn't make it to safety; she was killed by her husband. How do you reconcile your story with the facts, not that the book must be journalistic?

Sidhwa: Well, actually this book has two endings. It should have ended where she's hallucinating. She's scuttling across the bridge, and she realizes her husband is moving toward her. He kills her; it's tribal justice. It should have ended there, but I had lived with this girl in my imagination for three years. I'd identified with her. You do color every character by your own personality, by your own experience. And I felt it would be so futile to put the poor girl through all that I put her through just to have her die in the end. I did weep at that point, when this happened . . . so I changed the ending. She just barely survives, but at least she's alive.

DM: The amount of humor in your books changes. In *The Bride,* your first book, there is almost none.

Sidhwa: There's a bit of humor in the beginning . . . involving the wrestler Nikka.

DM: The middle book, *The Crow Eaters,* is just the opposite; it's filled with humor.

Sidhwa: Yes.

DM: Then *Ice-Candy-Man* is more of a mix. What happened between *The Bride* and *The Crow Eaters?*

Sidhwa: Well, it's very strange; the minute I write about my own community, the Parsis, straight away I'm into humor. I can't help it. And it's fun writing humor-ously. Perhaps it has something to do with my personality, but I find it a big strain to be solemn for too long. I was in a very good mood writing *The Crow Eaters. The Bride* was a much more difficult book for me to take. It made me morose. In *Ice-Candy-Man* there is Lenny, and again the moment she associates with Parsi characters, whether it's a group meeting or it's her godmother or a skinny aunt or a cousin, it just releases something in me to be humorous.

And I do feel that you can say a lot in humor without offending too much. It's gentler, yet it makes a stronger point than saying it seriously. I do feel strongly about things, and I very often make statements, but I disguise them in this way. I don't sort of sit down and say, I'm making a statement, but I know in the back of my mind it's something that I'm wanting to say and communicate. And I feel humor is a wonderful vehicle for this. Humor is especially effective in sex scenes. I mean, there's so much humor in sex which is seldom brought out in literature. So I've enjoyed using humor.

DM: Do you feel humor is more complete, in a way, or catches life more completely than, say, tragedy?

Sidhwa: Not really. I would say humor is a little more intellectual and wise, a little less emotional.

But I bring a lot of emotion to my writing. I feel emotion has a strong part to play. Maybe this has something to do with Urdu poetry, which is nothing but emotion and passionate complaint and touches deeply at the heart. I find this is suspect in Western writing, particularly these days. And it's perhaps that trait in Urdu which makes me want to deploy deep emotion in whatever I write: extreme tragedy, extreme anger, extreme jealousy, extreme happiness, all these factors. Of course humor can't depict everything. It can be poignant, sad, but not tragic. In *Ice-Candy-Man* I used both, comedy and tragedy.

DM: So there's more of a balance. Humor is so rare in world literature.

Sidhwa: I miss it myself, yes. I'd much rather read a book that makes me laugh.

DM: Do you see any other evolution in your three books, any other change that has taken place? What is the journey that you've made from *The Bride* to *Ice-Candy-Man?*

Sidhwa: They are all three very different books. Certainly, in *The Bride* I learned a lot about writing. It's the first piece of fiction I ever wrote, and it turned into a novel. I think I learned the craft from it, with the result *The Crow Eaters* came much more easily and much more spontaneously. In fact, *The Crow Eaters* was suspect in my eyes. It came so easily, I thought there must be something wrong. That's probably because I was so familiar with the subject, and I just allowed my bubbling subconscious to take over. A humorous streak took over.

Then, in *Ice-Candy-Man,* I was more politically motivated, certainly. And here I think I did try to manipulate situations to suit where I was aiming politically. And it wasn't always easy to do because I'm much more a sort of instinctive, spontaneous writer.

DM: Was one of these aims to describe the genocide the Sikhs carried out against the Muslim people?

Sidhwa: Well, the main motivation grew out of my reading of a good deal of literature on the partition of India and Pakistan. Not enough has been written about it in English. But what has been written has been written by the British and the Indians. Naturally, they reflect their bias. And they have, I felt after I'd researched the book, been unfair to the Pakistanis. As a writer, as a human being, one just does not tolerate injustice. I felt whatever little I could do to correct an injustice I would like to do. I don't think I have given a Pakistani bias to the book; I have just let facts speak for themselves, and through my research I found out what the facts *were*.

For example, one of the men I studied was an author called Penderton Moon, who was a British officer and an eyewitness of the partition. In writing his book, he said, "If I have a bias, it's a bias in favor of the Sikhs, because I was in charge of their regiment." And yet, time and again, he says that the Sikhs perpetrated the much greater brutality—they wanted the Punjab to be divided. A peasant is rooted to his soil. The only way to uproot him was to kill him or scare him out of his wits. Mountbatten flew over the Punjab during the riots and subsequently described it by saying that he saw the caravans of Muslims from East Punjab going to West Pakistan, and they were in a ragged state, without any belongings, without any cattle. You could see that they were decimated, scattered. Whereas the processions of the Sikhs, coming from the East to West Punjab, were walking in organized fashion with their bullock carts, with their buffalo, with their belongings piled on their bullock carts, and they appeared better organized to emigrate. The word had been passed to them. And here I also blame the politicians, the manipulations of people like Nehru and Gandhi, for manipulating the Sikhs. The Sikhs are, as far as I can see, both a very gullible and a violent people, and I have portrayed them as such.

You see, they were used for a long time as the military arm of the Hindus. The Hindus let them do all their dirty work, military-wise, violence-wise. And so they *have* had to be violent—that is, some of their sects.

DM: You said that there were points when you were writing *Ice-Candy-Man* where you felt you had to change something to follow your aim, your goal, politically. You also implied that it caused you some uneasiness as a writer. What tension did you feel?

Sidhwa: Well, it has to do with the point of view. Now, if I write in the same style I've used before, I find myself bored. So, in *Ice-Candy-Man,* I used the present tense and the first person. It had warmth and the capacity to create the atmosphere I wanted. I liked the voice that came out. But, at the same time, it was difficult to have this child be eyewitness to everything that was happening. And I think most people who write from this point of view have to make use of certain devices for that person to be present on most of the occasions and have somebody narrate them. At times it was a little difficult. I hope it's smoothened in the story. But

I did find myself asking: How is a child going to be witnessing this? Now I have to write something to show how she went there, how she witnessed it.

DM: Were there times when you disagreed with Lenny's point of view?

Sidhwa: With Lenny I don't think I was in much disagreement. Unless it was purposeful. Her point of view was serving a purpose.

DM: Can we talk about language itself for a moment? You speak several other languages—Urdu, Gujarati, and Punjabi.

Sidhwa: Punjabi, a little bit, not too well. I understand it pretty clearly.

DM: What part does each language play in your life? Are there tensions created between them?

Sidhwa: None at all, particularly when I'm in Pakistan. All of us there tend to speak a garbled mixture of languages. But, while in Pakistan, I thought: Oh, I speak English fluently. Then I came here and discovered that it was difficult for me to speak a string of sentences without putting some Gujarati or Urdu words in between. Because in Pakistan that's how we have become accustomed to talking. Listening to people who say they don't know any English, you'd be able to follow what they say because they're really throwing so many English words into the conversation.

DM: It's a patois or a salad of languages?

Sidhwa: Salad perhaps. I think you just juggle for the *best* meaning, somehow. And certain words are so much more expressive in another language. Something that is zestful comes out so much better said in Punjabi, or something that is emotional or romantic comes out better said in Urdu. Or certain Gujarati words carry so much more meaning. And you just automatically adopt this mixture to be more expressive.

DM: Is one language more dominant for you? Which do you consider your mother tongue?

Sidhwa: Gujarati, the language of the Parsis. My parents spoke it, and my husband and I, among our children.

Actually, it is a language of the Bombay area, the Gujarat area in India, because that's where we first came as refugees at the time of the Arabic invasion of Persia. The prince who let us stay stipulated we must learn the language of Gujarat. And so that became our tongue in India.

DM: And the majority of the Parsis live in Bombay?

Sidhwa: Yes. I think, there are about seventy thousand.

DM: And in Lahore?

Sidhwa: In Lahore we have now only ninety-two, but at the time of *The Crow Eaters*—that is, at the time of Partition—there were about three hundred.

DM: Are there any tensions between the Parsi and the Muslim communities in Lahore?

Sidhwa: No, I've not seen any tension, so far. Luckily, we've escaped that sort of thing. There's also a very enormous community of Hindus in the Sind, and fortunately, up to now, there have been no religious riots.

DM: Back to language; your books were all written in English. Does this cause any problems in Pakistan or India as far as representing your culture is concerned?

Sidhwa: No. I find myself comfortable writing in this language. My written Urdu is not very good, though I speak it fluently. As for Gujarati, hardly anyone in Pakistan knows the language. In Britain, of all places, people say, "Why don't you write in your own language?" And they bring very heavy political overtones to bear on this. But I think, well, the English don't have a monopoly on the language. It is a language of the world now. And it is a means of communicating between various nationalities and the most immediate tool at hand. So I use it without any inhibitions or problems, as far as I'm concerned.

In fact, it is of great advantage to write in English and be in Pakistan. My books are popular there. And Pakistan has pretty strong censorship. Strangely enough, you can get away with writing in English what you can't writing in Urdu. So, when it comes to translating into Urdu, I will have to modify certain passages that could be construed as obscene. (*The Bride* is to be translated.)

DM: How severe is censorship in Pakistan? There is press censorship.

Sidhwa: I think it's never been as free as I found it in the past two years, since martial law was lifted and replaced by a kind of grassroots democracy. I was amazed how much newspapers in English were permitted to report. In some respects, I think, they dared more even than the American press. But again that's in English.

But we do have this strong element of fundamentalist fanatics. And, because of them, everybody has to be on guard. When these people get agitated, nobody can control them, not even the government. They just burn the books, the newspapers, and wreck the newspaper offices, and nobody can control them at that stage. So I think everybody to some degree exercises a sort of self-censorship almost.

In the Urdu media the government comes down very hard on what it terms obscenity. Everything is obscene. Any of my sex scenes would be considered absolutely beyond the pale, and some political statements, too, if they were in Urdu. People go to prison for these things.

DM: In looking through an anthology of twentieth-century Urdu poetry, it quickly becomes clear that many of the poets have been imprisoned for some time or have been in exile.

Sidhwa: Yes, that's true, and for some it's a self-imposed exile. It's fashionable to travel to London. London has become a cultural center of sorts for the subcontinent now, strangely enough. And for most of them the level of comfort in politics is greater the further away from Pakistan they are.

I know the case of one woman writer who found this condition so intolerable that she left Pakistan and settled in India. She literally moved out of the country. And I think quite a few writers *have* found it so difficult that they have had to move out of the country off and on, like Faiz Ahmed Faiz. He spent a lot of time in Beirut and in the Soviet Union. He belonged to the group called the Progressive Writers at the time when communism was a great ideological fantasy for young people. You know, it was a new thing. He belonged to that generation. And, because of his belief, he suffered quite often.

DM: He wrote the introduction to *The Crow Eaters?*

Sidhwa: He wrote some delightful remarks on the back jacket of *The Crow Eaters.*

When he died he became very famous. Pakistan's publishing much more about him after his death than they did during his life. But that's the case with a lot of writers from our part of the world.

He liked *The Crow Eaters* very much. There was a rather dramatic incident connected to the introduction. When the galleys of *The Crow Eaters* were ready, in Pakistan Justice Javid Iqbal, the son of our mystic poet Alama Iqbal, removed the covers and distributed the book to a few writers for their comments and said, "What do you think of this?" It so happened that Faiz Ahmed Faiz was traveling beside my brother on a plane. And Faiz said, "I have this book written by a Parsi woman ... Do you know who she could be? The author's name is not on the book." And my brother said, "My sister, I think, writes. It could be her."

DM: Your brother wasn't sure you were writing?

Sidhwa: Well, you know, nobody was really aware I was writing. And then my brother read a little of it and said, "I think it is my sister's." And straight from the airport Faiz came over to the house. We had just one air conditioner in the bedroom. They came in there, and Faiz just sort of threw that shabby-looking book on the coffee table and asked if I'd written it. His praise was lavish, and I was delighted. Then he said a very funny thing. He said, "Yes, it's a very good, mediocre work"; he paused, while my heart shattered, and then he continued, "like Nardyan and [V.S.] Naipaul and the others. . . ." He named some other Indian writers. And I said, "Faiz Sahib, that's blasphemy. How can you compare me with them?" And he said, "Oh, yes, I can compare you."

DM: It must have been quite pleasing.

Sidhwa: It was quite pleasing, yes. Except that, you know, I didn't realize at that time how highly Naipaul was regarded. I was a little out of the literary fold. Living in Pakistan was living in a bit of a vacuum. So I had not taken it as that much of a compliment. But I did consider Naipaul a very great writer. And I didn't think it was justified to compare me with him. I certainly didn't believe I could write like him.

DM: Women in Pakistan—you have recently written an essay titled "Women Against the Mullahs." Is the Islamic fundamentalism that is spreading in the Mideast and Asia pushing women back into purdah?

Sidhwa: Into the medieval ages. But women are violently opposing it. What is very sad is that, you know, I don't think most of us were aware that the Hudood ordinance had been passed. And they are trying to bring the Sharia laws back, but the women are opposing it tooth and nail. Every time the mullahs open their mouths to talk of Islam, they end up saying, "Women should do this, women should not do this. This is how women should dress, this is how women should behave, this is how women should not bring pressure on them, and this is how women should not entice men." All those ridiculous things. They can't talk of Islam without talking of constricting women. And women are getting more and more fed up with this, because they have just a few hard-won rights. Very unfair things are happening in the name of the religion. Most men, when you talk to them, are opposed, and they see the injustice of it. Judges see the injustice of it much more clearly than anyone because they deal wtih these cases everyday. And I just hope now the Sharia laws are not passed. Although the fundamentalists are determined to have them passed.

DM: What do you think are the chances that they will be passed?

Sidhwa: It's so hard to predict. I don't know how strong the women are and for how long they can oppose the mullahs, who seem to be gaining in power. I don't know how long the rational elements in government will be able to oppose the Sharia laws.

This is not the same type of fundamentalism that Iran is facing. It was exacerbated by the Afghan crisis. Fundamentalism, religion, has been used to fight the war against the Russians. So the war gave fundamentalism an impetus. It became politically expedient to promote fundamentalism.

DM: And what legal steps are women taking?

Sidhwa: They are taking legal steps. But legal steps are dismissed offhand, because you go into unending tangles in the interpretation of the Koran. The men interpret it differently; the women interpret it differently.

There is an impatient element, and I myself belong to that element. But I'm not a member of the particular women's group known as the Women's Action Forum, which is making use of much more demonstrative methods of protest like protesting in the streets. In fact, most women's organizations are taking recourse to this strategy because it's the only way they seem to be able to draw attention to themselves and their causes. And they do a few things that, in the context of Pakistan, are very exceptional. They burn their veils or they shout on the road, which is, you know, very strange to see happen in Pakistan, and it does draw a lot of attention.

But these women are dismissed offhand by the religious element as being almost prostitutes: "These are loose women who do such things." Yet these women definitely belong to the elite of Pakistan because they are the only ones who can take such action, who are lettered enough and educated enough to do so. The poor women who belong to the lower or middle class aren't even conscious really of what's happening. They just suffer and suffer. They're in such turmoil they don't even have time to be conscious of what's happening to them.

DM: A book titled *Women of Pakistan* says that the rate of literacy among Pakistani women is 15 percent.

Sidhwa: Fifteen percent is a very exaggerated figure. I would say it's closer to 8 percent. Because, when you say literacy in Pakistan, it means if you can just sign your name you are considered literate. And a lot of women who go to school, let's say, up to the age of nine, or ten, revert to illiteracy. They totally forget what they've learned. It's much less than 15 percent.

DM: Obviously, then, there's great resistance to education for women.

Sidhwa: Pakistan has always had the potential to be a richer country than India. The GNP there is higher than in all the surrounding areas of the subcontinent. And those who are better off, particularly those in southern Pakistan, are seeing to it that their children go to English-speaking schools. They are very conscious of educating their girls, and this is a movement for the better. But among the lower-middle class and the nonmonied class there is certainly a sentiment against girls studying.

DM: Among the Parsis, there is no purdah?

Sidhwa: No, none at all.

DM: You mention in *The Crow Eaters* that, while there is no purdah in the Parsi community itself, you are surrounded by an atmosphere of repression, and this takes its toll on Parsi women as well.

Sidhwa: Well, the Parsis, wherever they have lived, have taken on the color of that country. Parsi women dress a little differently in Pakistan than those in Bombay. And they probably would even in England, let's say. In Pakistan that general repressive atmosphere for women naturally does have its effect on the values and attitudes which the Parsis hold there, with the result that a Parsi child might say, "Oh, Mommy, don't wear that sleeveless shirt. Don't come to my school without your shawl," or something like that. So to that extent it is very repressive, I feel, for girls.

DM: What does the word *purdah* or *chador* call up for you? Does it create a sense of frustration or anger or . . . ?

Sidhwa: Of sadness, because it is amazing how many women accept it. It is a part of their culture; they are accustomed to it. As little girls, they look forward to it. It's like a girl may want to wear high heels when she grows up and long to put on lipstick. A lot of very young girls think: Oh well, one day I will be very important, I'll wear a *chador*, I'll be adult. That's sad because it restricts their enjoyment of their bodies entirely. They're not free to cycle down roads or just plunge into water and swim or even be in the ocean, all these little gifts one has in life from nature, from God.

A woman's body is so constricted because of the attitude that also belongs to *burqa*. The *burqa* is different from purdah. Purdah is more associated with the segregation of men and women, particularly the segregation of women. The *chador* usually means you keep your face uncovered but cover the rest of your body. You just wear the veil but put it behind your ears. A *burqa* is quite different in that it's like a skullcap that fits on your head and falls like a tent to the floor. You just have a little netting over the eyes. As a teenager, I did once or twice wear it, you know, out of fun. And I found it very difficult to see through, to breathe through in the heat. It was a very restricting garment.

DM: In all of your books you do portray violence against women. In *The Bride* it's most apparent. Is this a taboo subject in that repressive society?

Sidhwa: No. Our papers are full of violence against women. It is continuously perpetrated, but it's trivialized. I mean, you just keep on hearing of instances where women have been killed for the merest suspicions of infidelity. And it's considered a crime of passion, and the men are exonerated. It's sort of part of the culture almost to permit that to happen to the women. I suppose this is a condition of poverty more than of attitudes. Attitudes, of course, play a very big part.

I think, on the whole, a Muslim woman is much better off than a Hindu woman. A Hindu woman is really degraded much more. She has no worth at all, in any fashion. Wife burning and all these things are so common in India. To treat the girl's part of the family very shabbily is again very common. Even in a marriage party, you just sense this "Oh, we are the boy's family." And they act like kings, and they bully the girl's family around. "The food is not good." They literally talk like that: "The food is not good. You're insulting our friends." The girl and the girl's family are denigrated.

In Pakistan it's a fairly common thing to kill a woman with your enemy and put them both naked in a field and say it's a crime of passion. This is a method of getting rid of your enemy.

DM: And in court the rules of evidence discriminate. The witness of one man is worth the witness of two women.

Sidhwa: Yes. Of course, it's so unjust. Especially in the case of rape, it leads to the woman being every time the victim of punishment. Every time the law works very unjustly against a woman who was raped.

DM: There have to be four adult male witnesses to prove...

Sidhwa: Yes, exactly—while in the woman's case the proof is there: She's got a big stomach, she's pregnant. She is there; no one needs to have four witnesses to prove her guilt—that she has had sex outside marriage.

DM: So, if there aren't four male witnesses, she is accused of adultery?

Sidhwa: Yes. Who's going to commit rape in front of four witnesses? In fact, right now there are about forty women in each of the provinces in Pakistan who are imprisoned under the Hudood ordinance for adultery, for sex outside of marriage. Most of these women are married. When a woman runs away with a lover, it's the husband who takes them to town, saying they're living in sin, and he has every right to say it, and both she and her lover are put in prison. If a girl runs away with another man—and this is very rare—her family takes it as a terrible insult, intolerable because very often a woman, a girl, is virtually sold and fetches a big price. Then the fathers and the brothers institute a case of adultery against her: There she's living with that man in sin. And straight away she comes under the Hudood ordinance. And all these poor women are facing the trial for adultery and death by stoning. Now, this is the absurd thing. Nothing of this sort has yet happened, and one hopes it will never happen. Every time a judgment of this type comes up, the whole government ministry intervenes. And the women make a big noise, and the sentence is withdrawn. But how many cases can they turn over, you know? It's ridiculous. And the poor people are suffering so badly.

DM: So there's punishment, regardless—persecution.

Sidhwa: Yes. Persecution is the right word.

DM: In *The Bride,* when Zaitoon flees, it's her mother-in-law who betrays her.

Sidhwa: Well, in fact, I gave the mother-in-law more compassion than she might actually be capable of having. At least she felt: Oh, everything is taking place for honor, and this poor girl is going to lose her life because of a code of honor that the men are practicing. In more probability, she would have been very much more angry at the girl because it's so ingrained now that this was a dishonor to her whole family and to her tribe. The women also are part of that code of conduct. And they also reinforce it. It's a man-made code of conduct, but it's how society functions there.

DM: Turning to *The Bride* again, the bridge in the story seems to divide two areas of law, the urban from the rural. Are there different laws in force for women on each side of this bridge?

Sidhwa: Well, no, not so different. It's got to do more with the structure of class in terms of wealth. Pakistan's is not a caste society like India's. It's a more egalitarian society, because Islam is egalitarian. But the classes come about with wealth. The richer families who can afford to educate their girls are kinder to their women, definitely. The poorer classes are not, whether they are in urban areas or in villages on this side of the administrative area where law and order by English standards are practiced. On the other side, in unadministrated territories, the women have to undergo almost equal hardship. There's no difference really. Women are just bullied.

I mean, how many even feel they can fight against big overt issues like the Hudood ordinance or the Sharia ordinance? They can't fight each individual case of brutality to women in their homes.

DM: Has the Zia government permitted the Islamization movement against women to go forward, and, if so, is this an attempt to win legitimacy from the fundamentalists?

Sidhwa: The fundamentalist movement is gaining strength because of political reasons and because of the Afghanistan situation. It is definitely very linked with that. We've had the war at our borders now for seven years, and, because of it, the government needs a lot of money and gets this from sources where there are fundamentalists also.

And how have the Afghans fought so long? There are countries like Yugoslavia and Czechoslovakia and Poland where the people couldn't resist the Russians even for *days* at a time. And these countries are, by our standards, a very developed and sophisticated, armed people. But here are these total primitives who carry homemade models of the Lee Enfield, who have given the Afghans so much fame in military terms for seven years. And there is a reason for this; they'd only be able to do this because of religion. Religion has played a very strong part in fighting this war. And this fact has been realized, and that is why fundamentalists have been promoted. They are the only force that could counter the Communist force there. It's so apparent, when they can resist for seven years while other countries can't for two days at a time.

DM: There are around four million Afghan refugees in Pakistan. Has this created a large-scale economic drain on the country?

Sidhwa: Not only economic. It's an ecological drain. We have very little vegetation in the northern areas of Pakistan because of the poverty, but now these people have taken over almost every tree for firewood. They've brought their goats and cattle to graze, and wherever goats graze nothing will grow for centuries because they eat up the seed from inside the soil. It's been an ecological disaster on a very massive scale.

DM: What other effects do you think the refugees will have if the war continues for several more years or if they stay in Pakistan?

Sidhwa: One terrible impact, which I've seen every time I've gone back during the past two years, is the proliferation of arms. My God, every household was a weapon now. And there were strict gun laws in Pakistan. Nobody had weapons; very few had licenses. And the other is the sudden outbreak and spread of drug use.

We are a very poor country, and now there's suddenly this enormous force of Afghans who are taking over the jobs of the poorer Pakistani. The Afghan, of course, through various forms of aid, is given a certain stipend every month. He's entitled to fifty rupees per head per month, plus food. Because of this, he can take on daily labor jobs for a much lower rate than the Pakistani can. So he's replacing the Pakistani. The Afghans are buying land; they're running this illegal drug traffic; they've changed the whole power structure of Pakistan. And they've done it overnight.

And they are a very ferocious, bullying, untamed people, you know. It's taken Pakistan thirty years to tame our own Pathans. The Afghans are totally a warrior people who suddenly descended on Pakistan with totally different values, very little consideration for life. They're liable to kill a person for ten rupees. They're being controlled, but with great difficulty. This doesn't reflect on all of them. When they've become entrepeneurs, they have more stake in the country, more stake in being peaceful.

DM: Moving to another border—the border with Iran. Pakistan is predominantly Sunni rather than Shiite. What influence has the Sunni Khomeini government had on the Sunni population in Pakistan or on the Shiite minority?

Sidhwa: I don't think the social revolution in Iran has made any change. There has been a little Shiite-Sunni tension for a very long time. This has not posed any threat for Pakistan. Iran is on our border, but I don't think Pakistan has ever felt threatened by it, because the fundamentalism there is different. And, so far, I've not seen it, because the Shiites are also a minority in Pakistan. They seem to be a fairly enlightened minority—don't seem to be those extremists.

DM: Pakistan also has a small border with China. What pressure does this exert on Pakistan?

Sidhwa: China has always been a very good friend of Pakistan, and we feel strengthened by its friendship. Pakistan feels China has been its only reliable ally. America has always been an ally but a very unreliable one. Whereas China, even if it's been able to help very, very little, symbolically it's helped a lot. Every time India, with its massive power on our borders, threatens Pakistan, China will come out with a humorous statement like: "Oh, the Indians have stolen eleven goats or eleven sheep, so we won't allow them to cross this area." They give India little threats like that that are a warning to leave Pakistan alone.

DM: When India was at war with China in 1962, the United States shifted support from Pakistan to India. How serious a shift in the balance of power was this in the region?

Sidhwa: The United States would much rather support India in every instance. But India plays a cool, nonaligned game and has valuable assistance from the USSR. This leaves the United States little option but the role it plays in Pakistan. India is very powerful. Pakistan feels very threatened by India because it's massive compared to Pakistan. And there are so many internal pressures within India also, you see, which could spill over and suddenly make India attack Pakistan or threaten the border. Pakistan is very uncomfortable in its relationship with India.

DM: And, of course, there's the nuclear problem. India did explode a bomb in 1974. [And in May, 1989, it tested a nuclear missile.]

Sidhwa: Yes. Once you pander to India, you abandon Pakistan. Pakistan feels it's just a small, kicked around, and bullied neighbor to India.

DM: It feels manipulated?

Sidhwa: Yes. And it is manipulated.

DM: Zulfiqar Ali Bhutto wrote a book called *The Myth of Independence,* which expressed that sense of being used by the superpowers.

Sidhwa: He had a point. No doubt about it.

DM: How do you feel about Bhutto's years in power?

Sidhwa: Well, for me, those years were an exhilarating experience as a woman and as a member of the minority. He had the sort of values most sophisticated people— in fact, he had the values most people in Pakistan agree with because he won by a huge majority in West Pakistan elections. And people were devoted to him, almost fanatically. At that time, during the elections, there was one party, which is still very much in power, called the Jamaat-e-Islami; they won almost *no* seats, whereas whoever Bhutto put up on the call of social reform and a very secular platform got elected by enormous majorities. And that same mood has prevailed.

DM: But it seems he became more and more isolated and defensive over the years.

Sidhwa: Somehow he became paranoid. He felt himself surrounded by enemies. And it wasn't really so much paranoia because he was beleaguered by superpowers. He was definitely targeted by America.

DM: He was executed by Zia in 1979. What did you think then?

Sidhwa: Well, when Benazir Bhutto appeared on "Sixty Minutes," she was asked what she thought of Zia and would she avenge her father's death. She answered something to the effect: "I don't believe in vendettas." Naturally, she was very moved by the question and the memories it recalled. But she blamed America as much as Zia for her father's death. Most people in Pakistan believe America was responsible for Zulfiqar Ali Bhutto's death.

DM: Does it seem inevitable that a progressive left-wing government will be followed by a right-wing, repressive government? Take Chile as a parallel where you have Allende followed by Pinochet, a very similar pattern, and Bhutto like Allende was elected.

Sidhwa: Yes, I think so, because of this great threat of communism. To counter communism, America will pump and pump money into Pakistan to not have communism.

DM: Thinking about cultural differences between East and West—first of all, are there differences in ways of storytelling? One reviewer has pointed out that *The Crow Eaters* is episodic, like an Indian folktale. Do you think a different manner of storytelling is used in the West? Or is there no difference?

Sidhwa: No, there is a very enormous difference, especially if you compare America and Pakistan. I think it's pretty true of most western European countries, too. In the West storytelling has been lost in the byways of verbal acrobatics and the need to be smart and innovative in writing. The story element is very often lost in what they call "literate fiction" in these parts of the world. And I'm not talking about writers who are minting money, telling stories with strong plots and all.

The Crow Eaters would be more in the style of my part of the world. It's telling a story. Then, again, I'm writing humor, and humor only comes out in *scenes* where you milk the scene for every ounce of its humor and drama. But *The Crow Eaters* is a novel. If you can call a lot of Naipaul's journalistic, self-indulgences a novel, this certainly is a novel.

DM: Is there a difference between East and West also in the attitude toward the individual in society?

Sidhwa: Oh, very much. In our part of the world, a person is generally a fatalist. There is so little he can do about the conditions in which he's born and the conditions in which he'll spend his life. I mean, in America it's inconceivable how much a man in Pakistan or India is mired by his birth, which they call destiny. You cannot sort of pull yourself up by the bootstraps and improve your life. No, if you are born into poverty, you will die in poverty 99.9 percent of the time. There's very little part anybody's will has to do with that. If anybody rebels, they'll be finished off by the society for rebelling, whether it's a man or woman. You can't move out of the strictures of those ingrained values there. And that is why people—no matter what happens to them—just say, what can we do? It's our fate.

Yes, I find a huge difference in America and in the Western developed world in that people feel they're in charge of their destiny. They don't have need for mystic powers of God. They can do away with these things. They feel much more in control. And that's a big difference in attitude.

Then, again, poverty has based our moral lives on family, and the structure of society reinforces this. People need to have the family network to support them. Actually, in Pakistan when a man is poor there is no social welfare; there is only his family to look after him. And everybody *is* looked after to that degree.

DM: You once mentioned that in Pakistan you write surrounded by people, and you find it somehow difficult to write in solitude.

Sidhwa: In absolute isolation.

DM: What does this mean to you?

Sidhwa: Well, you know, if I had isolated myself somewhere up on a hill in a house completely alone and unable to have people drop in, I would not be able to write a line. I cannot write living that way because that would give my life too much insecurity. I have become accustomed to having people around me.

In Pakistan society I'm a rebel in that respect. I want more privacy than most family members are willing to give. They think of me as very rude. I mean, it's inconceivable to say to someone, "I cannot see you because I'm writing." I can say, "I can't see you because I'm studying for an exam or because I am not well."

But here I find writers who lock themselves in their rooms and hibernate to write. I can't do that. I must have part of the family around me, interaction with friends. Otherwise, I'd just feel that I don't belong, I'm not rooted. I'd feel so unfettered I'd feel disembodied. So I do need a bit of both worlds to function.

DM: Are there differences in the way Pakistanis and Americans perceive your work?

Sidhwa: There I do find some difference. Instances in *The Crow Eaters,* which Pakistani and Indian readers took in their stride and found funny, were taken very seriously by some Americans. For example, when Freddy tries to kill the mother-in-law and burn his house but doesn't succeed. It is a fantasy, an act of imagination. But American readers have said, "How could you have somebody do this? We don't think of killing a mother-in-law or committing arson and then getting away with it." And it was just not seen in the make-believe light in which it was perceived so easily in other parts of the world. I think this has something to do with an older civilization that inclines one to a more accepting standard of "well, this is life" sort of attitude. Whereas, in America, there is still this new country idealism, which, in an way, is wonderful because it opposes something like that, and yet it's very hypocritical because much worse things happen all the time that are accepted here.

DM: In *The Bride* is a scene in which a crippled man is mocked and assaulted by some children. And the narrator makes the comment that, in the West, there is . . .

Sidhwa: The manufacture of deformities.

DM: Rather than...

Sidhwa: Rather than the mocking of one or two deformed people.

DM: Explain.

Sidhwa: This is a very serious difference because, in the West, there is often a very hypocritical stance adopted: "Oh, we wouldn't countenance jeering at a one-eyed man. We couldn't countenance making fun of a human being, let alone kicking a dog." You know? And, well, the Western society is very violent when it comes to war, the manufacture of war weapons. Its prosperity's based on selling arms, very often. They manufacture the means of deforming people, cause wars, and yet they're sort of aghast when they just see people being made fun of. I don't doubt that every society does have its little outlets of cruelty, but, I think, of the two evils, it's a lesser evil to jeer at somebody because they're deformed than to destroy cities, kill whole nations because they think differently from what you think.

DM: In *The Crow Eaters* Jerbanoo, the mother-in-law, is presented comically. In *Ice-Candy-Man* Godmother is not, and Lenny looks up to her. Yet, in a way, Godmother and Jerbanoo are very much alike. Has the attitude of the writer changed toward this type of woman?

Sidhwa: These are two different people, though with some similar characteristics. But Godmother has somehow been able to become empowered. She has come to a stage in life where she's not dependent on men. Godmother's old husband is feeble by now. He's been relegated to the background. He's had his day. And she has come into her own as a woman, whereas, in Jerbanoo's case, she is a widow and is still dependent for everything on her son-in-law. And, of course, the whole treatment of the story, the plot, the requirements of character, is different in each book.

DM: In *Ice-Candy-Man* the narrator makes some very funny observations on Ghandi— with his weaving and talking about his digestive problems—and says that Ghandi is "an improbable mixture of a demon and a clown." Later the narrator shows high regard for Jinah as a more reserved and serious politician. Do you agree with the narrator's point of view?

Sidhwa: Yes. This comes down to a statement I'm trying to make in the book that there have been films like *Ghandi* which have sanitized him into a saint. He's not human in that film. And I tried to humanize him. While watching *Ghandi*, I enjoyed it as a writer and a person who is interested in drama. I looked at him from the perspective of the film which portrayed him totally as a hero, and I enjoyed the film. But at the end of it—my daughter and her friend were sitting with me, and they were almost in tears. They said, "How could you like the movie, Mommy? Didn't you see what they did to Jinah?" And they felt that they, as Pakistanis, had been personally hurt the way Jinah had been treated in that movie. He was caricatured as a stick figure, as a very stiff villain of the piece. And I felt, in *Ice-Candy-Man,* I was just redressing, in a small way, a very grievous wrong that has been done to Jinah and Pakistanis by many Indian and British writers. They've dehumanized him, made him a symbol of the sort of person who brought about the partition of India, a person who was hardheaded and obstinate. Whereas, in reality, he was the only constitutional man who didn't sway crowds just by rhetoric and tried to do everything by the British standards of constitutional law.

Ghandi totally Hinduized the whole partition movement. This excluded the Muslims there. He brought religion into the Congress party. And Jinah, who was one of the founders of the party, found he had to edge away from it because it was changing into a Hindu party.

DM: Where are you heading now in your writing?

Sidhwa: Right now all the ideas I get have to do with people in America. I think if I write anything it will be now a humorous work of the interactions between Americans and immigrants, intermarriages, for instance, and funny situations. Humor and bathos. And I think I'm going to try to write a collection of short stories. I've not even written a single short story, so I will at least attempt to now. Everytime I've started a short story, it's turned into a novel.

DM: You have three grown children?

Sidhwa: Yes.

DM: And you began to write at the suggestion of a woman you met on a plane?

Sidhwa: Yes, an Afghan woman. I'm so fond of reading, and I used to think that a writer was some sort of a being who lives in another sphere. I never thought of the writer in human terms but almost as some disembodied power that automatically produced books. And suddenly, by telling me she was a writer, she made me realize that writers are very flesh-and-blood persons. And that did make me want to write. In fact, I then wrote just a short piece, which was published in a magazine with her help.

DM: Just one more question—a rather large one: What can the writer do? What makes writing important? In modern society where there is so much media, a flood of information, almost an overabundance of communication, what makes a writer necessary?

Sidhwa: Well, I don't think the writer can—not a writer of fiction—change the world. I don't think so at all—or, if so, very little in practical terms. There are exceptions. Certain writers maybe are able to do it. The poet Neruda is one example. It depends, I suppose, on what country you inhabit and at what time. But I do think that a writer can at least place facts so that people recognize themselves and stop taking themselves too seriously or start seeing themselves in a more realistic light. We all are so prone to see ourselves as a little better than the other person. Some readers have commented, "Oh, you made me see myself." Or "I'm an Oxford- or Harvard-educated person, and I find that really my thinking is no different from that tribal gentleman's in that tribal landscape you've portrayed." And I feel my writing is at least making some people aware of what they are. That's going to have some impact.

Then there are these incidents I can describe where I feel very concerned about injustices, whether it is the behavior of superpowers or the oppression of women or an injustice done to political leaders or to a country. At least, I think a lot of readers in Pakistan, especially with *Ice-Candy-Man,* feel that I've given them a voice, which they did not have before. They've always been portrayed in a very unfavorable light. It's been fashionable to kick Pakistan, and it's been done again and again by various writers living in the West.

DM: So a voice gives . . . ?

Sidhwa: It gives them a little self-esteem. This is a very strange thing, but the Western media has become so powerful that people in my part of the world are beginning to believe it. Their self-esteem *is* being eroded by their presentation as inferior persons. They're thinking less of themselves. And this has some strange results. When I was in Pakistan recently, I was suddenly struck by the fact that on a front page of a newspaper I saw an item saying: "Twelve Americans died, skiing in Colorado." Then somewhere locked up in the middle pages I saw a little item saying: "A bus fell down a gorge in the Karakorams, and fifteen people died." So, you know, we have been diminished, in our own eyes. And that *is* the power of the media. And I feel, if there's one little thing I could do, it's to make people realize: We are not worthless because we inhabit a poor country or because we inhabit a country that is seen by Western eyes as a primitive, fundamentalist country only . . . I mean, we are a rich mixture of all sorts of forces as well, and our lives are very much worth living.

From *The Crow Eaters*

Faredoon Junglewalla, Freddy for short, was a strikingly handsome, dulcet-voiced adventurer with so few scruples that he not only succeeded in carving a comfortable niche in the world for himself but he also earned the respect and gratitude of his entire community. When he died at sixty-five, a majestic grey-haired patriarch, he attained the rare distinction of being locally listed in the "Zarathusti Calendar of Great Men and Women."

At important Parsi ceremonies, like thanksgivings and death anniversaries, names of the great departed are invoked with gratitude—they include the names of ancient Persian kings and saints, and all those who have served the community since the Parsis migrated to India.

Faredoon Junglewalla's name is invoked in all major ceremonies performed in the Punjab and Sind—an ever-present testimony to the success of his charming rascality.

In his prosperous middle years Faredoon Junglewalla was prone to reminiscence and rhetoric. Sunk in a cane-backed easy-chair after an exacting day, his long legs propped up on the sliding arms of the chair, he talked to the young people gathered at his feet:

"My children, do you know what the sweetest thing in this world is?"

"No, no, no." Raising a benign hand to silence an avalanche of suggestions, he smiled and shook his head. "No, it is not sugar, not money—not even mother's love!"

His seven children, and the young visitors of the evening, leaned forward with popping eyes and intent faces. His rich deep voice had a cadence that lilted pleasurably in their ears.

"The sweetest thing in the world is your *need*. Yes, think on it. Your own *need*—the mainspring of your wants, well-being and contentment."

As he continued, the words "need" and "wants" edged over their common boundaries and spread to encompass vast new horizons, flooding their minds with his vision.

"Need makes a flatterer of a bully and persuades a cruel man to kindness. Call it circumstances—call it self-interest—call it what you will, it still remains your need. All the good in this world comes from serving our own ends. What makes you tolerate someone you'd rather spit in the eye? What subdues that great big 'I,' that monstrous ego in a person? Need, I tell you—will force you to love your enemy as a brother!"

Billy devoured each word. A callow-faced stripling with a straggling five-haired moustache, he believed his father's utterances to be superior even to the wisdom of Zarathustra.

The young men loved best of all those occasions when there were no women around to cramp Faredoon's style. At such times Freddy would enchant them with his candour. One evening when the women were busy preparing dinner, he confided in them.

"Yes, I've been all things to all people in my time. There was that bumptious son-of-a-bitch in Peshawar called Colonel Williams. I cooed to him—salaamed so low I got a crick in my balls—buttered and marmaladed him until he was eating out of my hand. Within a year I was handling all traffic of goods between Peshawar and Afghanistan!

"And once you have the means, there is no end to the good you can do. I donated towards the construction of an orphanage and a hospital. I installed a water pump with a stone plaque dedicating it to my friend, Mr. Charles P. Allen. He had just arrived from Wales, and held a junior position in the Indian Civil Service; a position that was strategic to my business. He was a pukka sahib then—couldn't stand the heat. But he was better off than his memsahib! All covered with prickly heat, the poor skinny creature scratched herself raw.

"One day Allen confessed he couldn't get his prick up. 'On account of this bloody heat,' he said. He was an obliging bastard, so I helped him. First I packed his wife off to the hills to relieve her of her prickly heat. Then I rallied around with a bunch of buxom dancing-girls and Dimple Scotch. In no time at all he was cured of his distressing symptoms!

"Oh yes, there is no end to the good one can do." Here, to his credit, the red-blooded sage winked circumspectly. Faredoon's vernacular was interspersed with laboured snatches of English spoken in a droll intent accent.

"Ah, my sweet little innocents," he went on, "I have never permitted pride and arrogance to stand in my way. Where would I be had I made a delicate flower of my pride—and sat my delicate bum on it? I followed the dictates of my needs, my wants—they make one flexible, elastic, humble. 'The meek shall inherit the earth,' says Christ. There is a lot in what he says. There is also a lot of depth in the man who says, 'Sway with the breeze, bend with the winds,'" he orated, misquoting authoritatively.

"There are hardly a hundred and twenty thousand Parsis in the world—and still we maintain our identity—why? Booted out of Persia at the time of the Arab invasion 1,300 years ago, a handful of our ancestors fled to India with their sacred fires. Here they were granted sanctuary by the prince Yadav Rana on condition that they did not eat beef, wear rawhide sandals or convert the susceptible masses. Our ancestors weren't too proud to bow to his will. To this day we do not allow conversion to our faith—or mixed marriages.

"I've made friends—love them—for what could be called 'ulterior motives,' and yet the friendships so made are amongst my sweetest, longest and most sincere. I cherish them still."

He paused, sighing, and out of the blue, suddenly he said: "Now your grandmother—bless her shrewish little heart—you have no idea how difficult she was. What lengths I've had to go to; what she has exacted of me! I was always good to her though, for the sake of peace in this house. But for me, she would have eaten you out of house and home!

"Ah, well, you look after your needs and God looks after you . . ."

His mellifluous tone was so reasonable, so devoid of vanity, that his listeners felt they were the privileged recipients of a revelation. They burst into laughter at this earthier expatiation and Faredoon (by this time even his wife had stopped calling him Freddy) exulted at the rapport.

"And where, if I may ask, does the sun rise?

"No, not in the East. For us it rises—and sets—in the Englishman's arse. They are our sovereigns! Where do you think we'd be if we did not curry favour? Next to the nawabs, rajas and princelings, we are the greatest toadies of the British Empire! These are not ugly words, mind you. They are the sweet dictates of our delicious need to exist, to live and prosper in peace. Otherwise, where would we Parsis be? Cleaning out gutters with the untouchables—a dispersed pinch of snuff sneezed from the heterogeneous nostrils of India! Oh yes, in looking after our interests we have maintained our strength—the strength to advance the grand cosmic plan of Ahura Mazda—the deep spiritual law which governs the universe, the path of *Asha.*"

How they loved him. Faces gleaming, mouths agape, they devoutly soaked up the eloquence and counsel of their middle-aged guru. But for all his wisdom, all his glib talk, there was one adversary he could never vanquish.

Faredoon Junglewalla, Freddy for short, embarked on his travels towards the end of the nineteenth century. Twenty-three years old, strong and pioneering, he saw no future for himself in his ancestral village, tucked away in the forests of Central India, and resolved to seek his fortune in the hallowed pastures of the Punjab. Of the sixteen lands created by Ahura Mazda, and mentioned in the 4,000-year-old Vendidad, one is the "Septa Sindhu"; the Sind and Punjab of today.

Loading his belongings, which included a widowed mother-in-law eleven years older than himself, a pregnant wife six years younger, and his infant daughter, Hutoxi, on to a bullock-cart, he set off for the North.

The cart was a wooden platform on wheels—fifteen feet long and ten feet across. Almost two-thirds of the platform was covered by a bamboo and canvas structure within which the family slept and lived. The rear of the cart was stacked with their belongings.

The bullocks stuck to the edge of the road and progressed with a minimum of guidance. Occasionally, having spent the day in town, they travelled at night. The beasts would follow the road hour upon hour while the family slept soundly through until dawn.

Added to the ordinary worries and cares of a long journey undertaken by bullock-cart, Freddy soon found himself confronted by two serious problems. One was occasioned by the ungentlemanly behaviour of a very resolute rooster; the other by the truculence of his indolent mother-in-law.

Freddy's wife, Putli, taking steps to ensure a daily supply of fresh eggs, had hoisted a chicken coop on to the cart at the very last moment. The bamboo coop contained three plump, low-bellied hens and a virile cock.

Freddy's objection to their presence had been overruled.

Freddy gently governed and completely controlled his wife with the aid of three maxims. If she did or wanted to do something that he considered intolerable and disastrous, he would take a stern and unshakeable stand. Putli soon learnt to recognise and respect his decisions on such occasions. If she did, or planned something he considered stupid and wasteful, but not really harmful, he would voice his objections and immediately humour her with his benevolent sanction. In all other matters she had a free hand.

He put the decision to cart the chickens into the second category and after launching a mild protest, graciously acceded to her wish.

The rooster was her favourite. A handsome, long-legged creature with a majestic red comb and flashy up-curled tail, he hated being cooped up with the hens in the rear of the cart. At dawn he awoke the household with shrill, shattering crows that did not cease until Putli let the birds out of their coop. The cock would then flutter his iridescent feathers, obligingly service his harem, and scamper to the very front of the cart. Here he spent the day strutting back and forth on the narrow strip that served as a yard, or stood at his favourite post on the right-hand shaft like a sentinel. At crowded junctions he preened his navy-blue, maroon and amber feathers, and crowed lustily for the benefit of admiring onlookers. Putli spoilt him with scraps of left-over food and chapati crumbs.

Quite hysterical at the outset of the expedition the cock had, in a matter of days, grown to love the ride. The monotonous, creaking rhythm of their progress through dusty roads filled him with delight and each bump or untoward movement thrilled his responsive and joyous little heart. He never left the precincts of the cart. Once in a while, seized by a craving for adventure, he would flap across the bullocks and juggling his long black legs dexterously, alight on their horns. Good naturedly, Freddy shooed him back to his quarters.

Freddy's troubles with the rooster began a fortnight after the start of their journey.

Freddy had already devised means to overcome the hurdles impeding his love life. Every other evening he would chance upon a scenic haven along the route, and raving about the beauty of a canal bank, or a breeze-bowed field of mustard, propel his mother-in-law into the wilderness. Jerbanoo, barely concealing her apathy, allowed herself to be parked on a mat spread out by her son-in-law. Sitting down by her side he would point out landmarks or comment on the serenity of the landscape. A few moments later, reddening under her resigned and knowing look, he would offer some lame excuse and leave her to partake of the scene alone. Freddy would then race back to the cart, pull the canvas flap close and fling himself into the welcoming arms of his impatient wife.

One momentous evening the rooster happened to chance into the shelter. Cocking his head to one side, he observed Freddy's curious exertions with interest. Combining a shrewd sense of timing with humour, he suddenly hopped up and with a minimum of flap or fuss planted himself firmly upon Freddy's amorous buttocks. Nothing could distract Freddy at that moment. Deep in his passion, subconsciously thinking the pressure was from his wife's rapturous fingers, Freddy gave the cock the ride of his life. Eyes asparkle, wings stretched out for balance, the cock held on to his rocking perch like an experienced rodeo rider.

It was only after Freddy sagged into a sated stupor, nerves uncurled with langour, that the cock, raising both his tail and his neck, crowed, "Coo-ka-roo-coooo!"

Freddy reacted as if a nuclear device had been set off in his ears. He sprang upright, and the surprised Putli sat up just in time to glimpse the nervous rooster scurry out between the flaps.

Putli doubled over with laughter; a phenomenon so rare that Freddy, overcoming his murderous wrath, subsided at her feet with a sheepish grin.

Freddy took the precaution of tying the flaps securely and all went well the next few times. But the rooster, having tasted the cup of joy, was eager for another sip.

Some days later he discovered a rent in the canvas at the back of the shack. Poking his neck in he observed the tumult on the mattress. His inquisitive little eyes lit up and his comb grew rigid. Timing his moves with magnificent judgment he slipped in quietly and rode the last thirty seconds in a triumphant orgy of quivering feathers. This time Freddy was dimly conscious of the presence on his bare behind, but impaled by his mounting, obliviating desires there was nothing he could do.

His body relaxed, unwinding helplessly, and the cock crowed into his ears. Freddy leapt up. Had Putli not restrained him he would have wrung the fowl's neck there and then.

When the whole performance was repeated a week later, Freddy knew something would have to be done—and quickly. Afraid to shock his wife, he awaited his chance which came in the guise of a water buffalo that almost gored his mother-in-law.

At dawn they had stopped on the outskirts of a village. Jerbanoo, obedient to the call of nature, was wading into a field of maize with an earthenware mug full of toilet water, when out from behind a haystack appeared a buffalo. He stood still, his great black head and red eyes looking at her across the green expanse of maize.

Jerbanoo froze in the knee-high verdure. The domestic buffalo is normally very docile, but this one was mean. She could tell by the defiant tilt of his head and by the intense glow in his fierce eyes. Cautiously bending her knees, Jerbanoo attempted to hide among the stalks, but the buffalo, with a downward toss of the head, began his charge.

"Help!" screamed Jerbanoo, dropping her mug. Lifting the skirt of her sari with one hand, she fled towards the cart.

"Get to one side, change your direction!" yelled Freddy, gesticulating with both arms.

Terrified into imbecility, Jerbanoo continued to dash in a straight line ahead of the buffalo.

"Move this way, move away!" shouted Freddy, waving his arms east and west and running to her.

Just then a man popped up from the maize stalks and, bellowing for all he was worth, waving his shirt to attract the attention of the buffalo, diverted the stampeding animal. Being the owner of the beast, he quickly brought it under control.

Distraught and disarranged, Jerbanoo fell sobbing into Freddy's arms. It was the last time he ever felt a wave of tenderness and concern for his mother-in-law.

Putli was grateful and pleased with Freddy's gallant effort in rushing forward to help her mother. Taking advantage of her sentiments, Faredoon delicately presented his case for the elimination of the rooster.

"God has saved us from a great calamity today," he declared after supper. "We owe Him thousands, nay millions of thanks for His grace in preventing bloodshed. As soon as we are settled near a Fire Temple, I will order a *jashan* of thanksgiving at our new home. Six *Mobeds* will pray over enough holy fruit, bread and sweetmeats to distribute amongst a hundred beggars . . . but it might be too late! We have been warned, the earth thirsts for blood! I intend to sacrifice the cock tonight."

Putli gasped and paled. "Oh, can't you sacrifice one of the hens instead?" she pleaded.

"It has to be the cock, I'm afraid," said Freddy, permitting his lowered head to sink sadly. "We all love the charming fellow, I know—but you cannot sacrifice something you don't care for—there is no point in it."

"Yes, yes," agreed Jerbanoo vehemently. After all it was her blood the earth thirsted after—her life they were talking about!

Putli nodded pensively.

Next day they ate a succulent chicken and coconut curry.

But the dashing sprint had proved too much for Jerbanoo's sluggish muscles. Her body ached horribly, and her initial gratitude was replaced by a sullen rancour. She blamed Freddy for having undertaken a journey that exposed her to the buffalo charge and to many subsequent vicissitudes.

Jerbanoo had been against the journey from the very start. Unnerved by the uprooting and by the buffalo, by the imperturbably polite stance adopted by her unfeeling son-in-law, she had ranted, moaned and finally resigned herself to martyrdom. Arms akimbo, black vindictive eyes snapping, she never failed an opportunity to castigate him. And the journey, fraught with mishap and mild disaster, had given her plenty.

As on that pitch black night when the wooden wheel of the cart collapsed on the outskirts of the Rajastan desert—and a jackal suddenly howled into the stillness.

Jumping from the cart, palms on hips, Jerbanoo planted herself solidly before Freddy. Her winged eyebrows almost disappeared in her hairline. "So, now we are to be devoured by wolves! Why? Because your majesty wishes it! We are to spend the night in this forsaken place, at the mercy of wild beasts! Why? Because our simple village ways were not good enough for you! But don't imagine I'm going to dance to your tune all the time. I've come for my daughter's sake and I'm not going to stand this nonsense any longer! You turn right back! You hear me?" she bawled, her eyes shining triumphantly in the glow of the lantern swinging from Freddy's hand.

Freddy turned away silently.

"You obstinate fiend, have you no idea how we are suffering? Have you no care for your wife and child? Oh, how can they live at the mercy of your whims . . . you heartless demon!" she cried.

Putli slept through unconcerned. Her mother's screeching tirades had grown so commonplace that the uproar hardly stirred her dreams.

Ignoring Jerbanoo, Freddy set about repairing the wheel. The slighted woman bounced back into the cart and sat quivering on her mattress.

The jackal bayed, his mournful notes amplified by the nocturnal stillness.

Jerbanoo's spine grew rigid and out of sheer disgust and frustration, she howled back.

The jackal wailed, caterwauling eerily.

"Owoooo!" went Jerbanoo.

Excited by the discovery of a mate, the jackal launched an abysmal moan.

"Yieeee!" yowled Jerbanoo, and between the two rose the most ghoulish duet imaginable.

His flesh creeping, his beautiful white teeth on edge, Fardoon leapt on to the cart and scrambled into the hut. Hurling himself within an inch of his mother-in-law's face he hissed, "Stop it...Stop that horrible noise or I'll leave you right here...I swear!"

Jerbanoo subsided at once. Not so much at the ominous pledge as at the demented gleam in his eyes.

Within two hours they had resumed their journey, soothed and lulled by the hollow toll of the bell hanging from each bullock's neck.

At other times the child had dysentery, Jerbanoo got cramp bathing in a canal, and Putli, stung by a scorpion, almost fell into a well. On these occasions, attracted by Jerbanoo's strident, scolding outcries, the entire populace of several villages was entertained mercilessly to the shortcomings of her son-in-law.

Tiring of this, Freddy addressed himself exclusively to his wide-eyed, diligent wife, and Jerbanoo slumped into a restive, martyred silence.

Two dust-grimed, mosquito-bitten months later, Freddy led his worn beasts into the fertile land of the Five Rivers.

They passed through several villages, green with wheat and gold with mustard. They spent a few days in the golden city of Amritsar and finally came to Lahore.

Faredoon Junglewalla fell in love with Lahore straightaway. His mother-in-law, the corners of whose set mouth had drooped progressively as the journey had gone on, surveyed the bustling, steaming city with bleak eyes. She withheld, for the moment, her comment, glad of a chance to rest her rattled joints.

Freddy toured Lahore all day and each hour strengthened his initial love of the ancient city. That evening they parked the cart beneath a shady tree near the Badshahi Mosque. The horizon cradled the sun in a pink fleece, touching the poetic assembly of white domes with a blush, filling Freddy's senses with serenity. The muezzin's cry, suppliant, plaintive and sensual, rose in the hushed air among the domes. Bells tinkled in a diminutive Hindu temple, snuggled in the shadows of the mosque. A Sikh temple, gold-plated, gleamed like a small jewel in the shadows and Freddy, responsive to all religious stimuli, surrendered his heart to the moment.

In the morning, having decided to adopt the city and try his luck, Freddy approached his wife for the gold. Putli, who had been laying out feed for the bullocks, glanced around with wary eyes.

"Even trees," she advised sternly, "have ears."

Placing a cautionary hand on Freddy's arm, she led him into their room on the bullock-cart.

The baby slept in one corner and Jerbanoo sat cross-legged on her mattress, battling the enervating heat with a palm-leaf fan. At Freddy's entrance she wrinkled her nose at the bazaar smells assailing her nostrils and, fanning herself into a froth, mutely advertised her displeasure of the city.

Freddy's heart trilled in his chest. Jerbanoo's disfavour set the seal on his inspired decision. Like hens settling on eggs, Freddy's mind settled on a smug clutch of smiling thoughts. Right there he took a silent oath that he would never leave Lahore so long as he lived.

Turning his back upon his mother-in-law's pointed histrionics, Freddy watched his wife unbutton the tight bodice beneath her sari blouse. Putli barely came up to his chest. Secure from prying, thieving eyes, she removed the cache that had pressed the flesh of her breasts from the onset of their travels. Carefully handing the cache to Freddy, she began buttoning herself back into her flattening cotton bodice. Freddy eyed with chagrin the buoyant little breasts as they disappeared. He reached stealthily for a last-minute touch but her censorious stare, warning him of his mother-in-law, stayed his hand.

There was a certain fixed quality to Putli's humourless eyes, set well apart in the stern little triangle of her face, that often disconcerted and irritated Freddy. The only time he saw her unwavering gaze dissolve was in bed. Then her long-lashed lids grew heavy with sensuality and there was such dogged and hedonistic devotion in her eyes for him, such a readiness to please and be pleased, that he became her slave.

As soon as Freddy left, Putli flung herself into an energetic orgy of work. In no time at all she had watered the bullocks, started a fire in the coal brazier and set a colander of vegetables and lentils to simmer. All this she did with such economy of motion and efficiency that her mother roused herself guiltily to give a hand. Taking the plate of rice from Putli she began to feed the child.

Freddy systematically found his way to the homes of the four Parsi families settled in Lahore: the Toddywallas, the Bankwallas, the Bottliwallas and Chaiwallas. None of them practised the trades suggested by their names. The Toddywallas, a large joint-family, were the proprietors of a prosperous tea stall, and the Chaiwallas ran a bar. Mr. Bottliwalla was a teller in a bank, and Mr. Bankwalla conducted classes in ballroom dancing.

An endearing feature of this microscopic merchant community was its compelling sense of duty and obligation towards other Parsis. Like one large close-knit family, they assisted each other, sharing success and rallying to support failure.

There were no Parsi beggars in a country abounding in beggars. The moment a Parsi strikes it rich he devotes a big portion of his energies to charity. He builds schools, hospitals and orphanages; provides housing, scholarships and finance. Notorious misers, they are paradoxically generous to a cause.

The four families were delighted by Freddy's visit and enchanted at the prospect of another family come to swell their ranks.

In two days Freddy had ensconced his family in a flat atop his brand-new provision store in one of the most busy and commercially prosperous areas in town.

The very next evening, rigged out in a starched white coat-wrap that fastened with bows at the neck and waist, and crisp white pyjamas and turban, he drove his cart to Government House.

Parking his splendid bullocks next to restive tonga horses, Freddy strode confidently up to the resplendent guards at the huge iron gates. The guards allowed him in almost at once and Freddy signed his name in the Visitor's Register.

Having thus paid homage to the British Empire, established his credentials and demonstrated his loyalty to "Queen and Crown," Freddy was free to face the future.

Carolyn Forché

Carolyn Forché, born in Detroit, Michigan, in 1950, published her first book of poetry, *Gathering the Tribes* (1976), as a winner of the Yale Series of Younger Poets Award. She won the Lamont Prize for her second volume of poetry, *The Country Between Us* (1981), which included poems based on her experiences as a journalist in El Salvador from 1978 to 1980. Her books of translation include *Flowers from the Volcano* (1983) by Claribel Alegria and *The Selected Poems of Robert Desnos* (1990), cotranslated with William Kulik. Her work-in-progress is a long poem presently titled "The Angel of History." She is also editing an anthology, *Against Forgetting: Twentieth-Century Poetry of Witness,* to be published in 1992. She won a Lannan Fellowship in 1990 and currently teaches at George Mason University in Virginia. She is married and has one son.

This interview took place in December, 1987, in Provincetown, Massachusetts. In November, 1990, I asked Forché about the relative silence surrounding the political murders in El Salvador (including those of six Jesuits, their housekeeper, and her daughter) and the clamor surrounding free elections in Czechoslovakia. She commented as follows.

I want, first of all, to qualify that it appears that the slaying of the Jesuits was carried out by death squads operating within the Salvadoran military.

Last May I was able to meet my family in Czechoslovakia, and, for the first time, my aunt Ana Borovska, who was exiled internally by Stalin to Brno, an industrial district about two and one-half hours from Prague. It was very moving for me to find her. She was active in supporting the Partisans in Czechoslovakia and was also active in a network of people who sought to shelter and protect Czechoslovakian Jewry during World War Two. For this she was arrested by the Nazis, imprisoned, and sentenced to be deported to Auschwitz. The story is complicated, but she escaped and later helped to resist the Communist regime, resulting in her internal exile.

I was also able to meet Eda Kriseovar, who is an advisor to President Havel and a member of Civic Forum and who is herself a writer and journalist.

So my contact with Czechoslovakia has been both familial and political. But because I have been reunited with family there, I've become very aware that since the revolution they have had to face a terrifying collapse of the national and local economies, a collapse of structure which, though they support this collapse politically, they find very difficult. They are enduring a transition. So I find myself in a condition of urgency with regard to them.

In respect to El Salvador, last year I was involved in bringing a defector from the Salvadoran army into contact with the media and the U.S. congressional commission investigating the murder of the Jesuits. He was offering testimony that alleges it was his unit that, after his defection, carried out the murders. He was very helpful in the investigation, although I have yet to see justice done because of the suspension of our own culpability for aiding and abetting a certain portion of the Salvadoran military.

Though I don't think "assimilate" is quite the right word here, and I don't like to use it in this context, I've found myself yet to assimilate events such as these in Czechoslovakia and in El Salvador. It's very difficult to find one's voice within the pressure of these conditions.

So my poem-in-progress, "The Angel of History," has been somewhat held in abeyance because of the intrusion of these events.

Yet I would never want to try to find a reason for the silence of others about such events as those in El Salvador. It's a silence I don't think I understand—although younger poets in the United States seem to be rather irritated at their elders and are not afraid to address the political in their work. I think we're seeing a flowering of this kind of writing.

We're in the midst of a cataclysmic change. We're seeing the demise of the American economy and, because of its links with other free market economies, the demise of the economy of the West. And we're seeing the political collapse of totalitarianism. I'm very interested in what will transpire, especially as countries in Europe and the Soviet Union come to terms with their nationalist and ethnic tensions. We'll see whether or not they will find a way to overcome these tensions with a social, political, and economic structure that might resemble what we respect as a political democracy. The world is under terrible pressure. As we go to press, this could all change.

As far as the poetic task at hand, I think these times are very exciting and promising. In my own work, I feel very challenged. I almost feel inhabited by a fiery spirit.

I did give a reading while in Prague last May. Miroslav Holub has translated some of my poems, and his Czech versions were read with the English versions. I found this a very moving experience.

David Montenegro: What happens to language when it is used—even almost photographically—to describe brutalities that are terrible to describe? What kind of weight does this place on language? Does this change language?

Carolyn Forché: An unbearable weight. Odysseus Elytis, whose work I have been recently studying, cautions poets not to attempt to compete with events nor endure their experiences once in life and a second time in art. I doubt that we "use" language other than "to describe," but I have found it very difficult to transform such events as those to which you refer, and I'm not certain I've done so to the degree I would wish possible. It isn't enough simply to *recount,* in the linear sense of legal discourse, because the work must also be somehow *redemptive,* and the narrative restructured. I now believe that to write of conditions of extremity is the most difficult. Well, no. To write *out* of conditions of extremity is the most difficult. Paul Celan, in his "Geschichter Fügue" might be one of the few who have found a way. But that way isn't found except by passing through almost unendurable pain, as is apparent in his work.

DM: Does language, then, reach a boundary where it can't cross over into certain areas of experience and come back whole?

Forché: It's interesting, the idea of boundaries. If you view langauge as a means of reporting and recording, then, yes, there are boundaries everywhere. If language itself is a force that has created our consciousness, that *is* capable of generating a world, then there are no boundaries.

Again, turning to the work of Paul Celan, what happened with language? *Within* Paul Celan, what happened? It emerged broken, fragmented, possible, suggestive, in agony. That is why his language is to be trusted. He is never facile. The boundary that I perceive has to do with one's intentions. As one moves farther from events, they become more apparently complex. And it becomes impossible to say *one* thing, which would not only be reductive, but exclusive, and would therefore create a notion of privilege within the poem.

The other difficulty is with the position of the speaker, with the creation of the fictional, first-person voice that then attempts to speak about things. Very often this voice is most especially speaking of its own sensitivity and positing a "self" to be regarded. That might be an inappropriate act, if the self derives its authority from its privilege over the "other," whether this be the privilege of knowledge or experience, and whether the "other" be the implied reader or the one to whom the poem is addressed. That is not to say that witness mustn't be borne, that testimony mustn't be attempted. Within the poem, or the language, or the text, it is possible to question this voice, or to permit a dialogue of selves, or at least to render the artifice apparent. Lately I've had difficulty with the first-person, lyric, narrative, free verse poem. I began by questioning the idea of closure, which almost always implies linearity, and then to contemplate the idea of resolution, and this has provoked a revolutionary change in my thinking and in my own work. In my new work I have been attempting to rupture that voice and to critique it from within in order to expose its artifice.

For five years I wrote fragments and notes, which I kept in a binder. The binder grew to two or three reams of paper. I hadn't a poem. I thought with some amusement that I'd been abandoned by the Muse, who suspected me of infidelity because I had spent too much time doing other work. But I *had* written every day, and I did have these reams of paper. There's a proverb: "Whatever keeps you from doing your work has become your work." I looked at this material and realized that it constituted the beginning of my new work. I wasn't writing the poem I had written in the past, and the only leap I needed to make was to acknowledge that fact. So I'm attempting to honor and continue this new form rather than dismissing page after page as mere notes toward "the poem."

There is another proverb: "When the student is ready, the teacher will come." I began to discover other poets and thinkers who were of great help to me. I read the work of Jacques Joubert, translated by Paul Auster. Then I rediscovered Evan S. Connell, his *Notes in a Bottle Found on a Beach in Carmel,* then his *Points for a Compass Rose,* and, finally, *St. Augustine's Pigeon.* I began to read Jean-François Lyotard and Walter Benjamin, then the works of René Char. I've also been translating, with William Kulik, the *Selected Poems* of Robert Desnos. One work has led me to another and another. I feel that I've broken through something, and there is new territory, and there are new guides. That's what seems to have happened.

DM: Are you talking about "The Angel of History"?

Forché: Yes. Well, that's a tentative title. The work shows no sign of coming to a last page. It's already one hundred and fifty pages long. It's composed of sequences. I wouldn't say that there are individual poems. The title comes from Walter Benjamin, from his work *Illuminations:*

> This is how one pictures the angel of history. His face is turned toward the past. Where we perceive a chain of events, he sees one single catastrophe which keeps piling wreckage upon wreckage and hurls it in front of his feet. The angel would like to stay, awaken the dead, and make whole what has been smashed. But a storm is blowing in from Paradise; it has got caught in his wings with such violence that the angel can no longer close them. The storm irresistibly propels him into the future to which his back is turned, while the pile of debris before him grows skyward.

I began the new work on April 4 of last year, and within a few days it was coming of itself. There were six voices. One of them was an interrogator, or a simple questioner. And one of them I recognized as a woman who had shared a hospital room with me in the Hôtel Dieu in Paris two years ago. We were together for a week. She was a German Jew who had spent the war years hiding in barns in Europe, making her way farm to farm. The first night when I was brought into the hospital, I was very depressed, particularly at having to leave my husband and newborn son. I was given a room with Elie. She was awake in the middle of the night, sitting at the edge of her bed, peeling her skin from her body. She had acute eczema. She turned to me and asked, "And *what* are you?" She didn't say: Who are you? or What is your name? So I answered, "I am a poet." And she responded, "I am also a poet." We talked all night and all the next day and next. Her voice later entered this work. Some of the other voices I am uncertain of— one seems to be the voice of the poetry itself and not a human being.

I'm immersed in this work completely. I've been working daily in Provincetown, in two separate residences, both facing the bay. When I leave this place, my voice and the voices of the others also depart. So the condition of the work is such that it has to be completed here, I think, where it began.

If events occur in the work, they are perceived from their periphery. The events are not central. The work is "about" history, time, and perception more than about lives or occurrences.

DM: Yours is often a poetry of conversation with friends and relatives, present or absent. It seems that the conversations are almost a means of survival. What is making them happen?

Forché: Dislocation. When I was very young, I was deeply affected by Czeslaw Milosz's *The Captive Mind* and, in particular, by the assertion that: "If a thing exists in one place, it will exist everywhere." In this passage he describes a village in which everyone is going about their business—going to work, pedaling bicycles, with baguettes and newspapers and so on. Everyone is very preoccupied with the day's activities in the day's beginning. And the village is bombed. The next day in the rubble someone is trying to find a spare potato buried in the ruins. And so this provokes from Milosz a discussion about assumptions having to do with the "natural" order of things.

I began in childhood to be very disturbed by that idea. I was first aware of it in 1955, when *Life* magazine published an essay of the first photographs documenting the liberation of the camps by the Allies. I took this magazine to my mother, and I asked her to explain the photographs. There was one taken before the liberation, in which two soldiers were beating a woman with a chain. I asked my mother why they were doing this, and she answered, "Because they are Nazis." I asked her what Nazis were, and she decided that I was too young for an answer.

She took the magazine away and hid it from me because she thought I was too young for such photographs. But I found it and put it between the mattresses and took it out at different times in my childhood.

My grandmother Anna had often spoken of this kind of dislocation. She talked of coming to this country, of things that occurred in Europe before she came, of her father who was turned away at Ellis Island because of a sore on his leg. She never saw him again. When I was nineteen I married—but it's difficult for me to talk about this. I've always harbored a dark sense that the world is at risk.

DM: The word *nothing* appears relatively often in your poetry—for instance, in "The Island" and in "Ourselves or Nothing."

Forché: It's dangerous to try to explain some of these things because I doubt that I really know what they mean. I'm not making excuses. I remember reading a transcript of Joseph Brodsky's trial in the Soviet Union, and I remember him saying, when asked where his poetry came from, that he thought it came from God. I have the usual difficulties with God, but I would say that I felt very sympathetic to his answer in that context.

DM: Remembrance plays a large part in your work. In a sense your poetry is a rosary of names, as you said of Claribel Alegría's poetry. Memory—is it loss, an obstacle? Is it a source, nourishment?

Forché: Terrence Des Pres, in his book *The Survivor: An Anatomy of Life in the Death Camps,* spoke of survivors as men and women who simply kept watch over life. Memory must be kept alive; those who perish at the hands of others must not be forgotten. I'm not sure anymore if holding the memory before the eye, before consciousness, is in itself redemptive, but this work of incessant reminding seems to arise from the exigencies of conscience. In my own life the memory of certain of those who have died remains in very few hands. I can't let go of that work if I am of that number.

DM: You grew up outside of Detroit?

Forché: My first five years were spent in Detroit, then my father worked in Dearborn, and we lived in Farmington Township. My aunts and uncles remained in Detroit.

The city has changed dramatically since I was there. Its appearance has changed. The underlying reality hasn't—the extreme poverty, the racial segregation, racism, and violence. Since the demise of the automobile industry, things have gotten worse. I went back a few years ago and drove around alone, not realizing that this was no longer a wise thing to do. Perhaps because of my naïveté or my stupidity I had no problems. But sections of Detroit reminded me, physically, of Beirut.

DM: How does that make you feel?

Forché: As if I were always on my way to Beirut, from the beginning. It was strange, and very sad. On the other hand, for me Beirut was one of the most beautiful cities in the world, even in ruins. The most passionate and intense and vital of cities.

DM: From Detroit, a very industrial city, to San Salvador to Beirut to Johannesburg to Paris and the other cities you've been to—how does this all fit together?

Forché: I don't think you are speaking about geography now, as much as about the matter of socioeconomics. I was born in Detroit and was the eldest of seven children. My father was a tool-and-die maker and my mother a mother. Had it not been for President Johnson's "Great Society" programs, and my father's labor and willingness, and my mother's interest and encouragement, I would never have gone to a university. I wouldn't have imagined it possible. None of my friends, no one I grew up with and knew well, went to a university. All of my brothers and sisters later attended. I went to the only possible school, the very large state school, and became lost there in the beginning until a few professors read my work and took me under wing. They gave me the kind of attention usually given as a matter of course to students in smaller, more elite schools. I'm deeply grateful to them.

When I look at photographs of my younger self, I want to tell her—and she does seem often someone other than myself—not to worry, that she would one day travel and understand more about life, and perhaps even something about that horrifying photographic essay in *Life*.

I was very sad as a child. It was a sadness of the soul and had nothing to do with my upbringing. I return to Detroit once or twice a year if I can. And every time I go back I'm in a familiar world again, but farther from that world. When *The Country Between Us* became the Lamont selection, my mother baked a cake and decorated it with flowers and wrote in icing "Happy Lamont," and lit a candle, and my family sang the birthday song.

My childhood friends are poorer now than they were when we were growing up. They've suffered terribly this past decade, and it isn't getting better. We're talking about something very painful. It isn't possible for me to understand why I'm here in Provincetown in this rented house by the sea writing poetry while they are there, working and suffering.

DM: Does poetry feel, in some ways, superfluous or like a luxury?

Forché: No, no, never. Never a luxury. I didn't mean that. I meant that I have the luxury to think and write, yes, but poetry is a necessity. It has been written and spoken by those who work and suffer as well as by those who live in rented houses on the sea even for brief periods of their lives. If it is true that language creates consciousness, then the self is constituted in language. Poetry is a necessity, not a commodity, a necessity. The only danger is that this "self" will be constituted in a hegemonic discourse—

But it is poetry's great good fortune that it could never be commodified in this culture.

DM: So it won't be corrupted or used?

Forché: It seems difficult to corrupt something that has no value, as value is consigned by the culture.

DM: Does our culture's valuation of the poet and poetry, though, reflect its sense of people, since poetry often is people speaking more openly than usual?

Forché: Do you mean does the lack of value given to poetry reflect upon the lack of value given to person?

DM: Yes.

Forché: Probably it has to do with a lack of understanding of the human being. If someone wants to understand what a human being is, they should spend time with a corpse—the corpse of someone they knew; it is then less possible to make a mistake about what a human being is. This culture does not value the human body.

DM: Is there a type of numbness in our culture? In your poem "Return" you mention an absence of recognition.

Forché: It isn't numbness. It's ignorance. I used to believe more firmly in goodwill. I now suspect that goodwill is more precious and more rare than I'd previously supposed. I think that Americans want to be considered "good." There is an inherent sense of true morality in the American culture, almost inversely proportional to its manifestation. But it is there.

The source of this morality is historical and nearly always accompanied by the desire to occult American complicity in crimes against conscience.

For non–Native Americans, America is a nation of exiles in search of a homeland, and, now that this need for homeland has become interiorized and is experienced as interior exile, the homeland sought has become figurative.

Last week, during the summit [United States–Soviet summit conference held in Washington, December, 1987], I was reading the English translations of the poetry of Yunna Moritz before audiences in New York and Washington. Yunna Moritz was traveling as part of a PEN-sponsored delegation of Soviet writers visiting the United States. After one of these readings some of us were talking about the Russian idea that anyone who leaves the Motherland, for whatever reason, is a traitor. And the retort, of course, was that we were a country of such traitors, a people who, by that definition, are descended from traitors or are traitors ourselves. I exclude from this definition those brought here by force. This might be considered in any discussion having to do with the national character.

DM: The Vietnam War casts a shadow in some way over your work.

Forché: Over my life.

DM: What is that shadow?

Forché: That of my first husband and that of my childhood friend Joseph. The two. We grew up together. Joseph was three years older, but we were quite close. He left for Vietnam when I was sixteen and, at some point in his tour of duty, refused to do anymore fighting and was put into a stockade. He wrote letters to me from the stockade. His life when he returned from Vietnam was very harsh, with moments of respite which he spent in a Trappist monastery. When I was nineteen I married a man deeply scarred by the war. Many of the boys in my class in school—we were a class of eighty-seven students who had gone through grades one through twelve together—many went to Vietnam. A few died. Others were injured. The boy who kept pigeons returned a heroin addict.

During our high school years we were supportive of the war. We were fooled. We felt deeply patriotic, and we believed that the boys were dying for something worth fighting for and were to be supported. We were emotional and sentimental about ourselves and the war.

When I went to the university I discovered for the first time the other view, and I became, as a result of what had happened to my husband, very active in the antiwar movement, committed to nonviolent resistance. Because of my class background (or, some would say, despite it), I was uncomfortable with extreme radicalism. I suffered no estrangement from my parents and wasn't at ease with those who had. I didn't trust anyone who had the luxury of jeopardizing their education, an option I didn't perceive for myself.

Michael Herr says that Vietnam is what we had instead of happy childhoods. I think the war marked my generation, and I would define that generation as anyone, man or woman, who reached conscription age during America's involvement in Southeast Asia. No one of that generation was untouched by the war.

Sometimes, in the course of speaking about Central America, the subject of Vietnam is raised by a member of an audience. I have asked then how many people died in Vietnam. The hands go up one by one, and finally the answer is given that more than fifty-seven thousand died. The question was not how many North American soldiers, but how many people? More than two million. It isn't a trick, something to shame or fool an audience, but simply a means of reminding ourselves of what is easily forgotten here.

I suppose every writer is more marked by what happened in the earliest years. And for me those years include the war. I don't know that I'll ever be able to write directly about it, or certainly not until I'm older, which might be the reason why relatively little poetry has been written out of Vietnam. Bruce Weigl's work is the notable and fine exception. He is a veteran. Perhaps it takes longer for those who didn't fight—

Our writing reflects our concerns. Our consciousness, our sensibility is *in the* text. When something is missing, we note the omission. The war, for many of us, is missing.

DM: Can we talk a moment about violent imagery? Is there a danger in the gratuitous use of such imagery by people who have not been at risk? Can it become a sort of counterfeit poetic currency applied to language to add a supposed intensity?

Forché: Perhaps, but I would feel reluctant to suggest such a caveat, if by implication we are valuing the human imagination any less. It might be possible to counterfeit such experience, but never successfully, and there might be a danger, too, in relying upon the intensity of a grotesque image to compensate for a lack of intensity in the work, but then we would be speaking of falsification, distortion, and the poet's failure to honor the language.

The danger has more to do, I think, with assumptions the poet makes about the experience, and his or her ability to achieve empathetic imagination, which is never easy. Inherently dramatic material presents difficulties for the poet and challenges the poet's ability to mediate, or transform, the experience through the work. It is to this difficulty that Elytis refers, I think, when he speaks of the uselessness of competing with events.

It's said that Americans are inured to images of violence, but I don't think this has been caused by an inundation of images of *true* violence. We've been numbed by counterfeit images of violence and by our own insensitivity, our own inability to react. We've made of violence an abstraction. If we truly perceived the pain of a particular image—and let's refer to a photographic image now rather than a poetic one—such pain as is apparent in a photograph of a maimed victim of a Salvadoran death squad would be too excruciating, if truly perceived, to contemplate or regard.

In situations of extremity, rather than our becoming numb to pain, the pain worsens and lessens our ability to endure. Each death seems more difficult than the last, and each inflicts its wound on the survivor, who remains tender from that wound when the next is inflicted, when the next loss is suffered.

To write out of such extremity is to incise, with language, that same wound, to open it again, and, with utterance, to inscribe the consciousness. This inscription restructures the consciousness of the poet.

What has happened in America has less to do with violence itself than with the way such images of violence are read and with the desire to abstract the violence, as a means of anesthetization. As Americans, we cling, however precariously, to the myth of our staunch individualism. We are inclined to view ourselves as apart from others. Perhaps we do this because we are haunted by the past, by the occulted memory of the founding genocide. If it were true that we imagined ourselves as connected to others, as part of a larger human body, it would no longer be true that we would suffer the lack of feeling in ourselves which we now describe as the condition of being inured to images of violence.

I've read poetry that fails in its attempt to speak for the suffering of others. But it might have been the attempt itself that was wrongly thought, and the work was then doomed from the beginning. It's a question of where you position yourself with regard to others. Grace Paley suggests that we write and then take out all the lies. Sometimes it's difficult to recognize them—the lie, for example, of our own moral superiority.

DM: Do you think there is any kind of censorship operating in this country?

Forché: No, not in the strictest sense.

DM: Of neglect or omission?

Forché: In that sense, yes, of neglect *and* omission. And the censorship of crude self-interest, which has to do with the idea of what poetry is, not poetry but publishable poetry, grantable poetry. Such calculation engenders mediocrity.

There is evidence of a measure of self-censorship in the cyclical uproar about the question of the relationship between poetry and politics, which wouldn't even be taken seriously in any other country.

DM: El Salvador and South Africa—the differences in the political situations are obvious. You've been in both countries. Were there any particular differences *or* similarities that struck you while in South Africa?

Forché: I was in each place under different circumstances. I went to El Salvador in 1978 on January 4 at the invitation of a member of Claribel Alegría's family, who believed that it would benefit me to spend the period of my Guggenheim grant in Central America. This was before the period that is known in this country as the war. I didn't journey to a dangerous El Salvador but to a Salvador in silence, the silence of misery. Death squad activity was just beginning. While there, I was in contact with Michael McClintock, then of Amnesty International's international secretariat in London. We corresponded as Amnesty began to study the situation in El Salvador regarding human rights. I was a correspondent. Later I worked with the woman who was then the voice of Monsignor Romero's radio station YSAX. We collected information and provided that information to various human rights organizations by various means. I made several trips to Guatemala and returned to the United States from time to time. I left El Salvador for the last time on March 16, 1980. I've spoken elsewhere more extensively about this.

When my husband was assigned to return to Lebanon as photographic correspondent for *Time,* I accompanied him, having already experienced waiting here for his return. During that period I was often unable to reach him by phone and, on one occasion, was told by an international operator that his hotel had been shelled. When contact with the hotel management was established, I was informed that his room had been among those destroyed, and it wasn't until several hours later that I learned he had taken refuge in the basement during the shelling and was alive. I didn't want to relive those hours. When he told me he was going back, I said "not without me." I got a job with National Public Radio's "All Things Considered" program, through Noah Adams, and was assigned to broadcast from Lebanon via satellite to NPR, which I did.

In South Africa I was a housewife and wouldn't have received my visa otherwise. I was pregnant and accompanied by husband, who was a credentialed member of the foreign press. I've written previously in the *American Poetry Review* about my activities there. I had determined that my task would be to record everything I saw, to make a document, and to assist my husband with the documentary work of preserving photographs and testimony that would never reach the public through mass media but would remain available through alternative media groups.

My experiences were in great part determined by these various contexts. I don't want to make facile comparisons between the political situations of Central America and Lebanon and South Africa. I will say that in none of these countries was the United States perceived as a friend of the common people, the people whom I met, the working people. That condition unites my experience in these countries: Americans were not perceived as friends, and to be an American in that context is very instructive. My personal conditions usually had nothing to do with nationality, so I am speaking more about lessons regarding the perception of my country as a nation-state.

DM: In El Salvador and in South Africa you have seen the often painful effects of history and politics on people's lives. How has this affected *your* life?

Forché: History and politics affect everyone's life, everywhere, always. Any difficulties I've experienced have been relatively minor. There is no comparison between the experience of an outsider (such as I was) and the experience of someone whose own country is under seige or who is engaged in a struggle against injustice.

I wouldn't say that I am unaffected, however. In the context of my life here in the United States, I would say that it's true for both my husband and myself that there have been periods quite painful for us, in which we've found reassimilation difficult. We sometimes experience dislocation.

Experiences of extremity are not necessarily assimilated over time. In 1981, while attending a human rights conference for writers which was held in Canada, I had the occasion to talk with Jacobo Timerman. My experiences of El Salvador were still very fresh. I walked out into a hallway during a cocktail reception and found Jacobo Timerman alone. We walked a little. He said, "It's rather difficult for me to attend these things sometimes." And then, "My terror is that, even after twenty years, it might not be possible to forget." He explained that he did not mean, by "forget," to relegate his experience to oblivion but to be able to live in certain moments, *as if* he had never endured that particular pain.

For my husband and myself the most difficult period was in South Africa. If it weren't for the threat of abduction, we would rather have returned to Beirut. We would rather have been shelled again, would rather have stayed in West Beirut, even again through the attacks of the American battleship USS *New Jersey* than bear the psychological terror of South Africa, even as whites. What we felt there was absolute and, for us, unendurable because we didn't have the psychological stamina for it. We're in awe of those who have been conditioned to endure such a horror and still preserve their humanity.

When we left South Africa to give birth to our son in Europe, rather than on South Africa's soil, our plan had originally been to return there. We'd committed ourselves to two years of work, but I would say that we weren't unhappy when our applications for visa renewals were denied by the South African government. It wasn't as if we weren't expecting the denial. We were half-expecting it. But we were relieved to receive it. We'd become parents, and we were at a crossroads ourselves. We decided against further subjecting ourselves to conditions of war voluntarily, as we had done for several years. My husband had been a war photographer for twelve years. He'd lived through the war in Nicaragua against Somoza, then was in El Salvador until 1982, then in Beirut until 1984, and then in South Africa until 1986. In the profession of war photography there are two ways out: death or early retirement. Most don't retire. My husband had come perilously close to death on many occasions, and we felt within ourselves this new responsibility, not only to our baby and each other but to the work which we imagined we had to do. And so we believed that, because we were older, and war photography is a profession for young men and women who believe in their immortality, that he might not be as equipped for it, as agile, as lucky as he'd been in the past.

Also, he had lost his sense of immortality, which is in itself a kind of shield.

I should add that I am not, by nature, a courageous person and was always afraid, and my fear manifested itself in different ways.

DM: One or two more questions. Would you mind talking a moment about Terrence Des Pres and about your friendship with him over the years?

Forché: It hasn't been a month since he died. He was one of my dearest and oldest friends. He was my mentor, my brother, my confidant, and, more than once, my defender. Although he himself was not a Jew, he so deeply entered the body of survival testimony in his work on the Holocaust that I imagine when he died there were six million souls to receive him.

We began our correspondence in 1976. I had contracted viral meningitis, and his book was among the few I read during convalescence. Later we became friends, and he guided my work for eleven years. He also guided my life and thought in a very particular and special way.

In 1979 and 1980, during one of my trips home from El Salvador, we visited each other. He'd been having difficulty after completing the book and was casting about for something that might so move him that he could commit himself to it fully. I had box of poetry books in the trunk of my car. Nazim Hikmet was there. We read "On Living" together and moved from book to book, most of them of contemporary poets in translation. Terrence was very deeply moved by the poems and so began his next long work. The book, *Praises and Dispraises,* was completed before his death and will be published in August [1988]. The subject of the work is the relation between poetry and the political, and it is a deeply intelligent work.

I will miss him much more than I could ever say. He was the only person with whom I was always in contact, during my time in El Salvador and beyond it. If I want to know now what I was feeling in those years, I have only to go to his fireproof safe in upstate New York and read the letters he preserved for me.

He was morally brilliant and luminously intelligent. Among his friends, he is irreplaceable.

DM: In your poem "Selective Service" you write, "In what time do we live that it is too late / to have children?" You now have a son. How has having a child changed your life?

Forché: For Harry, I think, it was the beginning to his self-preservation. In many ways, the beginning of a new life. It was his way of saying *no* to the evil he had seen. For me it was the fulfillment of a long desire. I think that the idea that it is "too late to have children" was an intellectualization, substituting for an explanation for my refusal of that desire, whether because of the circumstances of my life or my own self-absorption. Sean Christophe's arrival in our lives profoundly changed us and is the most wonderful thing that has ever happened to us.

He may not have a full human life if the earth ... if *we* do not protect his generation. Our decision to be receptive to his conception had nothing to do with any assurance we felt about human survival. But our children must also desire to be with us—I'm already speaking as if there were two of them, and there isn't a second yet—that is how much I hope.

The Colonel

What you have heard is true. I was in his house. His wife carried a tray of coffee and sugar. His daughter filed her nails, his son went out for the night. There were daily papers, pet dogs, a pistol on the cushion beside him. The moon swung bare on its black cord over the house. On the television was a cop show. It was in English. Broken bottles were embedded in the walls around the house to scoop the kneecaps from a man's legs or cut his hands to lace. On the windows there were gratings like those in liquor stores. We had dinner, rack of lamb, good wine, a gold bell was on the table for calling the maid. The maid brought green mangoes, salt, a type of bread. I was asked how I enjoyed the country. There was a brief commercial in Spanish. His wife took everything away. There was some talk then of how difficult it had become to govern. The parrot said hello on the terrace. The colonel told it to shut up, and pushed himself from the table. My friend said to me with his eyes: say nothing. The colonel returned with a sack used to bring groceries home. He spilled many human ears on the table. They were like dried peach halves. There is no other way to say this. He took one of them in his hands, shook it in our faces, dropped it into a water glass. It came alive there. I am tired of fooling around he said. As for the rights of anyone, tell your people they can go fuck themselves. He swept the ears to the floor with his arm and held the last of his wine in the air. Something for your poetry, no? he said. Some of the ears on the floor caught this scrap of his voice. Some of the ears on the floor were pressed to the ground.

May 1978

Return

for Josephine Crum

Upon my return to America, Josephine:
the iced drinks and paper umbrellas, clean
toilets and Los Angeles palm trees moving
like lean women, I was afraid more than
I had been, even of motels so much so
that for months every tire blow-out
was final, every strange car near the house
kept watch and I strained even to remember
things impossible to forget. You took
my stories apart for hours, sitting
on your sofa with your legs under you

and fifty years in your face.
                              So you know
now, you said, what kind of money
is involved and that *campesinos* knife
one another and you know you should
not trust anyone and so you find a few
people you will trust. You know the mix
of machetes with whiskey, the slip of the tongue
that costs hundreds of deaths.
You've seen the pits where men and women
are kept the few days it takes without
food and water. You've heard the cocktail
conversation on which their release depends.
So you've come to understand why
men and women of good will read
torture reports with fascination.
Such things as water pumps
and co-op farms are of little importance
and take years.
It is not Che Guevara, this struggle.
Camillo Torres is dead. Victor Jara
was rounded up with the others, and José
Martí is a landing strip for planes
from Miami to Cuba. Go try on
Americans your long, dull story
of corruption, but better to give
them what they want: Lil Milagro Ramirez,
who after years of confinement did not
know what year it was, how she walked
with help and was forced to shit in public.
Tell them about the razor, the live wire,
dry ice and concrete, grey rats and above all
who fucked her, how many times and when.
Tell them about retaliation: José lying
on the flat bed truck, waving his stumps
in your face, his hands cut off by his
captors and thrown to the many acres
of cotton, lost, still, and holding
the last few lumps of leeched earth.

Tell them of José in his last few hours
and later how, many months later,
a labor leader was cut to pieces and buried.
Tell them how his friends found
the soldiers and made them dig him up
and ask forgiveness of the corpse, once
it was assembled again on the ground
like a man. As for the cars, of course
they watch you and for this don't flatter
yourself. We are all watched. We are
all assembled.

            Josephine, I tell you
I have not rested, not since I drove
those streets with a gun in my lap,
not since all manner of speaking has
failed and the remnant of my life
continues onward. I go mad, for example,
in the Safeway, at the many heads
of lettuce, papayas and sugar, pineapples
and coffee, especially the coffee.
And when I speak with American men,
there is some absence of recognition:
their constant Scotch and fine white
hands, many hours of business, penises
hardened by motor inns and a faint
resemblance to their wives. I cannot
keep going. I remember the American
attaché in that country: his tanks
of fish, his clicking pen, his rapt
devotion to reports. His wife wrote
his reports. She said as much as she
gathered him each day from the embassy
compound, that she was tired of covering
up, sick of his drinking and the loss
of his last promotion. She was a woman
who flew her own plane, stalling out
after four martinis to taxi on an empty
field in the *campo* and to those men

and women announce she was there to help.
She flew where she pleased in that country
with her drunken kindness, while Marines
in white gloves were assigned to protect
her husband. It was difficult work, what
with the suspicion on the rise in smaller
countries that gringos die like other men.
I cannot, Josephine, talk to them.

And so, you say, you've learned a little
about starvation: a child like a supper scrap
filling with worms, many children strung
together, as if they were cut from paper
and all in a delicate chain. And that people
who rescue physicists, lawyers and poets
lie in their beds at night with reports
of mice introduced into women, of men
whose testicles are crushed like eggs.
That they cup their own parts
with their bedsheets and move themselves
slowly, imagining bracelets affixing
their wrists to a wall where the naked
are pinned, where the naked are tied open
and left to the hands of those who erase
what they touch. We are all erased
by them, and no longer resemble decent
men. We no longer have the hearts,
the strength, the lives of women.
Your problem is not your life as it is
in America, not that your hands, as you
tell me, are tied to do something. It is
that you were born to an island of greed
and grace where you have this sense
of yourself as apart from others. It is
not your right to feel powerless. Better
people than you were powerless.
You have not returned to your country,
but to a life you never left.

1980

Derek Walcott

Derek Walcott was born in 1930 in Saint Lucia near the Caribbean island of Trinidad. He is prominent as both a poet and playwright. His many volumes of poetry include *In a Green Night: Poems, 1948–1960* (1962), *The Castaway and Other Poems* (1965), *The Gulf and Other Poems* (1970), *Another Life* (1973), *Sea Grapes* (1976), *The Star-Apple Kingdom* (1979), *The Fortunate Traveller* (1981), *Midsummer* (1984), *Collected Poems: 1948–1984* (1986), and *The Arkansas Traveller* (1987). His most recent is his book-length poem *Omeros,* published in 1990. He founded the Trinidad Theater Workshop, and his plays have been widely produced in the United States. He was the recipient of the 1971 Obie Award for *The Dream on Monkey Mountain.* His books of plays include *The Sea at Dauphin* (1954), *Ione* (1957), *Ti-Jean and His Brothers* (1958), *The Dream on Monkey Mountain* (1967), *O Babylon!* (1976), *Remembrance* (1979), and *Pantomime* (1981). He has three children and teaches at Boston University.

This interview took place in September, 1987, shortly after his return from a summer in Trinidad. We spoke in the living room of his apartment in Brookline, near Boston University. On the walls hung several bright watercolors of the sea and shore in the Caribbean. In a bookcase nearby stood Joseph Brodsky's *Less Than One.*

In November, 1990, I briefly interviewed Walcott again. His comments are appended to the end of this interview.

David Montenegro: Could we start with "Another Life," your longest poem, and, in particular, with Part One, "A Divided Child"? Would you talk about the divisions, beginning with painting, since in the poem you start with painting and, in a sense, end by choosing poetry as a vocation?
Derek Walcott: I didn't give up painting. I do a lot of storyboards for the filmscripts and the plays and do them in a lot of detail. I draw carefully, though a storyboard merely dramatizes an incident or focuses on a different angle, and so on. I still do a fair amount of watercolor painting from nature. I haven't done—as I thought I would have—much oil painting on canvas.

Last summer I strongly resolved that I would go back to the rigidities of drawing and painting, and that I'd give myself a heavy schedule for doing them daily. But that got broken again. When I'm in the Caribbean, my prime attraction is toward representing it in painting. So I think there is still a dual attraction for me to painting and poetry.

The division one talks about I don't think is ultimately a sort of career decision between becoming a painter or a poet. You can't, obviously, put words into paintings, but, on the other hand, I had the absorption of the visual that is part of poetry and can be very strong, and I think that must be present in the sort of *frame* of work on a line or even a stanza sometimes. On the other hand, I have a quite different approach to what I'd like to achieve in painting. I think it's perhaps not as—I wouldn't say ambitious—not as arduous perhaps, not as sweaty or industrious as with the writing.

There's more to it than that though. The older I get I realize that I'm a pretty competent draftsman, and I'll get better with practice. And the watercolors are getting better. But all I'm after really is a visual representation of a thing that I see in front of me. I am very square when it comes to painting, especially watercolor, because in watercolor you can't really muck around with abstraction. It's too delicate a medium. Oils can be very rhetorical, in that sense, very pretentious sometimes, especially abstract painting. So I love watercolor because it's harder really than oils. It's less egotistical.

So I haven't given up the idea of painting. I suppose, in "Another Life," the section I'd refer to would be the one that talks about what exists in the wrist of a painter—the true painter—which is a very confident flourish, a feel for the weight of the paint and how it's confidently manipulated that I didn't think I had. I don't think now that that's necessarily a condemnation. There are different kinds of painters. There are those who layer and build and those who slash and mount and increase the surface of the canvas by strokes. There is a big difference between even, say, late Rembrandt and Degas. So I may have said once that I don't feel I have the life inside my wrists to be a painter because at the time I may have been comparing myself with other painters whose style was much more vehement than mine.

DM: Is part of your attraction to watercolor the way watercolor can catch nuances of light?

Walcott: Watercolor's an extremely difficult medium in the tropics. It's more or less a temperate medium, though not entirely, because you have obvious exceptions in Winslow Homer and Hopper, for instance. In the tropics, the division that exists between the horizon and the bottom of the horizon, in other words between the sky and the foreground, is extremely dramatic. It's almost complementary, in terms of the hues that are there. The incredible blue that is there in the tropics is almost impossible to get—the *heat* of that blue—in watercolor. And it may be silly to think it's because the paint is made in temperate countries. That's maybe a facetious attitude to have but look at the palette that exists for watercolor in the tropics, where shadows are black, black-green, or contain black, which you can't use really in watercolor. And the fact that you saturate the surface of the paper sometimes with a tone on which you can dip the paint is not quite useful in the tropics. I mean here the lines are hard, but there the lines are hard-edged, and you have a very hard time manipulating them into any kind of subtlety. If you see a negative of the tropics, you realize why cameramen always find it much harder to photograph in tropic light than they do in the magic hour at twilight or right after dawn.

One other thing that astonishes and exasperates painters from the north is that what they see in front of them is a lot of green, basic hues of green, green and red. I remember I was going out to do some painting, and there was a German tourist in a small hotel where I was staying. He said he couldn't paint there because it was *too green*. I think it's the way he looks at the color. Obviously, there is subtlety, an immense amount of variety in tones of the green that exist in front of you. And there is haze in the rain or early morning, and so on. But, in a way, forms in the tropics are almost emblematic; they're very hard and bright. I think that to try to capture that on paper means that the words have to be used almost as heavily as strokes are used in paint. Just to put down "blue" or "green" is not enough, because that's a postcard. What matters is how you manage to get into that blue whatever other variations and subtleties and orchestrations that one tries to get in the *words* so that you can feel the sensuality, the presence and the texture of, say, water and crisp sand, of going into cool water, that sudden change of temperature that exists between light and shade in the tropics.

DM: So it's a problem of very strong contrasts and maybe too much light?

Walcott: Well, if you say it's too much light, it means God has made a mistake, you know. There can never be too much light. It's the glare that is there. No one runs away from glare in terms of what's to be depicted. That's like saying in the Arctic it's all white. But it's all ice. I don't know, it leads to a kind of literature of indolence, a concept of lethargy, you know, of the siesta, of decay, of afternoon languor that is really more theatrical than real. It's just *literary*, that idea of the tropics, really.

DM: You mentioned different types of blue. Is it that there is not a language for the different shades of blue, or the *particular* shades of blue, and, in a sense, through words you are trying to identify those shades that have not been named?

Walcott: A passage I always quote when I'm teaching is the first chapter of *A Farewell to Arms* in which the model is really a combination of Gertrude Stein and Cézanne. Sometimes I point out to the class certain effects Hemingway achieved by watching Cézanne. One was to let the stroke of the word *blue* appear very late in the first few paragraphs. So that the first startling stroke of the word *blue* comes much later after the dust and the leaves and so on, and the waters swiftly moving are blue in the channels. Now, *what* blue is not described, but the point is that the stroke is put down with exactly the same cubic area that a Cézanne stroke is put on a bleached background. Or, say, the rocks or trees are skeletally or sparingly indicated, and then that stroke appeared next to another hue—a blue or a lilac, and so on. Hemingway's technique comes from a scrutiny particularly, I think, of watercolor.

DM: What stereotypes do you have to break through in language to bring out the reality of the tropics?

Walcott: Well, you know, every truth becomes a cliché after a while. I came on a break this summer from Saint Lucia to Boston. On the first or second day I thought my body would burst from the humidity. The acute, implacable discomfort that I felt in the house was nothing compared to the kind of heat that exists in the tropics. It can be fierce, scorching sun there, but you've got only to step into the shade to be cool. And that contrast is—in terms of temperature—melodramatic. So when people give an image of the tropics as a place of swelter and indolence and exasperation and languor and idleness and so on . . . well, I was devastated by the humidity of a northern summer. Now if we amplify that kind of cliché to say, well, in hot countries nothing is ever produced, we would have to say that for the bulk of the time that summer represents in all northern countries *nothing* can be produced. And it should not be, if you're going by that kind of geographic description of what is expected of certain locales. Whereas more can be produced in the summer in the Caribbean because it's cooler. So that concept of the tropics being a place of intense heat where nothing happens and nothing stirs makes for good fiction, but it's not true.

But I'm going deeper than simply the climate. I'm thinking of an attitude that's both geographic and historical. Hot countries, until the emergence of the Latin American novelist and poets, were not supposed to produce anything. It's a sort of Graham Greenish fantasy about the tropics that was perpetuated. But Greece is a hot country, and you've got to ask: What has Greece produced?

DM: What other divisions have come into play in your life besides painting/poetry, light/sound?

Walcott: I suppose the biggest cleft, the biggest division, the biggest chasm, is cultural, in a way. Obviously—however jaded a subject it is, and I do feel jaded talking about it—race is an enormous one. Not for *me.* I look at the chasm; I don't share it. But it's obviously here. And it seems to have widened every day in America. As an observer, I think the reality of saying this is a further fact that the Constitution of the United States is so democratic. Not only is the Constitution almost defensive in its democracy, it seems to say daily that, *despite* this or that, people are equal. And it's the despite part, I think, that I experience watching active day to day now. And that is quite frightening.

Not just racism. I think the examination that is required is to ask: Is one inhabiting a kind of fallacy or fantasy, a sort of suspended Constitution within one's daily life that is not enacted by various races, whether it's by the Italian or the Jew or the black or the Puerto Rican? And what holds that fantasy together? It's basically fragile. It's more like a rotten string than anything that really binds all the various races around the concept of democracy. And that is, I think, perhaps the most frightening aspect of America. As absolutely beautiful and true as the ethics of the Constitution are, the reality of them moves further and further away daily, I think. And one must, of course, adhere to and believe in the principles that are there. But they have been turning into a kind of gospel as opposed to a reality. You read the New Testament and see the same thing—that men must love one another, and Christ is the example, and so on—but nobody lives the New Testament. And it may be that, in this democracy, the equivalent of the New Testament is in the Constitution. So one does not actually live it; one can only believe that it exists and pay homage to it, as a sort of inside faith, but not in practice. I've spent some years in America now, and that separation is as if the Constitution were a church that you go into from time to time and come out of. Monday morning you don't adhere to it; the citizens do not go by that faith.

DM: So a person pays homage but goes away without being held to practice?

Walcott: No, I'm not saying it's not practiced. There are some fantastically astonishing things in the practice of democracy in America that continue. Among them, the press's relentless, self-adoring idea of justice is useful. *Many* things work and keep the bonds strong. But it's the one Constitution that says you must do *this.* It's the closest thing to the New Testament instruction that exists. But now, I think, it's become as remote, in a way, as the concept of brotherly love. It's not a *paradox;* it's just a frightening kind of fantasy.

DM: It seems almost as if, because of the diversity of cultures and races in this country, people have become gradually *less* tolerant of difference.

Walcott: You have to go into a very deep reason why that is so. It would have to do, perhaps, with the economic structure of the country, in a place where the width between those who have property and the people out in the street, the homeless, is staggering. The multiracial aspect of the society can be visually exciting, as it is in New York. But in a city like Port of Spain in Trinidad, you see a more active multiracial tolerance practiced in what is supposed to be a backward, smaller country than you would in any city in the States and certainly in New York now. But I don't think it's simply because of the size; I don't think it's simply because of the hustle and the competition and the capitalism and all that. I think that there's a lot more to be said for the excitingly real variety of races from all over the world that exists in the concentrated place called Port of Spain. I'm not pretending that there isn't a lot of hostility and prejudice—if you wish to call it that. But I do not consider it to be really profound. I think the day-to-day exchange between the Indian, the Chinese, the Portugese, and Syrian, the black, and so on has historical depth and guilt attached to it, et cetera, but the daily practice of that life in that city is not one that contains any threat of violence. You're always on the edge of violence in every city in America—of racial violence. And why is that? I think it's got to do with money; it's got to do with who protects those who have money.

You can use the same argument, I imagine, in the ex-colonies. But there's also a way of life that is different. There's a sort of elation about life, I think, an enjoyment of it that is totally separate. And if you want to talk about division, *that's* a division to me when I come here. When I come back here I find that I'm clenching my teeth a little more, I have to shout a little harder, I have to keep pointing out that I'm not ready to take shit from anybody, and it's really a backup attitude, you know. Not because I'm black, but because I think it's the average experience of anyone in the city.

DM: Your work is dominated by poems that are set out-of-doors. Much poetry in northern countries is indoor poetry. This suggests a different relationship to nature.

Walcott: No, I don't think that entirely. The closeted and hermetic poets that exist now in northern poetry may have as much to do with syntax as with climate. The sort of tight-sphinctered, monosyllabic thing that passes for good verse these days is not only a matter of weather, of people staying inside. The pages of a lot of great American poets like Frost and Whitman are ventilated by wind and by weather. And it's very easy to call them nature poets—any of these adjectives that come before poets just to be dismissive. *All* poets are nature poets—or poets by nature, which is the same thing really. But I know what you mean, that there is a kind of closing in of American poetry that I don't think has really to do with the outside or the inside because you can get stanzas written by people who may be in Montana and the poetry still feels closeted; it still feels tight. It's some sort of screwing tight of the mind that has happened, I think, which may be derivative of a *mis*reading of William Carlos Williams, a misreading of Japanese or Chinese poetry. A lot of people who practice what they think is Chinese poetry forget the *width* of the thing and think it's all minimal and modest. There's a great epic width to Chinese poetry. It's an immense country. And when somebody talks about a river in China, it's not a brook up in Vermont.

I *do* feel that American theater is closeted and chambered and dark and small and so on. But why is that? I think what's missing is a kind of width of the imagination that very few American playwrights have. Alien subjects aren't approached. They aren't wild enough, I find, for the size of the country. If you measured the height of American theater—when I say height I mean in terms of its concept and what it dares—you'd imagine that it was written in a country no bigger than, say, half of Wales.

DM: So it's almost agoraphobic?

Walcott: Well, it's enclosing; it is shuttered. There are a lot of themes that are just not approached by American writers. One of them, obviously, is the epic of the Indian or the epic—in theater—of crossing the country. I don't just mean the Western; I mean something with a scale and width to it like Whitman's poetry. You don't get that feeling of scale in American theater. And it doesn't have any *tribal* power. It's all very hermetic and private and individualistic and diaristic. It's very prosaic and journalistic, in that sense, and very conservative in form. I suppose why I say that is to point out that, when one talks about an outdoor theater, there's no outdoor literature. There's no reason why American literature shouldn't have that width to it.

DM: In northern literature is there a feeling of having been pulled up by the roots?

Walcott: I speak from a position of luck and privilege, because I share two climates, but perhaps the fact that poets keep wearing shoes, you know, gives them small feet or tight feet and corns. A lot of modern poetry is like having corns. It hurts. It's tight and small.

And I don't mean just going barefoot up on the Cape. What I mean is to be barefoot in spirit. Maybe I'm being too Gravesian, but I think if that doesn't happen poetry dies. If a man keeps walking on leather, on concrete every day of his life, and if you take that to represent the spirit of poetry, then it's going to get corns, it's going to get withered and chilblains. I think the poet goes unshod, and that's for the whole feel of the thing. To walk about barefoot, like Whitman said, really is the first need.

And the shape of the human foot is not a matter of style. A lot of modern poets are stylists. It's French prose poetry or it's Williams or it's Southwest or whatever. It's like different cuts of shoes, styles of shoes.

DM: In *Midsummer* you say: "No language is neutral." Could you expand a little on this?

Walcott: Well, I think the surrounding text may help. Obviously, when you enter language, you enter a kind of choice which contains in it the political history of the language, the imperial width of the language, the fact that you're either subjugated by the language or you have had to dominate it. So language is not a place of retreat, it's not a place of escape, it's not even a place of resolution. It's a place of struggle.

DM: So, particularly in colonial countries, *any* choice of words—this is an exaggeration—is, in a sense, a political choice, or there is a stance involved?

Walcott: Well, in a way, it's only the proportion of stress that matters. It's surely more theatrical for people to say to what is called the Third World: Well, you have inherited this language, and how do you feel *in* it, and that sort of nonsense. But, obviously, in a country of tyranny there is a political choice involved. The next word you write could get you in jail, really. You avoid the next word or you put it down at the risk of whatever happened to all sorts of poets in that totalitarian regime. And, in a sense, if you expand that and intensify it within yourself and you make yourself your own regime, when you're as dictatorial and as threatening to yourself as you are, it's the defiance of that inner regime that makes you choose and not cower in the courage of using the right word.

If you use a political metaphor, I would say that every poet is imprisoned in a system that is himself, that he is *jailed* in himself, and that that effort to get out of that jail is the struggle he has or the defiance he has in having the guts to use the next word without the safety or the cliché of repetition. And that inner political action of the choice of the next word, if it were broadened and taken out into a visible arena, is not any different than being on the witness stand in front of a regime. And the regime that is rigid is the one that says inside himself: Are you bullshiting, or are you talking the truth? Are you conforming to a tradition that is a regime or being outré and fake revolutionary to astonish the regime, or are you simply writing as honestly as you can without self-astonishment, without self-congratulation, without self-heroism or even martyrdom, and continuing by the process and the line that you think is true to the language that you are working in? The inner prison that exists is one that's outside and yet is inside the totalitarian regime. I consider that to be obvious in our time. And whether it's Mandelstam or Herbert or Milosz or even Seamus Heaney in the conflict in Ireland, there *is* an inner prison that one recognizes in oneself, and one is both judge and prisoner. But you don't plead and you don't whine; you state the condition.

DM: And, in a sense, you're always guilty.

Walcott: Well, guilty until the next time (*laughs*). But, no, you don't stay in guilt. I really think that—not for the poet but obviously for the race in the twentieth century—poetry has never been more urgent than it is now. What we have are regimes that are not just opposed to the idea of poetry as something effete but as something that is really threatening. We're in a time of ideas, *heavy* ideas, not ones that are as emblematical or as simple as, say, the church versus the state. We are in a whole area of conscience that is articulated, that has to be articulated within the regimes themselves. Looking at a poet like Seamus, for instance, it would be very easy for him not to concern himself or to concern himself on a level where his conscience is not so tortured. It would be very easy to write a kind of poem that is abstract and that is theoretical. But to share, to be involved in—take someone like Adam Zagajewski—is not only physical. There is a small community of conscience that exists all over the world now which brings poets closer together into a very small brotherhood. They may come from anywhere, from India or Poland or wherever. But it's like a concentration camp.

DM: Is there another danger of oversimplifying, of taking an issue at face value and writing a poetry that has a pro and con?

Walcott: Exactly. Those choices are even more demonic than those raised by the average, say, nature poem—if you want to call it that—because the temptations are enormous. One can then move into being bard, spokesman, martyr, even coward as a role. And all of these are roles offered by the regime, by the *exterior* regime, and the poet can be tempted, without knowing that he has been tempted, to become any one of those. I think a lot of great poets at some point move into that kind of high flatulence in which they may be believing at the time that they are absolutely necessary, that their voice, that particular pitch of the voice is necessary for the time. It exists in all great poets, but it's just that part of the great poet that you turn from and say sometimes: Oh, give me a break, knock it off, cool it down, you know—whether it's the "prophetic" vision of a bitter prophecy or whatever it is. Unless it has that kind of *total* devastating light or blight that exists in Blake, for instance, who is talking the truth. You sometimes hear it in Yeats, you hear it in Virgil, you hear it in Frost. It is that bardic voice that, after a certain age, a poet is attracted to without knowing that he is on a platform bellowing.

DM: Is it as if the pronoun *I* invaded the pronoun *we* without the poet intentionally taking on a collective voice?

Walcott: Well, there are kinds of egotism that are wonderful. There is an exhilarating egotism in Whitman. You know: I embrace everybody. And that's great because it's unabashed variety in the man. It's in Joyce. And it may be in the nature of the poet to be like that. It's often that sometimes a poet who has written great things may feel that, well, it's time for the big work, it's time for the big theme. And Joyce said it: to create the uncreated conscience of my race. Stephen says it, and then Stephen/Joyce goes ahead and does it in *Ulysses.* That's a sort of wonderful vanity or apparent vanity that's exhilarating because it is really a humility that is undertaken. There's no more humble, self-annihilating person than Walt Whitman. The "I" in Walt Whitman is not Walt Whitman. The "I" is you, the reader; the "I" is Whitman, but it's also you; it's man, a pair of eyes only.

It's the other kind of moment that's political. This may be a terrible thing to say, but there are moments in which a race may be undergoing a terrible amount of persecution and may require a great deal of physical fortitude and spiritual strength, and somehow the ages pass that moment by, and there's no poetry out of it. It isn't because poetry is above suffering; it isn't that poetry is something that just swallows up suffering, but there's always a very thin little light that may be there, a little crack in the door that is much more important than all the blaring trumpets or the beating on the chests and the wailing. Mankind has wailed about itself for centuries, and nothing has changed. And the poet, no matter what the condition, knows this, that it hasn't changed. The rivers run into the sea, and the sea is not full. But it's that knowledge, in middle age I think particularly, that attracts the bardic tone. I suffer from it. I get bouts of it, and I have evidence that I've been tempted by it to my embarrassment. It's not the high pitch I'm talking about either. Sometimes the thing opens and there's a total ventilation of the mind, and it's genuinely wide and a part of what you feel. That's very different from the putting on the mantle and prophesying or putting on the thorns *and* the mantle and suffering.

Every poet is full of it. Every poet is full of pompous or modest bullshit. It alternates. You can look through any contemporary poet—or any poet almost—and say: Oh, yes, this is a scuffling and a lowered-eyebrow kind of "I'm not fit to be, et cetera," which is the reverse of ambition, or you can get the other thing, that I alone know what's happening.

DM: Much of your poetry is filled with contradictions; it gives the feeling that there is no safe ledge to lie on.

Walcott: What I'm about to say I perhaps wanted to say, and this will sound very stupid. I've just written a book called *The Arkansas Testament,* and I almost wish that it would be ignored, in a way. Really, I almost wish that nothing was said about it, nobody reviewed it, nobody wrote a long essay about it, nobody said the same old things. I wish it were there just like a tree was there, you know, or a stone was there. We don't go around reviewing trees and stones. I think, when you talk about simplicity, it's a process that all serious poets undertake, and the simplicity not only of style but of soul. And it may be very pompous, but in the same way I wouldn't like anyone to review my soul. Nobody has the right to, any more than they have the right to review a stone or a tree. I'm not comparing the book to the natural grandeur of a tree or a stone; I'm just saying that now I think it should just be there, without commentary or without exegesis or whatever.

DM: Joseph Brodsky, in his essay "The Sound of the Tide" in *Less Than One,* mentions that some critics have attempted to label you a regional poet or a black poet from the Caribbean in order to reduce the scope of your work. Do you agree?

Walcott: Yes. I don't feel victimized by it, but of course that's been true. It's true because, as I've said before, you can take *one* of us seriously—you can take Naipaul seriously or you can take me seriously or you can take Eddie Brathwaite seriously—but if you took more than one of us seriously, you'd have to take the entire Caribbean seriously. And people are not prepared to do that because it's just too much work. That's all. It would mean not looking at the West Indian writer as an isolated freak; it would mean admitting that there's possibly something called a culture in the Caribbean, which would mean taking everything else on the level that we as writers individually are taken on now.

DM: Brodsky also mentioned there that the colonies are not where the empire ends but where it unravels. Are you saying that, if people take Caribbean literature seriously, they must also take what happened in the Caribbean seriously?

Walcott: No, not the past. The past is easy; the past is slavery. The problem is to take what's happening now in the Caribbean seriously.

DM: What do you think, for example, about the invasion of Grenada?

Walcott: I'm not ducking, but I think it would be a long, long answer. It's in the play I'm writing. We could take it as a larger question. Whenever people talk politics, they run the risk of sounding pompous, especially when you talk about conscience and crisis and power. But I think the flush of democracy has gone from America. It's very hard to say that. It is like the flush of revolution. If we had enough strength, we'd look hard at all—as Traherne calls them—"the dirty devices of the world." You'd then become an adult; your sins become more visible; your innocence, or even your awareness of the simplicity of original sin, is lost.

In America's case what you have is an empire that became an empire with extreme rapidity, in just a little over two hundred years. Now if you say—as you would in a five-year plan—the first flush of a revolution lasts two years, and the next three is getting down to work and having the junta take over and the leaders shot and the poets jailed and the journalists repressed, then where America is now is at the stage of cold reality. After the dawn, mid-morning or late afternoon begins to happen. And it's a *very* anguished stage.

You know, Larkin has a phrase—and he speaks about England: "When will England grow up?" Now, he's talking about a country that is allegedly—in terms of civilization—hundreds of years old, which may be nothing in a culture. And he's talking about Whitehall, the solemn sinister rubbish of Whitehall, and about the parades and laying wreathes on the tombs and all that. "When will England grow up?" If Larkin can ask that of England, imagine what one can ask of America.

Now what one sees is a terrible crisis of what you could call necessity. In other words, can this empire do wrong in the name of good? That's the crisis. Can an evil action or wrong action be committed for the right reason? Obviously, the answer is no. The answer is no in human conduct, and, if human conduct multiplied is politics, then the answer *has* to be no. Because then you can reverse the answer and say the invasion of Afghanistan by Russia, the invasion of Czecho-slovakia by Germany, is, from their point of view, a wrong but necessary action that will ultimately justify what happened.

In the case of Grenada, obviously, what seems moral and righteous is to come in and rescue a country from a junta that is worthless. That was right, in a sense. To me, as a West Indian, it was right. To me as someone else—or maybe as the same person—it was wrong. It was a violation of the sovereignty of the country. And you can back up and say: Well, so was Bishop's takeover of the previous regime a violation of sovereignty. But, for that matter, the American Revolution was a violation of sovereignty. There was a king, and they were violating sovereignty. But it's not that confusing. It really comes down to a simple Greek formula that says: If the gods say do this, who is to be blamed, man or the gods? This empire is not a maniacal empire that says, like the Spanish or the British or the French empires did, that we are doing this in the name of God. We aren't that evangelical. Luckily, we just give some very pragmatic reasons for doing X or Y.

But there is a kind of evangelical fury in this country now about principles of democracy that will not listen to any other kind of argument about democracy. And the definition of democracy that America describes has to be *its* definition only. If that definition only is what America means as an empire, it will continue to lose ground all over the world, because the definition of Nicaraguan democracy is a definition of democracy by Nicaraguans, and they have a right to define it. And that, I think, is the crisis of an empire, when it *has* to—and that's the tough part—harden, to get tough. Perhaps—as Oliver North has said really—America should cut out the pretense of being democratic. That's what the Iran-Contra affair has been all about. It's a challenge, a crisis, that says: This is an empire; empires act in a certain way. The fantasies of democracy may exist in the Capitol and at home; they do not exist outside the frontiers of the empire. That is what America has become, for us out there and for me here watching it. And that's what I think the invasion of Grenada was about.

DM: So, the Iran-Contra hearings were a kind of unmasking of the real workings of our democracy?

Walcott: What it obviously points out is the dissatisfaction of the government—the official government—with Congress, which led it to a point where an army was being built up within the government. That army may not be an armed army, but it is an army of *opinion.* It's an army, that is, whose opinion is shared, whose power is shared by a lot of people who admire North and what's being done. And what is back of that admiration? Behind that admiration is the opinion that, yes, this country has got to do certain things, and not only to protect itself, you see.

The fallacy of protecting oneself is another excuse that is *always* being used by empires. Germany said it about Russia; Russia said it about Afghanistan; India can say it about Burma. We have to protect ourselves, and, therefore, if we protect our boundaries by invasion, we enlarge our frontiers. That's a very old argument. Now, you can look at it and say it's frightful or, with ordinary historical cynicism, what's so new about that? The problem lies in a resolution of a doctrine that has to say, yes, this is clearly a democratic *empire*—which is a contradiction in terms, from the beginning. How does a democratic empire operate? Does it do things undemocratic in defense of that democracy? Soon you get to the argument of necessity. Once you get into the argument of necessity, you get into that easy rhyme with necessity: Nazi. You know, you move from that to that. It's very easy to slide from one into the other. And that's a perilous position.

But, of course, the great thing is the safeguards and the watchdogs that exist here that expose and flay and bring to light and hopefully to justice that kind of threat. That's what's great about the system. Nobody could criticize the system were it not a democracy. Yet this does not obliterate the threat that exists in the empire exercising its right as it feels, whenever it does. There's nothing to prevent America from invading my own island tomorrow on the pretext that it needs to straighten out the politics there. And that was the example of Grenada.

DM: What about Trinidad itself? A few days ago was the twenty-fifth anniversary of its independence. How do you feel about Trinidad's changes up to now? Have new problems developed? Have the promises of, say, Dr. Eric Williams been carried out?

Walcott: Trinidad is going through the trauma of being broke now. The oil money is gone. There is fantastic, astonishing corruption in the government. In the previous government there was a spending spree beyond belief. There is a sort of—not really what you call inflation—a greed that went down from the top to the last person and is very infectious. You know, overcharging people. You overcharge me, and I'll overcharge you. If I charge you forty bucks for a canvas bag, I'm afraid you'll have to charge me sixty for a pack of cigarettes, and so on. It isn't that the money has decreased in value; it goes into a kind of whirlwind swirl, and suddenly it's gone. And so Trinidad is now in a state of shock from not having any money to grow by. That's one side of it, and you can hardly separate the day-to-day life of a country from what that country is supposed to be.

But I was just there for four or five days last week working with actors and dealing with a lot of people. Incidentally, apart from this, I felt certain obscenities of experience, among them, a lot of abuse from my friends—not friends but people who turn into enemies overnight—about my being away and being a sellout, or whatever I am, which didn't bother me, though I looked at it and heard it and so on. There was a little bit of that. On the very strong side, though, what I felt and what I continue to feel when I go back there is a vigor I can describe. I can *detail* that vigor. I'm not talking about a sort of tropical exuberance and a new world coming and all that about the Caribbean man. I'm talking about an intellectual precision that I've found in the Caribbean. There was some conversation among moderate but pretty astonishing people. In terms, for instance, of conversation, the syntax of the Caribbean—the intellectual syntax and not just the dialect rhythm— the *exchange* that happens just in language alone and the rhythm of language, indicates a culture that has no idea how acute it is in terms of either its humor or its balance. A strong balance, I think, exists—a knowledge of where one is that is very *rooted* in the Caribbean, very secure.

DM: Hard won to survive?

Walcott: Well, not only to survive. There, you see, there isn't this daily confrontation of identity, of "Who are you; what am I?" I don't understand that. What am I? I'm a black man. What am I? And so forth. This doesn't happen, as it does to minorities who have to live in the cities every day. In Trinidad people know where they are; they know who they are, and it gives them an immense amount of vigor in terms of their direction.

DM: So people aren't reduced to categories?

Walcott: Well, in one room, for instance, in one evening, you'll see the same kind of thing you might see in New York. But the point is that I'm not making distinctions while I'm there. If I begin to make those distinctions, I'm less than the experience in the Caribbean. If I'm in a room, and if I say this person is Chinese or has the linaments of being Chinese, then it turns out you stop at the face. In another place you do the whole body: This person's face is Chinese; this person's skin is . . . and so forth. It's of superficial importance ultimately. There is something absolutely astonishing about the concentration of races in Trinidad which cannot be suppressed. It doesn't matter what individual pessimism is; it doesn't matter what the wreckage of the political economy is; it is irrepressible.

DM: The theater gives you satisfactions that poetry might not or allows certain parts of your voice to express themselves that poetry does not.

Walcott: Well, there's a bit of sadness about poetry. Once a poem is finished and it goes away, it's severed from you; it's not yours. Whereas in the theater the playwright is the one who takes all the blame and the burden. And, of course, there's the sharing of that elation or that despair by several people. Twenty people, thirty people could be in that boat together. So, in a sense, yes, the personal elation, when it's multiplied, can be ecstatic. But also, by contrast, so can the personal despair for which you are responsible. Multiplied by twenty—right?—this makes you twenty times more depressed than if you wrote a bad poem (*laughs*). If you write a bad poem, you just throw it away or hope you realize it's a bad poem.

If you write a bad play, you never know it's a bad play until you really hear the groans.

DM: What about the line itself; when the actor begins to speak the line, does it lift itself off the page and change into something else?

Walcott: No. The poetry that survives in the theater survives by itself. It isn't *made;* it can't be *created.* If it's there, it's there; if it's not, no amount of lighting effects and terrific acting can make it happen. I sometimes give my students exercises in which they read their own lines. If you take a lyric poem and treat it dramatically, the embarrassment you can feel in reading a line that is not on the page but is coming out of the human mouth is acute. So I do a lot of that with the writers in the class. You learn a good deal either way. You learn that a line that may pass by the ear and be forgiven and slide by *grates* in the theater. Of course, the other threat is pomposity because you can elevate theatrical speech into making it sound extremely good, but that's the voice getting up on a platform, you know, and performing.

DM: In your poem "Nearing Forty" you implied you were trying to strip your style: "the household truth, the style past metaphor." In your recent book *Midsummer* you seem to be more spare, almost impatient with artifice, almost impatient with poetry itself, and yet these poems are extremely concentrated.

Walcott: But there can be *clear* concentration. I mean a drop of dew is clear concentration, because it can reflect an entire universe. In the little window in a dewdrop you can have that. The clarity that one wants and never *will* get but one lives all one's life for is, I think, to become an element, if it were possible. To become water, you know, to have no coloring, no obvious source, no artificial source, no frame. And, in a way, as one who is dealing with time, you think of the component of water, the element of time in the stillness of water. In a sense, that's the kind of simplicity that one strives for. I mean you wish to live to be ninety so you can try to be as clear as that in the effort. Larkin has a poem that says: "If I were made to construct a religion, it would be of water." Pasternak says it about water, about simple nouns. Or Rilke says it—just to put that word down as if it were the first time, as if it had an element of simplicity. And I think there are periods in the epochs of English poetry in which again one comes back, as Wordsworth did, at a certain point to something that is not illiterate and not dumb but *clear,* a simplicity that may contain a lot of knowledge in it, like Blake's has. The simplicity of Blake is a profound simplicity that has all the cosmology and myth that is in his head. But when he gets down to putting down his monosyllables, that's the clarity that one is talking about, something that is an elemental, unmeasured, unscannable kind of clearness. And one is talking, I think, about memory really. How direct is the word to human memory? The word put on the paper should be not *read* but *remembered* when it is read. The moment of reading is a moment of remembering, not a moment of learning.

DM: Distillation, in a way, and expansion at the same time?

Walcott: Yes, it's Blake's grain of sand.

DM: In your poetry some words seem to have a different meaning than in most poetry in English. Take the word *sugar,* for example. The costs of sugar, the human costs are alive in the poetry, which makes the word new, in a sense, or reveals what the word really means.

Walcott: Well, the word *wheat* for me will always be a literary word. It's a word out of poetry; it's not a word out of agriculture for me. It's not a word that I know—it's not a world or word that I know. When you plant wheat, that's work, but wheat in tapestries, wheat in literature, becomes a pastoral word that has no work in it, in a sense. I think that may be the difference, because sugar is not a pastoral, though it may appear to be a pastoral thing. The fields of sugar in the Caribbean are divinely beautiful, are supremely calm and so on, but there's a lot of blood and sweat in the earth for it. I think the same is true of wheat, and when a northern writer writes about wheat, he's writing close to the idea of bread, of survival. The wheat in the Bible is hard-work wheat; it's not a literary word. The same thing would be true, I imagine, of olive oil in Greece or, if you change places, of the coconut. For one person it's picturesque and archaic and literary. For another person it's something that smells and grows.

DM: What voice leads you from line to line?

Walcott: I was thinking today, at fifty-seven I may have not wanted to be a poet but an anthology, which I don't mind, because I enjoy so many voices that my own is irritating. So what you ask, what leads me from line to line, I *hope,* is any poet who is inhabiting the next letter. If poets can shift like shadows and an *A* may belong to Dante and a *J* to Homer or Pasternak, those letters aren't my property. And I just hope I don't have the vanity to believe that they are. So what leads me, I imagine, leads anyone who is serious and admits the generations that precede the word, and one is only adding, if one can, to that general sound with a very small sound of one's own. I think every poet of any modesty hopes to make just a small contribution to the sound of the world's hum and does not by any means wish to be individual or be praised for his style or whatever.

Just to come to a conclusion, and not because he's my friend, I think Seamus, for instance, could have done a very nimble thing. He could have danced away conspicuously and with great levitation and skill from the haunting shadow of Yeats and turned into something very aggressively different. But he knew that gradual absorption *would* lead to his own voice. And, for instance, in the phase that he's now gone through in his last book, *The Haw Lantern,* his use of the abstract noun as a whole territory and not just as an abstraction is very different from the way Yeats emblematically used abstract nouns. Seamus uses a language now that is not concentrated and fine and provincially exquisite or right, but one that is passing into a language of understanding, of exchange in a territory where the *blocks* of the polysyllables exist as solidly as if they were nature. And how does that happen? It happens because Heaney allows the voice in.

Poets who frantically try to escape any accusation of sounding like anyone else, who bloat themselves up, are the ones who have eventually sort of foundered.

DM: In your earliest poems there's already a maturity in the voice. Somehow your poetry doesn't evolve, in a sense, as if you were whole at the beginning. And yet there are many changes. What would you say the changes are over the span of your poetry?

Walcott: I agree with that. I'd say only the suffering is different, the quality of the suffering is different. You see, one can have an unembarrassed conversation and say at fifty-seven, without any fake humility, that I was a prodigy in the sense that I wrote very well very young. *Tonally,* it sometimes amazes me that I don't seem to be any different from when I was eighteen. You know, it seems to me to be the same person talking. Now that may be an imitation, because there may be no wisdom there. But it may be in my nature, and may be in the nature of the eighteen-year-old writer, to *avoid* wisdom. There's a kind of prerogative attached to wisdom, which has to do with style. There are certain great poets who achieve wisdom, and it's very inseparable from style. Yeats and Eliot are two who are full of wisdom, but you can't separate the wisdom from the style. The wisdom of Eliot is the style of Eliot; the wisdom of Yeats is the style of Yeats. But the wisdom of the Bible is wisdom; the wisdom of Isaiah is wisdom, and so forth.

I think that openness is what I've always had. I have been very flattered, as opposed to being insulted, when I've been told that I sound like someone else who was great. I always considered that to be an honor and not an accusation. You see—and maybe I have a medieval mind—I'm really part of a *guild.* I don't consider myself to be an individual. And if I were working as a stonemason in a guild, that would be my contribution to the cathedral. If I was an apprentice to Leonardo, I would feel terrific if someone said, "This is as good as Leonardo," or "You got this from Leonardo." Obviously, I'd say, yes, thanks very much. But the twentieth century—and especially in this country—is obsessed with the idiosyncratic genius, the doing your own thing, having your own style. It's like the movies. It turns everybody into a movie star. TV extras. There are no extras in American poetry.

DM: In "Sea Grapes" you say: "The classics can console but not enough." Does this need any explanation?

Walcott: Well, I don't think so. All of us have been to the point where, in extreme agony and distress, you turn to a book and look for parallels, and you look for a greater grief than maybe your own. You can immerse yourself for awhile in that tragedy and hope there will be some elation, as tragedy's supposed to provide. And it does. It provides a distance—the distance of character, of experience—and you can distance your own experience through this. But the truth of human agony is that a book does not assuage a toothache. It isn't that things don't pass and heal. Perhaps the only privilege that a poet has is that, in that agony, whatever chafes and what hurts, if the person survives, produces something that is hopefully lasting and moral from the experience.

DM: Do you think now language is in a rather precarious situation in the shadow of nuclear weapons? Do these weapons have an effect on our confidence in language?

Walcott: I don't think so. You see, the callous thing about poets is somebody would say have the war; it would make a great poem. You know, really, who cares which soldier killed which, at the time of the Iliad? Whom do we remember? We remember Patroclus; we remember Achilles. That's the callous beauty of great art. It's that the individual does not count. The beauty of great art is not totalitarian; it is not. It is just a domination of time, an idea of the eternal.

I don't think language is threatened by nuclear war. I think language is never really threatened. I never feel that language is threatened. I feel the spirit is threatened, and if the spirit withers, the language will wither. But the spirit, you know, pops up in various places. It's very elusive. The fact that American poetry or British poetry may be in lousy shape may be the consequence of the British spirit and the American spirit. Poetry's not to be blamed. The times are not to be blamed. Other areas of the world flourish; another kind of exuberance grows up in one place and withers, and that's the state of time and the world. The error that is made, of course, and which is preserved by critics, desperately preserved by critics, is that they have to feel that their particular corner on language is the center; otherwise, they're out of a job.

DM: Just a few more questions. Looking back over your poems, is there any one in particular that makes you feel it was a watershed, that in it you crossed something?

Walcott: No. It's treacherous, in a lovely sense—poetry. You have a period in which you say this is the only shape that poetry must take, that a poem should take. And you're totally convinced of it. And then the other thing happens; the demon happens and says, but there is this shape. And you go on to that.

And it isn't that one contradicts the other. I'm still almost convinced that what I'm doing now is a betrayal of what I did in my last book, The Arkansas Testament, a betrayal and an orchestration of that book's belief in the quatrains and all of the truth about the shape of a poem, that nothing recasts a certain measure of the breath. It's a belief that the instinctual line is irrepressible and indigenous to the craft and that it's a narrow stream, not a big river and not a sea. It's a belief that, after all of Greek mythology, that line's just a little brook up in the mountains somewhere, a spring—and a cold, clear spring, very narrow.

And then you're tempted into something of epical width, and you have to ask yourself: Well, is that the old ambition saying, you know, flex your muscles, expand your line? Is it that you feel you've gotten important? Or is it genuinely another different rhythm of breathing inside your body that begins and says: Well, this is equally true. And so, recently, I've been writing something totally different— and almost a contradiction of what I've done in that book. I don't really feel that I've betrayed what I felt then, but I'm a little angry that it should be happening (*laughs*). I mean blessed and angry that it should be happening.

DM: May I quote some of your own lines to you from "North and South"?

> and the side streets of Manhattan are sown with salt,
> as those in the North all wait for that white glare
> of the white rose of inferno, all the world's capitals.

Metaphor—what happens? Is there a resolution, or is something revealed? What connections are made? What does metaphor do?

Walcott: Well, again, whenever you have a situation where there are question and answer, the answer is always on a platform above the question. And it leads to a sort of pompous modesty or, vice versa, modest pomposity.

I don't think of the word *metaphor* at all. I have to use it, say, if I'm teaching. I might use it. I hate to use any of those terms. Metaphor is muscle, I think. And I don't mean like flexing your torso or whatever. It's the muscle of thought, it seems to me. And if the line is proceeding along the right rhythm the metaphor comes. A lot of the stuff written about poetry claims that metaphor is vision. It's not been so much a matter of vision, I think, as a matter of meter. Metaphor may be meter because, as the rhythm progresses, you solve a rhythmic perception that is not necessarily saying something. There is a rhythm that makes a thing be seen; it is not the thing that is seen that makes the rhythm. So I think metaphor evolves out of the beat. It may come out of a succession of alliteratives that may suddenly make the words see next what's happening. Of course, a metaphor can be clear, and it can be startling, but it's *self*-startling. And that's what's astonishing about metaphor, that it startles the self as it proceeds. When it comes, it's startling to the writer. It's not like a planned camera shot of an image that happens.

There are Auden's wonderful lines, which I often quote in class:

> Oh, dear white children, casual as birds
> playing among the ruined languages.

This is a vast, astonishing device. Auden didn't see. What he saw was columns, what he saw was terraces, what he saw was temples or whatever. But *languages* is better. And that's *not* a metaphor. It now goes into something beyond a metaphor. It's both abstract and concrete. It's all of Greek and Latin and Pompeian and Roman and Egyptian civilization among ruined languages. "Columns" would have kept it down to Greece. But "playing among the ruined languages" is just—well, that's the furthest almost that poetry can go.

DM: Is there one more thing that you're reaching toward? What seems insufficient to you?

Walcott: What seems insufficient—just to be glib—is the respect of my peers (*laughs*). Well, I would really like to please. And this is very intimate, but it's true. It's been true, historically true. I mean, as crappy as this may sound, poetry is in a way a performance for another poet, really. It's to please Joseph Brodsky, it's to please Seamus Heaney. One performs for another poet basically.

DM: So the audience is . . .

Walcott: The audience is the other poet, who doesn't stand for bullshit (*laughs*).

DM: One you respect.

Walcott: Well, or love, yes—or whose work you love. The intelligence that one poet brings to another's work is a radical, severe intelligence because all the tricks are known. And to do it without tricks, to see *that,* when it comes—and it's shared, you know—is very, very rare, actually. But now everybody can say: Oh, I see, you write for other poets, or you write for this little clique. But if poetry were a progressive thing, numerically every age, by geometric progression, would produce one thousand then two thousand then three thousand poets. It doesn't work like that. There can be an age with none—of any quality.

DM: A last question. You've never had to deal with any type of censorship, but is the lack of an audience—aside from other poets—a type of, not censorship, but of silencing by neglect or indifference? What does this do to the voice, the silence of not being heard, in a sense?

Walcott: Well, I've always wondered about the sense of isolation of the American poets that is *so* acute in contemporary American poetry, especially the generation of Lowell and Berryman and Jarrell and the others. How come there was such adulation and yet such isolation at the same time? And how come so many made almost a frantic claim to the right to be poets in a culture? I'm not an American, so I don't go through that. I really, in the Caribbean, am not treated like a literary figure. And it's extremely healthy because, in a way, I'm really left alone. It makes you very much your own judge and your own applauder—unfortunately, your own audience. At the same time it also does not make a social crisis out of the idea of being a poet, as it does here.

I think the thing about being a poet in America, or even a young poet in America, is the poet is almost crying out for the society to be hostile to him, to repress him, to take notice, to imprison him—or her, I mean both him and her— to pay attention, in a sense. But what happens is suddenly or quietly there is a very wide blandness that occurs in which the poet is subtly absorbed and given a name and an occupation and a trade *separate* from the society, maybe because of that naming. You are a poet, you write poetry, you get your books published, you're in magazines. And you don't go around with a cape and a rose, so you can't tell in this democracy how different being a poet would be. And I think that it is this real unnavigable but hospitable space ahead of the poet that finally makes a lot of them say "I'll just do something else." And that is another kind of death, really, that happens. It's not some big dramatic thing. It may not be like breaking your pen and fleeing into the jungle or something. But there's something that just quietly absorbs and deadens the spirit. And it's not inertia, because Americans are vigorous, industrious, honest—that's the quality of American activity—direct, forthright. Pay you what you deserve, reward you with what you get, et cetera. It's a just society and not a cunning one. And it isn't that you want more evil, but it may be a very, very spiritually satisfied society—or apparently spiritually satisfied society. It can't be disturbed. It's like making a lot of noise in a void room. And I think that, when that voice begins to sound as if it's being raised for effect or lowered so that attention can be paid to it, that middle ground is not found, you see. And then, in a way, the poet goes into a kind of isolation. He may be on the Pacific Coast or he may be alone on a farm in Iowa or he may be in a loft in New York or he may be teaching in Boston, but there's no *necessity* in him.

DM: Communication?

Walcott: Yes, he doesn't feel needed. By luck, by blessing, I feel needed. I feel very needed. In the Caribbean, meeting people anywhere, on a beach somewhere, talking to poor people, to fishermen, a guy in a store, anybody, I feel as if I could speak for them. When that is missing, it's deadening.

DM: I think I'll leave you in peace.

Walcott: Deadening is a terrible word to end on (*laughs*).

November 26, 1990

DM: With democracy now spreading in Eastern Europe and the USSR, what do you see as the pressure points in the current political climate, or poetic climate— the places where language and history cross, the points of greatest tension? Is there a corresponding new stress developing in some areas, while there is relief in others?

Walcott: I think there is a very scary ambiguity in a lot of the political changes we are now seeing. The spread of more democratic—capitalist democratic—regimes obviously contains immediate civic advantages: free elections, free expression, the cessation of the persecution of writers, et cetera. But sometimes these freedoms have a condition that is not overtly censorship but is still a condition or, even, in *some* cases, virtually a bribe. In other words, you can have freedom, provided that, say, foreign policy adheres to the foreign policy of America.

The fall of communism is a good thing since it was a tyrannical regime, but I think that collapse has also meant perhaps the collapse of the *idea* of socialism. All aspects of socialism are contaminated by the idea of communism, and contaminated in certain countries that have never had the chance to fulfill their economic balance or their own political ideology peculiar to *their* condition, which is usually or inevitably, in the Third World, one of poverty *and* of exploitation.

Then, when these freedoms are offered, that, yes, you can have free elections, you can have freedom of the press, et cetera, sometimes those offers are very guarded. I'm not sure that now in the Third World, if any regime offered what is very ordinary and necessary, such as programs that are state-supported, state-owned, nationalized, and not according to workings of free enterprise, that that is not repressing the idea of social justice. The fall of communism should not mean the fall of social justice.

It may be that if the language that is used to describe the political ideology of any particular country that is poor is categorized as socialist, then it will be categorized as Communist and therefore evil, *socialist* being an abused word in this country, an abusive word in this country, just as *liberalism* is an abusive word in this country now.

From the safety of a capitalist democracy like America it's easy to provide examples of freedom of expression, of criticism, and so on—although censorship is strangely enough beginning to happen in the States to a very curious degree, or maybe *not* so curious degree. The censorship of the arts is alarming, for instance.

So we may be back in a situation in which one says to poor countries, yes, you can be free, but you must under no conditions talk socialism. Now, by talking socialism, what may be meant is simply talking about providing social services to the poor. Yet you can't offer the poor free enterprise because they have nothing to invest. And it is not necessarily true that the systems, democratic systems, work the same in different societies.

I think that that whole question of the bureaucratic language remains the same with whoever is in power. The definition of the word *liberal* in America, in Washington, is not the definition of the word *liberal* in Hawaii or in Puerto Rico. One is continually fighting under this blanket of generic, political description that can smother an attempt that looks as if it's a return to an abandoned or ruined or passé ideology. The poor remain poor; the services are required. There *should* be medicine; there *should* be roads.

Unfortunately, the language of politics that is used has now become a standardized dictionary in which people are described with certain letters—like *s* for socialist, *l* for liberal... but those words do not vary according to the location in which they're used. There are revolutions. If a country is corrupt, and if a country is exploiting its people, and so on, the need for change and for revolution should not be threatened by these overall, generic ideas that emerge as described by Washington or London or Berlin.

So there can be something quite ironic in the fall of the Wall, in a sense. There is some curious area that says: Everyone is now free, and so on. But that's in Europe, and that's in America; that's not necessarily applicable in the Third World, since the people who control the strings and the banks are saying "We can't have any more of that kind of talk of such things as socialism." In fact, the economic opportunity has *never* been there in poor countries. I think any small country that now attempts to sound as if it were Communist or socialist is in a lot of trouble. The fall of the Berlin Wall and so forth means that the passion for justice is also threatened by this cooling off.

I've never identified myself politically, but I think if somebody asked me, since I come from very poor islands and I see what is required, what is so obviously needed in these islands, where there is that awful disparity that happens between the usual thing—the wealthy and the poor—I suppose I'd have to define myself as a socialist. And, I think, if I define myself as a socialist, as an American, I'll be immediately branded as a Communist. Whereas there's no other political position possible for anybody in the Third World than to say, of course: Naturally I'm a socialist. I believe that there should be socialized medicine. We don't have that pyramidal economy that exists here. How can you have a situation in which people couldn't afford to go to doctors in poor countries?

DM: Is this new stress in the political vocabulary transferred in any way into the personal vocabulary of poetry?

Walcott: As a writer, you don't use clichés that are provided by the bureaucracy, unless you're writing propaganda. Under a Communist regime, or any tyrannical regime, you use the counters that are provided for you by the bureaucracy that says: This is what you mean by freedom, this is what you mean by liberty when you use it. But, if you use words like *social justice,* or whatever, I'm saying that in poor countries these are no longer clichés but necessities. And such words are not out of a vocabulary that is legitimized by a bureaucracy. These are passionate and emotional responses to conditions that are there in front of you. So, every time you describe a condition like poverty which looks permanent and unchangeable, then you are not reinventing a cliché; you're talking out of a passion.

In what appears to be a free country, you can't say the word *justice* without sounding rhetorical. But if you go to conditions in which people are tortured and in which people are poor, and people have been exploited, and there seems to be no relief for their condition, then of course you are driven to words like *justice*. But to write the word *justice* in one country is not the same thing as to write it in another or in another political situation. The vocabulary that one has to struggle against is a vocabulary that is *given* to the writer to use in a tyranny. Whereas the writer rediscovers those passions and the words attached to those passions in the conditions that are different, the ones that are outside the frontiers of the tyranny.

You know, the whole ambience of Seamus's work now is exactly that gray area in which he's using the language *of* the bureaucracy in a strangely personal and ironic way. He's using the exhausted vocabulary to rediscover a condition that *is* tyrannical. But the writer is forced to use those counters as if he could rediscover, through the use of the clichés, some other kind of experience. It's very finely put in Seamus.

DM: Is there any overflow of what you've been talking about into the world of comparisons that is important in poetry? Are there barriers that have been broken, or are there walls that have fallen? Or on the contrary, have new walls appeared?

Walcott: The condition of poetry is always one of another kind of responsibility; another responsibility begins again with the shift of conditions. One has to be very guarded that one is not using an *old* responsibility in a situation that has to be looked at in all its ambiguity. For instance, the poets of Eastern Europe... one can say, well, what have they to write about now? Because the Wall is down, so they're okay, they can vote. They've got Havel and so forth. If you look at it superficially, you would say, well... it's like the spy novel. The spy novel is supposed to be dead. But the difference between poetry and the spy novel is that poetry is more concerned about a permanent condition of evil, so that does not make Milosz or Zagajewski or Brodsky or Herbert or any political writer limited to a regime in which they were repressed. And if they have been read that way, then they haven't been read profoundly. Because they're not simply describing a phase of European history. The best and deepest of them are asking: Why does this recur in European history? So that you can get very dislocated by a sense of comfort and relief and bracketing people in an epoch in which you would say, well, they wrote in times when expression was repressed. If that were *all* that there was to writers like that, then they themselves would be full of self-contempt because then they would be saying: I can only write under that kind of political pressure; my work only has meaning under political pressure. Remove the political pressure, and there's nothing to say. Well, first of all, the political pressure is *never* removed, the condition of evil in which mankind seems to revel is a permanent one, and it shifts—it shifts its strength. It's elusive. You cut off one head, and another head rises . . . It's a hydra-headed situation. So, if you say the Wall is down, there's another wall somewhere going up.

DM: Do you think there's a tie-in between the fall of the Berlin Wall and the censorship of the arts now developing in the United States?

Walcott: I don't quite understand what has happened here with censorship. But I know that I can't balance the idea of saying there's freedom in Eastern Europe and there's artistic censorship here. That seems to me a hell of an irony that you could rejoice at the Wall coming down and then put up another wall here for your artists.

DM: Poetry seems to be attracted to places of intensity. In political or artistic terms, where do you see poetry moving now?

Walcott: A great deal of poetry has lost its *first* responsibility, which is not perhaps to head either toward or away from what you call pressure points, but it's the celebration, and it is the veneration, not of man but of creation, of nature, the mystery of creation. That's always been the primal function of poetry. I think anything less than that is secondary and egotistical, and I include my own work, obviously. So, poetry does not necessarily have to do so much with pressure as with radiance. And it can be extremely quiet—it can be utterly contemplative, it can be away from the world, it doesn't have to be busy with the *business* of the world. So the idea to me of pressure may apply if you're talking of social responsibility and justice and articulate objection and so on. And certainly that is inevitable in terms of the propulsion of poetry toward articulating what is unjust. But there's a higher thing than that, obviously, which is that, if there were only one man left in the world and he were a poet, I think he would still be in awe of creation; he would not be in awe of the destruction of man. He would not be in awe of destruction but of creation. And when we are concerned, I think, about destruction and waste and man's inhumanity to man, and so on, really it's a secondary subject compared to man's responsibility to God. I mean, this may sound a little old-fashioned, as much as "liberal," "socialist," and "nature," and all that. Poetry's not a valve that releases pressure. It may be a state of being that . . . The supreme example, of course, is the traveling of Dante toward the light—*that* remains, the radiance that happens, a kind of sublimity that happens. And if the nations of the world, as all the prophets and all the religious leaders and so on in *all* the religions, insist that that is the direction of man, then war would simply be something that one would accept as the stupidity of man.

Midsummer

XXIII

With the stampeding hiss and scurry of green lemmings,
midsummer's leaves race to extinction like the roar
of a Brixton riot tunnelled by water hoses;
they seethe towards autumn's fire—it is in their nature,
being men as well as leaves, to die for the sun.
The leaf stems tug at their chains, the branches bending
like Boer cattle under Tory whips that drag every wagon
nearer to apartheid. And, for me, that closes
the child's fairy tale of an antic England—fairy rings,
thatched cottages fenced with dog roses,
a green gale lifting the hair of Warwickshire.
I was there to add some colour to the British theatre.
"But the blacks can't do Shakespeare, they have no experience."
This was true. Their thick skulls bled with rancour
when the riot police and the skinheads exchanged quips
you could trace to the Sonnets, or the Moor's eclipse.
Praise had bled my lines white of any more anger,
and snow had inducted me into white fellowships,
while Calibans howled down the barred streets of an empire
that began with Caedmon's raceless dew, and is ending
in the alleys of Brixton, burning like Turner's ships.

North and South

Now, at the rising of Venus—the steady star
that survives translation, if one can call this lamp
the planet that pierces us over indigo islands—
despite the critical sand flies, I accept my function
as a colonial upstart at the end of an empire,
a single, circling, homeless satellite.
I can listen to its guttural death rattle in the shoal
of the legions' withdrawing roar, from the raj,
from the Reich, and see the full moon again
like a white flag rising over Fort Charlotte,
and sunset slowly collapsing like the flag.

It's good that everything's gone, except their language,
which is everything. And it may be a childish revenge
at the presumption of empires to hear the worm
gnawing their solemn columns into coral,
to snorkel over Atlantis, to see, through a mask,
Sidon up to its windows in sand, Tyre, Alexandria,
with their wavering seaweed spires through a glass-bottom boat,
and to buy porous fragments of the Parthenon
from a fisherman in Tobago, but the fear exists,
Delenda est Carthago on the rose horizon,

and the side streets of Manhattan are sown with salt,
as those in the North all wait for that white glare
of the white rose of inferno, all the world's capitals.
Here, in Manhattan, I lead a tight life
and a cold one, my soles stiffen with ice
even through woollen socks; in the fenced back yard,
trees with clenched teeth endure the wind of February,
and I have some friends under its iron ground.
Even when spring comes with its rain of nails,
with its soiled ice oozing into black puddles,
the world will be one season older but no wiser.

Fragments of paper swirl round the bronze general
of Sheridan Square, syllables of Nordic tongues
(as an obeah priestess sprinkles flour on the doorstep
to ward off evil, so Carthage was sown with salt);
the flakes are falling like a common language
on my nose and lips, and rime forms on the mouth
of a shivering exile from his African province;
a blizzard of moths whirls around the extinguished lamp
of the Union general, sugary insects crunched underfoot.

You move along dark afternoons where death
entered a taxi and sat next to a friend,
or passed another a razor, or whispered "Pardon"
in a check-clothed restaurant behind her cough—
I am thinking of an exile farther than any country.
And, in this heart of darkness, I cannot believe

they are now talking over palings by the doddering
banana fences, or that seas can be warm.

How far I am from those cacophonous seaports
built round the single exclamation of one statute
of Victoria Regina! There vultures shift on the roof
of the red iron market, whose patois
is brittle as slate, a grey stone flecked with quartz.
I prefer the salt freshness of that ignorance,
as language crusts and blackens on the pots
of this cooked culture, coming from a raw one;
and these days in bookstores I stand paralyzed

by the rows of shelves along whose wooden branches
the free-verse nightingales are trilling "Read me! Read me!"
in various metres of asthmatic pain;
or I shiver before the bellowing behemoths
with the snow still falling in white words on Eighth Street,
those burly minds that barrelled through contradictions
like a boar through bracken, or an old tarpon
bristling with broken hooks, or an old stag
spanielled by critics to a crag at twilight,

the exclamation of its antlers like a hat rack
on which they hang their theses. I am tired of words,
and literature is an old couch stuffed with fleas,
of culture stuffed in the taxidermist's hides.
I think of Europe as a gutter of autumn leaves
choked like the thoughts in an old woman's throat.
But she was home to some consul in snow-white ducks
doing out his service in the African provinces,
who wrote letters like this one home and feared malaria
as I mistrust the dark snow, who saw the lances of rain

marching like a Roman legion over the fens.
So, once again, when life has turned into exile,
and nothing consoles, not books, work, music, or a woman,
and I am tired of trampling the brown grass,
whose name I don't know, down an alley of stone,
and I must turn back to the road, its winter traffic,

and others sure in the dark of their direction,
I lie under a blanket on a cold couch,
feeling the flu in my bones like a lantern.

Under the blue sky of winter in Virginia
the brick chimneys flute white smoke through skeletal lindens,
as a spaniel churns up a pyre of blood-rusted leaves;
there is no memorial here to their Treblinka—
as a van delivers from the ovens loaves
as warm as flesh, its brakes jaggedly screech
like the square wheel of a swastika. The mania
of history veils even the clearest air,
the sickly sweet taste of ash, of something burning.

And when one encounters the slow coil of an accent,
reflexes step aside as if for a snake,
with the paranoid anxiety of the victim.
The ghosts of white-robed horsemen float through the trees,
the galloping hysterical abhorrence of my race—
like any child of the Diaspora, I remember this
even as the flakes whiten Sheridan's shoulders,
and I remember once looking at my aunt's face,
the wintry blue eyes, the rusty hair, and thinking

maybe we are part Jewish, and felt a vein
run through this earth and clench itself like a fist
around an ancient root, and wanted the privilege
to be yet another of the races they fear and hate
instead of one of the haters and the afraid.
Above the spiny woods, dun grass, skeletal trees,
the chimney serenely fluting something from Schubert—
like the wraith of smoke that comes from someone burning—
veins the air with an outcry that I cannot help.

The winter branches are mined with buds,
the fields of March will detonate the crocus,
the olive battalions of the summer woods
will shout orders back to the wind. To the soldier's mind
the season's passage round the pole is martial,
the massacres of autumn sheeted in snow, as
winter turns white as a veterans hospital.

Something quivers in the blood beyond control—
something deeper than our transient fevers.

But in Virginia's woods there is also an old man
dressed like a tramp in an old Union greatcoat,
walking to the music of rustling leaves, and when
I collect my change from a small-town pharmacy,
the cashier's fingertips still wince from my hand
as if it would singe hers—well, yes, *je suis un singe*,
I am one of that tribe of frenetic or melancholy
primates who made your music for many more moons
than all the silver quarters in the till.

Isabel Allende

Isabel Allende, born in 1942, was a journalist in Chile until 1975, when she left with her family for Venezuela. There unable to practice journalism, she supported herself with "odd jobs." In 1981 she began writing *The House of the Spirits*. Since that time she has made her living as a writer, though she prefers the title of storyteller, or narrator, to writer. She has one son and one daughter and now lives in the United States.

She is the author of three novels, *The House of the Spirits* (1982), *Of Love and Shadows* (1985), and *Eva Luna* (1988). Her most recent book is a collection of short stories, titled *The Stories of Eva Luna*, published in 1990. She has also written children's stories and several plays that have been successfully produced in Chile.

This interview took place in April 1988, in New York. In November, 1990, Allende commented on the end of the Pinochet regime. These comments follow the interview.

David Montenegro: May we begin with September 11, 1973? A member of Salvador Allende's family, his niece, what happened to you on the day of the coup?
Isabel Allende: I think I should start by saying that the fact that I was a member of his family didn't make any difference. Millions of Chileans were affected by that day. There was much pain, much suffering, much fear. And my particular case is not very interesting because other people suffered much more.

Although I belonged to Allende's family, I was not living in his house. I had been with him a week before. We had lunch together. I loved and admired him, and I think he had a beautiful dream. But it's very selfish to talk about my own experience when it was the whole country that was experiencing such a terrible, historical event.

Well, I was a journalist at that time, and that day I got up very early in the morning, as I usually do. I prepared my children for school, like any day, and went to my office. I didn't realize there was a coup. I had no radio in my car, and I reached the center of Santiago. While driving, I saw that the streets were practically empty, except for military transports and trucks and soldiers everywhere. There was a sudden quietness in the air—something very strange. And since we had been hearing about the possibility of a military coup for several weeks—really months— I suspected that it would be that. But we had no experience of such a thing whatsoever; we had never seen that before in Chile. So I continued, and when I arrived at my office it was closed. There was nobody there. So I drove to a friend's house. She was married to a teacher, who would get up very early in the morning and go to his school to correct exams. When I got to her house she was waiting at the door, crying; she had heard on the radio about the coup after he had left, and she couldn't get in touch with him. So I said I would go and pick him up. I drove back to the center of the city where his school was, one of the oldest schools in Chile, the Institutio Nacional. I don't know how I could have crossed all those military barricades. Somehow I got through, but then we couldn't get out. From the school we saw all the bombing of the palace. We were alone in the school when we heard on the radio the last words of Allende. Then finally we could leave the building. Making a big detour, we got back to the upper part of the city where we lived. I couldn't get in touch with my house because it was practically impossible to call on the telephone. All the lines were busy. Maybe everybody was calling at that time. By two o'clock, more or less, I learned that Allende was dead and that many of my friends were in hiding; others were killed; others were in prison. But at that moment it was very difficult to realize exactly what was happening. It was a time of great confusion. And just rumors. On television we only had military marches and Walt Disney movies. It was so sur-realistic, so strange.

DM: Though there had been rumors of an approaching coup for months, you didn't expect one actually could happen?

Allende: No, we didn't expect it to happen in that way. People talked about the possibility of a military coup because half the population in Chile was against Allende's government. Really the country was divided. The economic crisis provoked by the conspiracy and supported by the United States had really damaged the economy of the country greatly. And the opposition was asking Allende to resign. When I had lunch with him the week before, he said, "I'm not leaving the palace. The people put me there, and I'm not leaving until my constitutional term is at an end, unless the people ask me." But he was talking already—and everybody was talking—of a military coup. We thought, since the armed forces in Chile had a tradition of democracy, and we were not a banana republic, in our case things would be different. That's what people thought. Allende knew better. In fact, in his last speech he announced prophetically what was going to happen because he knew his enemy exactly, precisely. But I think that very few people knew what was going to happen. I was a journalist. I was informed. I had the information, but I never expected it to happen.

DM: You are now a novelist. For you, is there a tension between being a novelist and being a journalist, between imagination and objective reporting? What brought you to make that transition?

Allende: Well, that transition was made over many years. After I left my country, I couldn't work as a journalist. I spent many years in silence, and I think that that silence was important for me, in many ways. Literature needs distance and ambiguity. If you are in the middle of the hurricane, you can't talk about the hurricane, not in literature, at least. You can do it in journalism but not in literature. And maybe those years of silence, which were very, very painful for me—those first years of exile with that paralyzing feeling, for example, of being rootless, of having lost all that was dear to me—were important, necessary. And the transition was very smooth because of those years of silence.

There *is* a great difference between journalism and fiction, but I use the techniques of journalism for literature: interviews, reporting, research, working in the streets with the people, participating in a community, talking and listening. That's what a journalist does finally, and that's what I do in literature, too. So sometimes I don't know where the borderline between fiction and reality is. My second novel, *Of Love and Shadows,* is based on a case that actually happened in Chile. Everything in the book was researched; everything is true. But, of course, it's presented as fiction, as a novel, and now I cannot tell you which of the characters is invented and which belongs to reality. I can tell you exactly where the bullets were in the bodies and how the bodies were found. These things I can say are true as I described them. The basic plot is not real; it's fiction, and I don't know any longer how much I invented of the story.

On the other hand, I was an awful journalist. I was always putting myself in the middle of the news and never being objective. I was very emotional, so maybe that helped, too.

DM: Did you feel something was missing in journalism? What does fiction add to the facts?

Allende: Interpretation only. In journalism you are not free to look at things from behind because you have to stick to facts. Nobody wants to listen to your interpretation of events. In fiction you feel free to interpret and to pull out the emotion, which, I think, is very much a part of reality. We are not reason only. Facts are never just what we see; there's always something behind, something beyond. And that is an invisible force—reactions, emotions that move us. I think one can put that in literature, and therefore sometimes fiction is more real than objective reporting.

DM: You mentioned the need for ambiguity in fiction. Is this what you also bring to the facts as a novelist? Does fiction show the complexity of a story and of people more fully than reporting?

Allende: At least in fiction you have a multiple vision. In journalism you don't. In journalism you're allowed one page, and in that page you have to put everything—when, what, who, and so on. In a novel you can have six hundred pages if you want, so you can tell the events in a much more complex and complete way, I think.

DM: You mentioned your silence during the first years of your exile. In *The House of the Spirits* Clara goes through a long period of silence. Is her silence related to your own? Also, what are the dangers of silence for a person?

Allende: Sometimes, when I talk of silence, it's a silence of women, who have had to obey the rule of silence for centuries. Now, recently, we have a voice. We are a choir of different but harmonic voices, feminine voices. We are writing; we are giving our own interpretation of the world on a big scale for the first time in many centuries. Of course, women have done this before, but they have been very isolated, and they have had to pay a big price. The punishment for being different was solitude. Now writing and talking don't mean solitude because we are many women together doing this. Maybe in the case of Clara in the book, and in my case, there is the danger of submission and solitude.

But silence can also enrich you very much. Maya Angelou talks about a long period in her childhood when she was silent, and during those years she turned evil into action. All the evil that had happened to her—she was raped—was turned into a positive strength, into energy, because of those years of silence. She reinterpreted the world, recreated reality. In a way, I think, that happened to me, too. Not as dramatically as it happened to her, but those years of silence were very necessary. Now that I've been talking and talking and talking in these lectures and in these seminars and courses and teaching, I have the feeling that all my energy is gone out, so I've decided that I will stop all interviews, all lectures. I will only do those I've already agreed to do. I will finish these obligations on October 1. And then it's my time of silence, because I need silence. Without silence I can't write.

DM: Silence puts the genie back in the lamp, in a sense?

Allende: Yes *(laughs)*.

DM: Chile is relatively exceptional for the amount of education available to women there. Until 1949, however, women could not vote in national elections. What is the progress of women's rights in Chile? And are there special difficulties for women in Latin American countries, where the culture is often paternalistic?

Allende: Patriarchal and *machista.* It's difficult to talk about Latin America as a whole. Every country is different. The law or the constitution is different in each; the race sometimes, the traditions, are somehow different. But more important than any other thing is social class. Everywhere in Latin America, if you belong to an upper-middle class of educated women, you are more or less equal to men— not equal, but more or less. But if you belong to the middle class or if you are a peasant or an Indian woman, the situation for you is much more difficult in every country.

In the case of Chile women have traditionally been very strong, although the law does not help them at all. We have no abortion, no divorce. Always, the father is the caretaker of the children, except in those cases where a judge determines that the mother will have custody of them. Women are not protected by the law or are less protected in Chile than in other countries. That makes them very strong, because you have to be strong to survive.

Chile's a poor country. Men have to travel a lot to get jobs. In the life of a woman there can be many men, and with each man she can have a different child. Sometimes women don't marry; very often they don't marry. I'm talking about poor women. And they learn very quickly to be strong. They are self-denying, very generous, very . . . with a great sense of motherhood. I would say that Chilean women are great mothers. They are not so only to their own children but to other people's children, too, and to their men. They always consider men as being a little bit childish. For example, you will always find among poor women in Chile the excuses for men. When a man abandons them, when he drinks, when he beats them, they have the feeling that he's just like a grown-up child, and they are very forgiving.

But they are very strong; they have organized themselves at the base of the society to set up soup kitchens, schools, and to care for the old and children. Because the state, the government, doesn't do much for them. On the contrary, authority is always the enemy—especially in a military dictatorship, which is the most macho society that you could possibly imagine. You can't imagine anything more macho than a soldier with impunity. And that is the government we have. In the slums, in poor neighborhoods, everywhere, in factories, in their working places, they have organized themselves, for survival.

And that organization, I think, will be extremely interesting, when we have democracy back. Because, until the military coup in 1973, we have had a legal, a political, democracy in Chile, but it was not really a *social* democracy. The democracy was not at the base of the society; it was more a political structure than a reality. Now I think we will be able to build a real democracy because, for survival, the society has organized itself in a very democratic way. People vote in the slums to choose their representatives to take positions. They can't vote for a president. They are living in a dictatorship, and yet they vote on every decision at the base of the society. And that's something that women have done.

DM: What other effects has the dictatorship had on women's organizations?

Allende: All social and political organizations in the country suffered greatly after the dictatorship began. Many were forbidden or eliminated. Women's organizations are part of that social and political process, so they have also had to suffer great repression. Women have been acting in the opposition very strongly. They are in the first line in the protests on the streets because they have nothing to lose. They have already lost everything. A man always has to take care of his job, if he has a job. Women have nothing, so they can risk everything. And they are usually very courageous.

The military dictatorship has taken away things that women had before, many things. There is a new morality, which I hate, a strange, old-fashioned puritanism, which is very hypocritical. It's very corrupt in its soul, I would say. And that has affected the women very much.

I think the worst part of the dictatorship is that it fragments society. Terror works, isolating people. It is effective, as long as you can't communicate, as long as you are isolated, as long as the society is fragmented. If you are a nuclear family sitting around in a small apartment watching TV, terror works. But if you can get together, unite with other people, talk, express your feelings out front, then you become strong. And that is what the dictatorship fears the most. Prisoners are isolated; people are isolated; gathering is forbidden, and that has affected the lives of women very much because, if women are not united, they are silent. They have had to become very strong in order to get together.

DM: Can you give an example of this and also of the puritan fundamentalism you mentioned?

Allende: Yes. For example, the very day of the coup, soldiers would cut the pants of women in the streets with scissors because they wanted ladies to wear skirts, which was proper. All movies that were considered erotic were forbidden. There was great censorship and self-censorship. Books ... *everything* was forbidden. And then on TV we had this sort of fundamentalist righteousness. That was the message. And at the same time you knew that they were torturing, raping, abusing, and that there was extreme corruption. It wasn't even hidden; it was *there,* obvious.

Women were supposed to stay at home and be quiet. How and when could they overcome silence? In the beginning it was very difficult, practically impossible. They were desperately trying to help their men, looking for the disappeared ones, burying the dead, visiting prisons—that's what women were doing, and surviving, working, trying to make a living for the children. Then, after this artificial economic boom that happened at the beginning of the dictatorship and lasted until sometime between 1981 and 1983, the economy collapsed. This economic boom occurred because the United States and other countries injected money into the country, and people could buy anything on credit. But when the minute came when they had to pay, and when, added to repression there was poverty, hunger, lack of jobs, well, the whole economy of the country collapsed.

Women then began protesting in the same way the opposition had protested against Allende—that is, by beating pots and pans. It's difficult to explain, but, when you have to go out in the street and protest in front of a soldier who has a gun, you have to be very brave. But if you are at home and you beat a pot and pan, and you know that your neighbor is doing the same and the other neighbor is doing the same and that it's impossible for the soldiers to stop it, because they can't bomb the city or shoot everybody inside their houses, that's a way of protesting that is somehow safe. And when you beat pots and pans and hear that everybody in your neighborhood is doing it, you know that you're not alone. Fragmentation of society doesn't work any longer. You become part of the community. You know that there are thousands feeling as you do, and so you become strong. And that's how the protesting started.

DM: So the silence and isolation were broken?

Allende: Yes. And now everybody knows in Chile that 80 percent of the population is against the dictatorship. They talk about it freely in the streets, in the buses, everywhere. If you go to Chile as a tourist, you will hear it everywhere because now people dare to talk. They didn't five years ago.

DM: In Chile censorship places strict limits on the media. Is there also an undefined censorship of the public that triggers self-censorship? When limits on speech are undefined, do people then become even more silent?

Allende: One of the main characteristics of this dictatorship is its ambiguity in certain aspects, which makes it even more dangerous. They can change the rules in one minute. What was allowed yesterday could be forbidden today, but what you did yesterday you have to pay for today. So the rules that were for yesterday do not keep you safe. For example, if you thought that you were allowed to speak against the government in your school yesterday and today the rule suddenly changes, you will be punished for what you did yesterday. That is very perverse because that means that people exert self-censorship to a great extent, I would say.

On the other hand, now there is a space that the opposition has won during these years, a certain space. For example, you can see very outspoken and very brave plays in theater. All books are now permitted. They're not published in Chile, but you can buy *Missing, Labyrinths,* Antonio Scarmetta's books, my books. You can buy them everywhere; you can read everything. There's no censorship for books.

Why? Because books are very expensive, and only very few people can read. But nothing is permitted on television because that's a great mass media. Very little is published in most newspapers but a lot in two newspapers and some magazines that the opposition has been able to keep alive. Why? Because they reach only a few thousand people, and the government believes that they are not really significant. That is an underestimation because they have been very important in the resistance. *But* the rule can change any minute. And the directors of any of those magazines can be killed any day or put in prison. And this has happened during these years. So you have to be extremely courageous to say: Okay, I'll go on and do it, even if I know that tomorrow I will have to pay the price. So it's a very subtle line, and the line moves all the time; the rules change all the time.

DM: Arbitrary rules?

Allende: Absolutely. And, with absolute impunity, they can do whatever they want.

DM: So people feel cornered, surrounded?

Allende: No. You learn how to live with that. I mean, after fifteen years, there's a whole generation that has been brought up in that situation. They don't know what it is to live in another world.

People have *learned.* They have learned through clues, a sort of special language. Chile's an extraordinary country. During these fifteen years of oppression and terror, there are many groups of people—although groups are forbidden—that are studying its own reality, studying the country, studying our history, studying the dictatorship, preparing for the future, working on an intellectual and, I would say, also emotional level for the future. So I have great hope that Chile will be a great country after the dictatorship. We've learned a lot about ourselves during these years. And the dictatorship has not been able to destroy those essential values that were always with us. Even if the government is a dictatorship, the society's democratic, multipartied, tolerant. It's only a group that was always intolerant that now has power; they were always brutal. We were afraid to see it. Those fascists were *always* in the society, but we—as people who are very tolerant—just lived with that. And we will continue living with that. And I think that, when democracy has come to Chile, there will be a spirit of forgiveness. Not forgetting, we will shout to have justice, but I am afraid that most people who have been so brutal during these years will probably be forgiven.

DM: As a writer, how have these fifteen years affected you? Is there an evolution in your work parallel to the political events?

Allende: I don't know. It's very difficult for me to talk about my own writing because I can't explain it. It happens as if in a state of trance. I've written three novels already, and always the first impulse to write is a deep emotion that has been with me for many years. I need years to internalize it. I recreate the pain or the anger or the love. Writing for me is always a very emotional process. So it's difficult for me to explain.

Sometimes I'm asked: Do you belong to the post-Boom? I don't know what that is. I never learned about it or studied anything about literature. And I don't even care to. I only want to communicate. I want to tell people what I think is true. I want to change the world. I know it's very ambitious and very pretentious, but that's what I want to do. I don't like anything else but that.

DM: In what way does writing change people or change the society we live in? How does the writer help?

Allende: Sometimes a writer is a foreteller of the future, has a prophetic gift, has the ability to speak for others who have been kept in silence. That's our job. I think it's a gift; it's something that simply happens to certain people. And if you have that, you have to use it. I'm aware that, in this world where the majority is illiterate, where only a few people can buy books and only a very small minority has the habit of reading, a book has very little impact. But sometimes it's a seed planted in fertile soil, and you never know what the effect will be or when you will be able to measure the effect.

Take the books of Charles Dickens. They told people about children working in factories. And many years later people realized that child labor was obscene and perverse. Or at a certain moment a group of writers talked and wrote about slavery. It was a seed planted in the souls of people. And all of a sudden we were able to reach an agreement; humankind was able to reach an agreement against slavery and say: This is obscene and perverse. I think we have the capacity to reach that agreement about war, for example. And I think in some years we will be able to look back at ourselves and say: How was that possible? We were building weapons for peace. It's like fucking for virginity. I mean, how could we be so stupid? Or we are going to say: Many years ago people tortured each other. That was obscene and perverse. How could we do that? And we will have the same reactions we have now against slavery. I think that a book can defy the passage of time and somehow change the mind of certain people, and that has an effect, if a small one, but it can grow.

I know some books that have changed *my* life. And if I can do that for one person, I have done enough. I received a letter the other day from a man who is eighty-six years old. He said, "I've read your books, and I've changed. It's not too late for me." Well, I've done something then. I mean, if by talking or writing I can reach a young person and tell him, "*You* have the responsibility as much as I have it of changing the world"—because we don't like the world as it is—and he believes me, he wants to do this with me, well, I've done enough. A lot.

DM: When you write a novel, you have to live with your characters for a long time. How do you feel about them? Do you feel differently about each of them? *Allende:* First of all, I have the feeling that I don't invent them. I don't create them; they are there. They are somewhere in the shadows, and when I start writing—it's a very long process; sometimes it takes years to write a book—little by little they come out of the shadow into the light. But when they come into the light, they are already people. They have their own personalities, their clothes, their voices, their textures, their smells. I don't invent them; somehow they are there. They always *were* there. I mean, half of those persons were very easy because they belong to my family, so I just had to recreate something that had existed or exists.

In *Of Love and Shadows* the story is real. I needed the characters to tell the story, but those characters could be real; maybe they are. And they were always there, waiting for me to bring them out into the light. The book begins with a small paragraph. I don't remember it by heart, but it's something like: This is a story of a man and a woman who loved each other so deeply that it saved them from a bare existence. I know that's possible—that a great love can save you from a bare existence. I know that there are courageous people who will risk their lives for truth and justice. I know that those people in that book, Irene and Francisco, were always there; I just had to take them out of the shadow, as I took that horrible plan of murder out of the shadow into the story.

But my third novel, *Eva Luna,* is a very joyful, extravagant tale. It's like *The Arabian Nights,* a story of a storyteller who saves her life by telling stories. And Eva Luna's character was always there. I know that the character was within me. She doesn't resemble me; it's not my biography. I'm not her. But somehow she was inside me, as if I were a glove and she were the hand inside the glove. By writing, the hand got out of me and existed by itself.

There's a character, for example, in that book called Raid Halabí. Raid Halabí is an Arab. He's completely invented, if you could say invented. That is, I didn't have a live model for him. First of all, I didn't have to invent the name; the name came to me, and when I wrote Raid Halabí immediately he appeared, and he had a cleft lip. Why was he like that, I don't know, because when I saw him I said: I don't *want* him to be like that. I want him to be handsome because he will have a very important role in this book. He's very important for Eva Luna, so I want him to be handsome. But he was not. He was ugly. I tried to change him, but I couldn't because he was already there. He was a presence in my house.

So that's my relationship with my characters—very strange and very powerful. At the beginning of the novel sometimes they are ambiguous, but by the end they are so real that my children play with the idea that they are living in the house. And we talk about them as if they were part of the family.

DM: Some of the characters still live, in a sense, after the book is finished. What, for example, would Irene from *Of Love and Shadows* be doing now or Alba from *The House of the Spirits?*

Allende: All of them are making love *(laughs)*. I'm joking. That's the happy ending for me *(laughs)*. Some characters live with me, like Clara, like Professor Leal in *Of Love and Shadows,* like Irene, Alba, Eva Luna. They travel with me somehow.

DM: Are there any of your characters you would rather not have imagined? You mentioned at the end of *The House of the Spirits* that Colonel Garcia is part of the whole, implying that he had to be included.

Allende: Yes. I think that all the characters have to be there. Some of them I don't love, but I know that they are necessary. And I always try to be fair with them. At least, if I don't like them, I try to understand them. And that's what I try to do with people in real life, too. I try to understand why people think and act the way they do.

In *Of Love and Shadows* I had one character that, when I finished the book, I felt was a stereotype—Gustavo Morante, Irene's fiancé. I hate militarists, and anyone who wears a uniform is scary for me. So I put in him all my prejudices. And when I finished the book I realized that was not a character—that was not a person. That was only all the bad things I thought about soldiers. So I looked for a real model, for a real militarist, someone I could learn to understand, maybe to love in certain aspects. I found someone, and I interviewed him for weeks until I got out of him...I think I got his soul, the way he moves, the way he acts.

DM: What did you find when you actually interviewed him over that long period of time? What did you discover as a writer about this person?

Allende: I discovered that there is a code of honor, a twisted and perverse code of honor, but it *is* a code. And I learned to understand why they act that way and how their brains work. I learned about all these ridiculous ceremonies, this childish attitude toward the world. These are people who have been trained for death and destruction yet think of themselves as saviors, as owners of the truth, as righteous people. I learned also that they don't act that way—most of them—out of being bad or perverse themselves; it's the system that perverts them, that trains them to think, to not see reality as it is but to interpret it in a perverse way. For a militarist the goal justifies the means, and that's perverse in its very soul. I don't believe in that. I believe that the goal is determined by the process. If you want to have peace, for example, you have to act peacefully. You can't have a war for peace. If you want to be loved by someone, you have to be loving. If you want someone to be violent, then you must accept violence somehow. It's a process. For the militarist it's not. The goal determines everything. And I think *that's* the greatest perversion of that system.

There's another thing that is also terrible about these people: obedience, blind obedience. You have impunity because you are not responsible. Someone else is responsible, someone who is above you.

And then there is the way they use words. Great words that for me have no meaning for them are everything, like—in Spanish, the word is *patria*—fatherland. Fatherland. What is *patria*? *Patria* is people. It's not a territory; it's not a flag; it's not a childish ceremony of soldiers walking in a straight line. That's not fatherland. Fatherland is a language, a tradition. We are all living on the same planet. We have no more land, no more territory than this planet. And we share it. So who cares if the boundary is here or there? Who cares about boundaries, about nationalities, about ideologies? That is crazy, absolutely crazy. And *that* is the perversion of the system. These people are brainwashed to think that that's important. They make wars, and they've been killing each other for centuries for this illusion of having control of a certain part of the globe which belongs to everybody. They will never own anything else but a little piece of this globe, and we *all* own it. We are all part of the same planet and the same human race. I think it's so childish!

DM: Your title *Of Love and Shadows* brings to mind Carl Jung, who says the "shadow"—as he calls the capacity to commit atrocities—is collective. How do you react to this? What do you think?

Allende: Yes, I think there is evil in every one of us, in the same way that there is good in every one of us, and therefore in the world, in the society. And there are moments in history and moments in our lives when evil seems to have control of everything. That happens during very violent processes or during a war. The Nazis are a very good example. The dirty war, or what has been called "the process," in Argentina is another. Those are moments in which evil seems to have control over everything. But I think that, just as we have that evil part in us, we have the capacity to control it. And there is a great force that can be opposed to that evil: love. You have to be loved when you are a child to overcome that evil. And you have to love all the time to be able to relate to other people in the world. *Love* is a word that has been so ill-treated that it sounds campy, kitsch, sentimental. You can't talk about it without sounding like a Christian or—I don't know what. Or people laugh, scorn you when you talk about it. But in my life—I'm forty-seven—I have experienced this force, this energy, this positive strength which love is in such a strong way that it's only fair that I talk about it all the time and I write about it all the time.

Of Love and Shadows was meant to be a book about death and torture, repression, crime, horror. And when I started researching and interviewing and talking with the people, the victims of that crime, I realized that I couldn't afford being angry or feeling hate because they didn't, because that was a story of love, of solidarity, of generosity. For one torturer you have a thousand people who have risked their lives for freedom, for justice, to help each other. So how could I talk only about the bad, about the evil, if in confronting that evil was so much good, so much solidarity, so much love? You have to talk about love. And that has been the experience of my life.

I didn't have a father. My father disappeared when I was so young that I have no memories of him. But I had a mother, and she loved me in such a way that I have felt love in my life always. I've always had men in my life that loved me; my children love me, my friends. I feel that I'm a good person because I've been loved. So I want other people to be good because they are loved. Evil is just lack of affection. In those moments evil takes power, takes control.

DM: At the end of *The House of the Spirits* Alba says, "And now I seek my hatred and cannot seem to find it. I feel its flame going out as I come to understand the existence of Colonel Garcia."

Allende: Yes. Hate, in my case, and fear are paralyzing emotions. But I've been able to overcome them when I've tried. Not before. And those years of silence were years of fear and hate—and anger. I think that anger is good. It's somehow above emotion. It brings action, if you can control it. If you can't control it, it can destroy you.

I think that this love, this understanding, is the only possibility we have to build a different world, a more gentle world, a more entertaining world, a more merciful society. If we give back all the violence that we have received, that only creates more violence. We can't torture the person who has tortured us because then it's a never-ending chain of fear and hate and anger and violence. We have to stop it because we are better. And I think that that is the great difference.

This is not something that I invented or I have felt myself. I learned it from other people who have suffered much more than I, who have *really* suffered, and those people don't have any wish for revenge. They want justice. They want to keep alive the memory of the Holocaust, for example, or of what happened in Argentina. They want the disappeared ones back. They want at least to be able to bury the corpses. They want graves so they can go there and pray—at least that. They want justice. They don't want to forget, but they want to forgive. They are not willing to kidnap the children of the kidnappers or torture the torturer or kill the criminal. No. Because they are better. And that's a great lesson. They are better. And I think the good ones are going to win finally.

DM: These atrocities, what do they do to the human voice? When you know of such things, is there any loss of confidence in language, since language seems to promise the best things for people, the ability to build, to envision the future, to make changes? When you describe a coup, for example, in your chapter "The

Terror" in *The House of the Spirits* or, in *Of Love and Shadows,* the discovery of the bodies in the cave, is there an undercurrent that brings language down?

Allende: No, I think it gives energy to language because at that moment one has the illusion that maybe by putting it in words it won't be repeated, that you will register history and therefore keep alive the memory and avoid the same mistake or the same evil. Of course, that's not the case, but sometimes it works. And, at least in my case, I have the feeling that language is so powerful that just by saying things you can provoke them or induce them.

Eva Luna—and, in a way, Clara does it too in *The House of the Spirits*—narrates the world. She has the feeling that by writing things down and narrating them she makes them real, that then they exist. There is an Indian tradition in some tribes in South America in which the Indians don't name certain things because they believe when they pronounce the word it becomes real. Don't name evil. Or name what is good to keep alive what is good. Language has a tremendous power, I think. So I don't feel that there is any contradiction between evil, between these atrocities, and the fact that we have to tell about them.

DM: What about the younger generation who have never experienced the democratic tradition in Chile? Has the dictatorship created a deep freeze for cultural and political life?

Allende: It's like a pressure cooker. The lid is tight, but underneath, you know, something is boiling. Young people who have been brought up in the dictatorship and don't know democracy can dream of it and invent it, imagine it. Most of the letters I receive are from very young people, people who couldn't be aware of democracy as it was when we had it because now they are nineteen, twenty, and they were very small children at the time of the coup fifteen years ago. But it's young people who are protesting, young people in the universities and the schools. They are very subversive; they are irreverent. They defy terror. So I think there is hope for that generation, great hope. Maybe that generation will overcome all the weaknesses and errors of the old political leaders in Chile. And then, as I pointed out earlier, there is democracy operating in the society, real in everyday life.

DM: In your books you seem to suggest a moderate political course. For example, in *Of Love and Shadows* Professor Leal goes to collect his son from the revolutionaries in the south. In *The House of the Spirits* there's a similar episode. Would it be correct to say that you believe a moderate course is the best way to achieve the return of democracy in Chile?

Allende: I think that's the case in Chile. But I have great respect for people who take arms against the status quo. I have great respect for those people who can't wait any longer. And there are certain moments in the history of humankind, in the history of certain nations, when the only alternative is violence. Take a look at the history of Nicaragua, for example. Nothing could be expected out of moderation. They have been invaded by the United States thirteen times in the twentieth century. They have had a tradition of dictatorships propped up by the CIA. How could they have anything else but a revolution?

Chile tried to do something very original in Allende's government. We tried to build up socialism within the democratic constitution, without changing the constitution. Allende was elected in popular elections, free elections, and he tried, within the constitution, to make profound reforms that would really mean a social, political, and economic revolution in the country, without eliminating any of the liberties, any of the rights that the constitution guarantees for any citizen in Chile. That was very original; that was a beautiful dream. And he could have achieved it, but the size of his enemy was too great.

I think that Chile has the tendency to moderation historically, so maybe we will get out of this dictatorship without violence, without more violence. Of course, we have had fifteen years of violence. Therefore, I respect the guerrillas in Chile, armed if Pinochet doesn't leave. If the plebiscite doesn't change anything, if he stays in power for another eight years, we will have a civil war in Chile. That's unavoidable, absolutely unavoidable. Violence will become greater and greater every day.

DM: What do you think the prospects are that he will leave?

Allende: I don't think he will leave willingly, that just because he's a nice grandfather he will decide to go and take care of his roses. No, that will not happen. The militarists only understand the language of force, of violence. That's a language they know; they don't know any other. So they will have to be forced out of power. But there are many ways of doing it, not only with weapons. There's a tremendous moral strength, moral force, growing in Chile. And there comes a moment when you can't oppose that with any army.

On the other hand, everywhere in the world the image of Pinochet and the dictatorship is awful. Even in the United States now. And, in spite of Reagan's administration, in spite of the CIA, people don't want Pinochet anymore. Of course, they would love to prolong the right-wing, conservative, military regime, but not with Pinochet. You can't defend Pinochet any longer. He's just awful. So there are many different forces that are conspiring against him at this point. And he's not immortal. He will also die. I hope that he will die very soon.

DM: Two other people, Chileans of a different type: Gabriela Mistral and Pablo Neruda—what do they mean to you?

Allende: Those two poets, and some others—I'm talking about poets, not novelists— have been the voice of the people in Chile. I don't know why, but they have been able to interpret the people much better than any other artist or intellectual.

Personally, I relate much better to Neruda because in Gabriela Mistral there is a metaphysical pain. She's always in pain. She's a solitary person, defeated by pain. And I'm a very sensuous person, usually very happy. I'm very energetic. For me very rapidly pain is transformed into something else. So I relate much better to Pablo Neruda because he has a very sensuous voice and a political voice.

When I left my country I could take only twenty kilos in my suitcase in the airplane. I took some clothes, a small bag of dirt from my garden, some photographs—of my grandmother and my grandfather and friends—and a book by Pablo Neruda, the only book that I took with me. And now fifteen years later, when I recently moved to San Francisco, I brought the same book with me.

Whenever I need to recover my landscape, the feel and smell of my country, I read Neruda. Somehow he represents it, synthetically. I don't know how. He describes Chile by saying, "It's a long petal of snow and wine." A few words—*petal, snow, wine*—that's it.

DM: Which book of his was it that you brought with you?

Allende: His *Obras completas,* but it was not his complete works because it was a very old edition. The last work is not there. I bought that afterward. But I love the book very much. I've read it so many times, I can find the pages in darkness; I can find *the* poem I'm looking for.

DM: Is there a particular poem that is most important to you? For example, *Canto general?*

Allende: No, some lines. It's more than a poem; it's a line or word, an image, a metaphor that all of a sudden opens a window to me. Sometimes it's the name of a tree that I had forgotten, and, when I read the word and I name the tree, the tree appears. The power of words; they make it real.

DM: You mentioned that one of the things you brought with you was soil from your garden. One of the characters does the same in *Of Love and Shadows,* which closes with the words: "We will return." What are your hopes about returning, and what are your feelings in exile?

Allende: I'm sure that I will return. I'm younger than Pinochet. And I will return to a wonderful country. We will be living a very special moment of our history. It will be a time of confusion and making many mistakes but also of creating, and it will be really a renaissance of everything. It will be a very joyful moment. I know that the country has changed very much, and I have changed very much. I don't expect to go back to the past. I will return to the future. We have to invent the future in Chile.

My feelings toward exile are very ambiguous. On one hand, I have this nostalgia for my country that I'm not aware of until I'm confronted with something—for example, a movie, a book, a name, a person, a photograph, a memory. Sometimes it's just something so stupid. For instance, at one time I went to Texas and happened to look at the flag, which is exactly like the Chilean flag. When I saw the flag it had this tremendous impact on me, and I said to myself: But you're stupid; it's only a piece of cloth; it doesn't mean anything. And yet it does.

So I have this nostalgia, but I also am very happy to have lived these years out of my country. Now I don't consider myself Chilean only. I have the feeling that I can speak for Latin America, that Latin America is my house, my home, and I have a responsibility to care for everything that happens on that continent to everyone, not only to Chileans. Our circumstances are very much the same. We have five hundred years of exploitation and colonization in common. We have the same Catholic religion, Spanish and Portuguese colonization, that heritage of Spanish and Portuguese cultures. We have the Indian cultures; we have the African. We have the same demons and the same nightmares and the same dreams. So I think that I've learned a lot. Before I thought that Chile was the beginning and the end of the world. Now I know it's not.

Afterword

November, 1990

Allende: The election was held in December, 1989. Since March of 1990 there has been a democratic government in Chile. But the old military and economic structure created by the dictatorship of Pinochet remains practically intact. So the democratic government must be very cautious. They can't provoke this structure, these people, because they are there, waiting in the shadows.

Immediately after the election, censorship ended, and there was a great sense of freedom, some sort of river of strength welling up, especially in the arts. Many writers had returned to Chile right after the plebiscite—José Donoso, for example, who has just won Chile's highest literary award.

I think, during all those years of the dictatorship, culture continued with astounding tenacity. In spite of all, it was impossible to destroy. Even though they could not publish or show their work, writers went on writing, painters went on painting. Now there is a kind of renaissance spirit, a very joyful spirit in Chile. This renaissance I can only compare with the time of Salvador Allende's government, when, even though there were difficulties economically, socially, and politically, there was a real renaissance of the arts and of folklore. People were in a very creative mood. People were in the streets creating things. Chile is a very creative country.

From *The House of the Spirits*

The Terror

The day of the coup the sun was shining, a rare event in the timid spring that was just dawning. Jaime had worked practically all night and by seven in the morning his body had had only two hours of sleep. He was awakened by the ring of the telephone. It was a secretary, her voice slightly agitated, who scared his drowsiness away. She was calling from the Presidential Palace to inform him that he should present himself there as soon as possible; no, the President was not ill; no, she was not sure what was happening, she had simply been instructed to call all the President's doctors. Jaime dressed like a sleepwalker and got into his car, grateful that his profession entitled him to a weekly ration of gasoline; otherwise he would have had to go by bicycle. He arrived at the palace at eight o'clock and was surprised to see the great square completely empty and a large detachment of soldiers stationed at the gates to the seat of government. They were in full battle dress, with helmets and guns. Jaime parked his car in the deserted square without noticing the soldiers who were motioning him not to stop. He got out of the car and was immediately surrounded.

"What's this, *compañeros?* Have we gone to war with China?" Jaime smiled.

"Keep going. You can't stop here. Traffic is prohibited," an officer ordered.

"I'm sorry, but I received a call from the President's office," Jaime said, showing them his identification card. "I'm a doctor."

They escorted him to the heavy wooden doors of the Presidential Palace, where a group of guardsmen were standing watch. They let him through. Inside the building, the commotion resembled that of a shipwreck. Employees were running up and down the stairs like seasick rats and the President's private guard were pushing furniture against the windows and distributing pistols to those who were closest to him. The President came out to greet him. He was wearing a combat helmet, which looked incongruous with his fine sports clothes and Italian shoes. Then Jaime understood that something momentous was taking place.

"The Navy has revolted, Doctor," the President explained tersely. "It's time to fight."

Jaime picked up a telephone and called Alba, told her not to leave the house, and asked her to warn Amanda. He never spoke with her again. In the next hour a few ministers and political leaders arrived, and telephone negotiations with the insurgents were begun in order to gauge the magnitude of the insurrection and to find a peaceful settlement. But by nine-thirty in the morning all the armed units in the country were under the command of officers sympathetic to the coup. In barracks across the country, purges had begun of all those remaining loyal to the Constitution. The commander of the national guard ordered his men at the palace to leave because the police had just joined the coup.

"You can go, *compañeros,* but leave your guns behind," the President said.

The guardsmen were confused and ashamed, but the commander's order was final. Not one of them dared to accept the challenge in the gaze of the Chief of State. They left their arms in the courtyard and began to file out with lowered heads.

One of them turned when he reached the door. "I'm staying with you, *Compañero* President," he said.

By midmorning it was clear that dialogue would not resolve the situation and almost everyone began to leave. Only close friends and the private guard remained behind. The President had to order his daughters to leave; they had to be removed forcibly, and they could be heard from the street calling his name. Some thirty people were left in the building, holding out in the drawing rooms on the second floor. Among them was Jaime, feeling as if he were in the middle of a nightmare. He sat down on a red velvet chair with a gun in his hand, staring at it blankly; he did not know how to use it. It seemed to him that time was moving very slowly. His watch showed that only three hours of this bad dream had passed. He heard the voice of the President speaking to the nation on the radio. It was his farewell.

"I speak to all those who will be persecuted to tell you that I am not going to resign: I will repay the people's loyalty with my life. I will always be with you. I have faith in our nation and its destiny. Other men will prevail, and soon the great avenues will be open again, where free men will walk, to build a better society. Long live the people! Long live the workers! These are my last words. I know my sacrifice will not have been in vain."

The sky began to cloud. Isolated gunshots were heard in the distance. At that moment, the President was speaking on the phone with the head of the uprising, who was offering him a military plane to leave the country with his family. But he was not the kind of man to become an exile in some distant place where he would spend the rest of his life vegetating with other deposed leaders who had left their countries on a moment's notice.

"You were wrong about me, traitors. The people put me here and the only way I'll leave is dead," he replied serenely.

Then came the roar of the airplanes, and the bombing began. Jaime threw himself to the floor with everyone else, unable to believe what he was seeing; until the day before, he had been convinced that nothing like this would ever happen in his country and that even the military respected the law. Only the President was on his feet. He walked to the window carrying a bazooka and fired it at the tanks below. Jaime inched his way to him and grabbed him by the calves to make him get down, but the President replied with a curse and remained erect. Fifteen minutes later the whole building was in flames, and it was impossible to breathe because of the bombs and the smoke. Jaime crawled among the broken furniture and bits of plaster that were falling around him like a deadly rain, attempting to help the wounded, but he could only offer words of comfort and close the eyes of the dead. In a sudden pause in the shooting, the President gathered the survivors and told them to leave because he did not want any martyrs or needless sacrifice; everyone had a family, and important tasks lay ahead. "I'm going to call a truce so you can leave," he added. But no one moved. Though a few of them were trembling, all were in apparent possession of their dignity. The bombing was brief, but it left the palace in ruins. By two o'clock in the afternoon the fire had consumed the old drawing rooms that had been used since colonial times, and only a handful of men were left around the President. Soldiers entered the building and took what was left of the first floor. Above the din was heard the hysterical voice of an officer ordering them to surrender and come down single file with their hands on their heads. The President shook each of them by the hand. "I'll go last," he said. They never again saw him alive.

Jaime went downstairs with the others. Soldiers had been stationed on each step of the broad stone staircase; they seemed to have lost their senses. They kicked and beat those coming down the stairs with the butts of their guns, as if possessed by a new hatred that had just been invented and had bloomed in them in the space of a few hours. A few of them fired their guns over the heads of those who had surrendered. Jaime received a blow to his stomach that made him double up in pain, and when he was able to stand his eyes were full of tears and his pants moist with excrement. The soldiers continued to beat them all the way into the street, where they were ordered to lie face down on the ground. There they were trampled on and insulted until there were no more Spanish curse words left; then someone motioned to one of the tanks. The prisoners heard it approach, shaking the pavement with its weight like an invincible pachyderm.

"Make way, we're going to run the tank over these bastards!" a colonel shouted.

Jaime looked up from the ground and thought he recognized the man; he reminded him of a boy he used to play with at Tres Marías when he was a child. The tank snorted past, four inches from their heads, amidst the hard laughter of the soldiers and the howl of the fire engines. In the distance they could hear the sound of war planes. A long while later they divided the prisoners into groups, according to their guilt. Jaime was taken to the Ministry of Defense, which had been transformed into a barracks. They made him walk in a squatting position, as if he were in a trench, and led him into an enormous room filled with naked men who had been tied up in lines of ten, their hands bound behind their backs, so badly beaten that some could hardly stand. Rivulets of blood were running down onto the marble floor. Jaime was led into the boiler room, where other men were lined up against the wall beneath the watchful eye of a pale soldier who kept his machine gun trained on them. There he stood motionless for a long time, managing to stay erect as if he were sleepwalking, still not understanding what was happening and tormented by the screams coming through the walls. He noticed that the soldier was watching him. Suddenly the man lowered his gun and came up to him.

"Sit down and rest, Doctor. But if I tell you to, stand up immediately," he said softly, handing him a lighted cigarette. "You operated on my mother and saved her life."

Jaime did not smoke, but he savored that cigarette, inhaling as slowly as he could. His watch was destroyed, but his hunger and thirst led him to believe that it was night. He was so tired and uncomfortable in his stained trousers that he did not even wonder what was going to happen to him. His head was beginning to nod when the soldier came over to him again.

"Get up, Doctor," he whispered. "They're coming for you now. Good luck!"

A moment later two men walked in, handcuffed him, and led him before an officer who was in charge of interrogating the prisoners. Jaime had seen him on occasion in the company of the President.

"We know you have nothing to do with this, Doctor," he said. "We just want you to appear on television and say that the President was drunk and he committed suicide. After that you can go home."

"Do it yourself. Don't count on me, you bastards," Jaime said.

They held him down by the arms. The first blow was to his stomach. After that they picked him up and smashed him down on a table. He felt them remove his clothes. Much later, they carried him unconscious from the Ministry of Defense. It had begun to rain, and the freshness of the water and the air revived him. He awoke as they were loading him onto an Army bus and sat him down in the last seat. He saw the night through the window and when the vehicle began to move he could see the empty streets and flag-decked buildings. He understood that the enemy had won and he probably thought about Miguel. The bus pulled into the courtyard of a military regiment. They took him off the bus. There were other prisoners in the same condition. They tied their hands and feet with barbed wire and threw them on their faces in the stalls. There Jaime and the others spent two days without food or water, rotting in their own excrement, blood, and fear, until they were all driven by truck to an area near the airport. In an empty lot they were shot on the ground, because they could no longer stand, and then their bodies were dynamited. The shock of the explosion and the stench of the remains floated in the air for a long time.

In the big house on the corner, Senator Trueba opened a bottle of French champagne to celebrate the overthrow of the regime that he had fought against so ferociously, never suspecting that at that very moment his son Jaime's testicles were being burned with an imported cigarette. The old man hung a flag over the entrance of his house and did not go outside to dance because he was lame and because there was curfew, but not because he did not want to, as he jubilantly announced to his daughter and granddaughter. Meanwhile, hanging on to the telephone, Alba was attempting to get word on those she was most worried about: Miguel, Pedro Tercero, her Uncle Jaime, Amanda, Sebastián Gómez, and so many others.

"Now they're going to pay for everything!" Senator Trueba exclaimed, raising his glass.

Alba snatched it from his hand and hurled it against the wall, shattering it to bits. Blanca, who had never had the courage to oppose her father, did not attempt to hide her smile.

"We're not going to celebrate the death of the President or anybody else!" Alba said.

In the pristine houses of the High District, bottles that had waited for three years were opened and the new order was toasted. All that night helicopters flew over the working-class neighborhoods, humming like flies from another world.

Very late, almost at dawn, the phone rang. Alba, who had not gone to bed, ran to answer it. She was relieved to hear Miguel.

"The time has come, my love. Don't look for me or wait for me. I love you," he said.

"Miguel! I want to go with you!" Alba cried.

"Don't mention me to anybody, Alba. Don't see any of our friends. Destroy all your address books, your papers, anything that has to do with me. I'll always love you. Remember that, my love," Miguel said, and he hung up.

The curfew lasted for two days, which to Alba seemed an eternity. On the radio they played martial music, and on television they showed only landscapes from around the country and cartoons. Several times a day the four generals of the junta appeared on the screen, seated between the coat of arms and the flag, to announce various edicts: they were the new heroes of the nation. Despite the order to shoot anyone who ventured outside, Senator Trueba crossed the street to attend a celebration in his neighbor's house. The hubbub of the party did not concern the soldiers patrolling the streets because it was a neighborhood where they expected no opposition. Blanca announced that she had the worst migraine of her life and locked herself in her room. During the night, Alba heard her rummaging in the kitchen and concluded that her mother's hunger must have overcome her headache. Alba spent two days walking around the house in circles in a state of sheer despair, going through the books in Jaime's tunnel and on her own shelves and destroying anything that might be compromising. It was like a sacrilege. She was sure that when her uncle returned he would be furious with her and lose all trust in her. She also destroyed the address books with her friends' phone numbers, her most treasured love letters and even her photographs of Miguel. Indifferent and bored, the maids entertained themselves throughout the curfew by making empanadas; all, that is, except the cook, who wept nonstop and anxiously awaited the moment when she would be able to go out and join her husband, with whom she had been unable to communicate.

When the curfew was lifted for a few hours to enable people to go out and buy food, Blanca was amazed to see the stores filled with the products that during the preceding three years had been so scarce and that now appeared in the shop-windows as if by magic. She saw piles of butchered chickens and was able to buy as many as she wanted even though they cost three times as much as usual, since free pricing had been decreed. She noticed many people staring curiously at the chickens as if they had never seen them before, but few were buying, because they could not afford them. Three days later the smell of rotting meat infected every shop in the city.

Soldiers nervously patrolled the streets, cheered by many people who had wished for the government's defeat. Some of them, emboldened by the violence of the past few days, stopped all men with long hair or beards, unequivocal signs of a rebel spirit, and all women dressed in slacks, which they cut to ribbons because they felt responsible for imposing order, morality, and decency. The new authorities announced that they had nothing to do with actions of this sort and had never given orders to cut beards or slacks, and that it was probably the work of Communists disguised as soldiers attempting to cast aspersions on the armed forces and make the citizenry hate them. Neither beards nor slacks were forbidden, they said, although of course they preferred men to shave and wear their hair short, and women to wear dresses.

Word spread that the President had died, and no one believed the official version that he had committed suicide.

Translated by Magda Bogin.

Joseph Brodsky

Joseph Brodsky was born in Leningrad in 1940. He left school at the age of fifteen, and worked in a factory to help support his parents. He began to write poetry several years later and to teach himself English and Polish in order to translate poetry. His poems quickly came to the attention of Anna Ahkmatova, who befriended him. In 1964 he was arrested for "social parasitism" and was sentenced to five years in a labor camp in the Archangel region of Siberia. His trial and sentence received worldwide attention. Akhmatova, among others, was instrumental in obtaining his early release after he had served eighteen months. In 1972 he was "invited" to leave the Soviet Union, without his parents and one son. After a brief stay in Europe he came to the United States, where he began teaching at the University of Michigan. He became an American citizen in 1977, and now teaches at Mount Holyoke College. In 1987 he was the recipient of the Nobel Prize in literature. He was named poet laureate of the United States in 1991.

His books of poetry in English translation include *Elegy for John Donne and Other Poems* (1967), *Selected Poems* (1973), *A Part of Speech* (1980), and *To Urania* (1988). His collection of essays, *Less Than One,* was published in the spring of 1986. At the time that he was awarded the Nobel Prize, his work was still virtually unpublished in the Soviet Union.

This interview took place in April, 1986, in the small kitchen of his house in South Hadley, Massachusetts.

David Montenegro: You've just published *Less Than One,* your first collection of essays. Do you find prose gives you a new latitude? What problems and pleasures do you find in writing prose that you don't find in writing poetry?

Joseph Brodsky: Well, to begin with, I simply happened to write those pieces over the years. On several occasions I've been commissioned for one thing or another, and I just wanted to do whatever was asked of me in each particular instance. What pleases me really about the book is that it's something that was never meant to be. Perhaps a collection or two of poems was in the cards, but a book of prose—especially in English—wasn't. It strikes me as something highly illegitimate.

As for the difficulties or differences, essentially the operations of prose and poetry are not so different. In prose you have a more leisurely pace, but in principle prose is simply spilling some beans, which poetry sort of contains in a tight pod.

DM: You once wrote that prose is hateful to you because it doesn't have poetry's discipline.

Brodsky: How shall I put it? To use an almost paradoxical term, that's one of prose's shortcomings. That's specifically what makes prose lengthy. What I value about poetry, if I can simply estrange myself to look with a kind of cold, separate eye at these things, is that in verse your mind—reader's or writer's—moves much faster, for verse is overtly final and terribly concise; it's a condensed thing. In prose there is nothing that prevents you from going sideways, from digressing. In poetry a rhyme keeps you in check.

Basically, my attitude toward prose—apart from its being the vehicle of making a living because, in fact, prose is paid for, if not more handsomely, at least more readily than poetry—the thing that I can say in praise of prose is that it's perhaps more therapeutic than poetry. For poetry's risk, its uncertainty, well, its anticipation of failure is terribly high. And after a while one gets rather edgy or bilious.

In prose, I think, it's harder to fail. You simply sit and write, and as the day passes you've written several pages, then the next day, and so forth. That in part perhaps explains why there are so many novels around. Prose gives a writer confidence, whereas poetry does exactly the opposite.

DM: Efim Etkind, in his book *Notes of a Non-Conspirator,* described you as a very modern poet. He said that even when you were quite young you were presenting problems to yourself and dealing with problems presented to you by your times. What new problems does the modern poet face unlike those faced by the nineteenth-century poet or even the poet prior to World War Two?

Brodsky: That's a big question indeed. Now, one of the main problems that a poet today faces, modern or not modern, is that the body of poetry prior to him—the heritage, that is—is larger, which makes you simply wonder whether you have anything to add to that body, whether you're simply going to modify some of your predecessors or whether you're going to be yourself.

But, basically, it's not so much the question asked at the threshold, whether you're going to modify somebody or not. You ask this subsequently, with the benefit of hindsight. It's a question you ask yourself because of the critics around. But it's precisely because you have such great people before yesterday who breathe on your neck that you have to go a bit further, where theoretically nobody has been before. It simply makes it more difficult to write, because you are quite conscious of not wanting to be a parrot. And the people before you were quite great. To think that you can say something qualitatively new after people like

Tsvetaeva, Akhmatova, Auden, Pasternak, Mandelstam, Frost, Eliot, and others after Eliot—and let's not leave out Thomas Hardy—reveals either a very enterprising fellow or a very ignorant one. And I would bill myself as the latter.

When you start writing you know less about what took place before you. It's only in the middle of your life that you come to amass this knowledge, and it can dwarf you or mesmerize you.

That's one thing, one problem for the modern poet. The other is obviously that the modern poet lives in a world where what had been regarded as values, as virtues and vices, say twenty or thirty years ago have, if not necessarily swapped places, at least been questioned or compromised entirely. A modern poet presumably doesn't live in a world that is ethically, let alone politically, as polarized as was the situation before the war. But I think the polarization is still quite clear. I don't really know what Etkind had in mind. Presumably, what he had in mind was a difference between the modern poet and a poet, let's say, of the turn of the century. Our predecessors perhaps had more to believe in. Their pantheon, or their shrines, were a bit more populated than ours. We are one way or another, in a sense, awful agnostics.

But there are agnostics and agnostics. I would say that the poet worships perhaps only one thing in the final analysis, and that has no embodiment except in words, that is . . . language. His attitude toward the Supreme Deity who is absent is more of a reproach for His absence than a pure jeering or else hosannas. Perhaps I am modern in that I am living in my own time, and to some extent I reflect— what I write reflects—the sensibility of the people who speak my language toward their reality. In that respect, of course, I am modern. What else could I be? Old-fashioned? Conservative? Well, I'm conservative in terms of form perhaps. In terms of content, in terms of the attitude toward reality, and the sensibility, I am fairly— well, I hope—au courant.

DM: You mentioned the polarization of good and evil. Do you think there's a blurring of those categories now?

Brodsky: Not for an attentive eye, not for an attentive soul. But blurring the distinctions has become, indeed, an industry. It's done either deliberately by the forces of evil—for instance, by a certain political doctrine and its advocates, by its propaganda outfits—or it's done by honest, self-questioning people. But ultimately it's done by those who thrive on questioning and compromising things, the smart alecks who try to turn every idea, every reality, inside out. And, of course, there's a great deal of gray area now. Well, that's fine by me. The greater the blur, the more glory to you if you manage to sort it out. It's always been the case—the blur, that is. But today, given the population explosion, we have a quantum increase in the number of devil's advocates as well. Doubt nowadays is more in vogue than convictions. To put it kindly: Doubt is a conviction. Basically, we live in a period that is quite similar in tenor to certain stages of the Enlightenment.

DM: The scrutiny of all the preconceptions . . .

Brodsky: . . . of all the preconceived notions indeed. Except a Russin differs here. The results of scrutiny by a Russian may yield results totally different from those of his Western counterparts. For example, during the Enlightenment scientific evidence led people to the denial of a Supreme Being. Certain Russians—for example, Lomonosov and Derzhavin—were saying exactly the opposite, that the abundance of this evidence testified to the intricacy of the world, which is a divine creation.

DM: As a poet, you're conspicuous in that you often use religious imagery. Do you think it's still effective? Is it a common language?

Brodsky: In my view, yes, it is. At least it's common vis-à-vis my Russian audience. And I'm either generous or cynical enough to think that my Russian audience is not that qualitatively different in the final analysis from my English audience. But maybe that's wishful thinking on my part. I think it's still a language comprehensible to a certain percentage of people, and that's enough. For no percentage of the people is merely a small one. How small are, let's say, ten people, or six?

DM: Marek Oramus, while interviewing Zbigniew Herbert, said that Herbert *corrects* mythology. How do you approach it?

Brodsky: You animate it; you try to make sense out of all of this, out of all that you've inherited. That's what you do. You're not really correcting it; you're making sense out of it. It's simply interpreted. It's the function of the species to interpret the Bible, mythology, the Upanishads, anything we have inherited, including our own dreams.

Basically, each era, each century, not to mention each culture, has its own Greece, its own Christianity, its own Orient, its own mythology. Each century simply offers its own interpretation, like a magnifying glass, in a sense. We're just yet another lens. And it simply indicates the distance that grows between us and myths, and I think the attempt to interpret is essentially proportionate to the distance.

DM: You mentioned in one essay—and I'll just quote you: "At certain periods of history it is only poetry that is capable of dealing with reality by condensing it into something graspable, something that otherwise couldn't be retained by the mind." What are some other functions of poetry? What is the power of language through poetry?

Brodsky: Poetry sells perhaps better as the record of human sensibility. To give you an example: the age of the Augustan poets. I think if we have a notion of Rome and of the human sensibility of the time it's based on Horace, for instance, the way he sees the world, or Ovid or Propertius. And we don't have any other record, frankly.

DM: This might not be pertinent at all, since the poet's fascination with language isn't with its utility, but what does poetry now provide that prose doesn't, that religion doesn't, that philosophy doesn't? How strong is language in fending off a sense of chaos, in defending people or their sensibilities from brutality?

Brodsky: Well, I don't really know how to answer this, except by pointing out the very simple fact that speech is a reaction to the world, some kind of grimacing in the darkness or making faces behind the bastards' backs, or else controlling your fright or vomit. It's a reaction to the world, and in that sense it's functional. Protective? Does it protect you? No, more than likely not. It really *exposes* you. But it's quite possible that the exposure leads to the real test of your quality, of your durability. To say the least, producing something of harmony today is tantamount to saying in the face of chaos: "Look, you can't break me, not yet." And "me" in the language stands for everybody.

I don't really know what the function of poetry is. It's simply the way, so to speak, the light or dark refracts for you. That is, you open the mouth. You open the mouth to scream, you open the mouth to pray, you open the mouth to talk. Or you open the mouth to confess. Well, each time presumably you are forced by something to do so.

DM: When you first arrived in the United States in 1972, you said one fear you had was that your work would suffer a kind of paralysis because you would be living outside the environment of your native language. But, in fact, you've been prolific. What effect *has* living here had on your poetry?

Brodsky: I don't know. I guess what I was saying then simply reflected my fears. Prolific I was. I would imagine that I would have been as prolific, if not more, with no less interesting consequences for myself and for my readers, had I stayed at home. I think that fear expressed in 1972 reflected more the apprehension of losing my identity and that self-respect as a writer. I think what I was really unsure of—and I'm not so sure today, as a matter of fact—was that I wouldn't become a simpleton because the life here would require much less of me, not as subtle an operation on a daily basis as in Russia. And indeed, in the final analysis, some of my instincts have dulled, I think. But, on the other hand, by being apprehensive about that sort of thing, you're trying to make up your own mind. And, after all, you perhaps break even. You end up as neurotic as you would have been otherwise—only faster, though you can't be sure of that either.

DM: Do you think being in another country gives you a sort of dual vision?

Brodsky: But, of course, if only because here a great world of information is available to you. I was talking not long ago with a friend of mine, and we were discussing the shortcomings of being away from our country. And we came to the conclusion that perhaps the usual apprehension of the individual as well as of his public or of his critics is that, once outside of danger, out of harm's way, one's instincts, one's pencil, get duller. One's notion of evil becomes less sharp.

But, I think, on the contrary, in fact you find yourself really in a rather remarkable predicament vis-à-vis, let's say, the evil . . . well, vis-à-vis the dragon. That is, you can observe him; you can ascertain and assess him in a better fashion. You can see with greater clarity—precisely because of all the data available to you here which wasn't there—all his scales, all his spikes, all his teeth. On top of that, you are not mesmerized. Your attention is not clouded by the fear of being grabbed by that dragon at any time. So, basically, if you are to take him on, you can find yourself as well armed as the dragon is. In fact, you establish a certain parity at this safe distance. And, on top of that, you have always suspected that you are, perhaps, as bad as the dragon yourself, and given the chance you would be just as nasty and monstrous as he is. That is, you have always suspected there is more of a monster in you than of Saint George. It's not customary for a certain type of writer to regard himself as a fallen angel. One would rather regard oneself as a devil, as one of the devils.

And maybe the fact that I stayed, as you say, prolific reflects simply the availability of data. Maybe it reflects simply the realization that monstrosity is everywhere, while in Russia I thought of it as being our local specialty.

DM: It sounds as if you're implying an identification of the victim with the assailant.

Brodsky: But of course. No, I would say simply your notion of the dragon becomes far more subtle. That is, you realize you may play Saint George ad infinitum because the animal is everywhere. And, in a sense, you become—your armor becomes—in the the the final analysis, your own scales. And clarifying these things on paper conspires to bring the subsequent charge of being prolific. Prose is a more natural medium for that sort of job, for pondering. And to answer your very first question, the thing that many fail to realize is that there is a great bond between a poem and essay writing. Both employ the technique invented, of course, in poetry by poetry, of montage. It's not Eisenstein; it's poetry. It's stanzas with those framelike shapes.

DM: It's the parts trying to become the whole?

Brodsky: Yes, exactly.

DM: In comparing two of your poems, "Elegy for John Donne," an early poem, and the more recent "Lullaby of Cape Cod," it's striking how similar they are in many ways but also how drastically different. Both are set at night; both are very solitary poems. The earlier poem seems to show a spiritual struggle. There's a definite battle going on. In the John Donne poem it seems you kept the categories clearer: spirit, flesh, and so forth. And therefore the struggle was much more intense. But in the later poem there's less certainty. There's a sense of exhaustion—maybe even a spiritual exhaustion. Instead of snow, there's heat. You repeat the word *stifling*. And also there's the sheer weight of the material world. Despite the list of objects, in the earlier poem there's a sort of resurrection. In the later poem everything seems to be drugged, heavy, as if it can't wake up. What do you think of this reading?

Brodsky: There is some similarity, come to think of it. I never thought about it. I don't really know. Perhaps this is a valid comparison and a valid observation, and perhaps there is some sort of a genealogy of the kind that you're talking about. But I don't think so. I think the only thing it testifies to is, at best, not so much the evolution of the views as the consistency of the device.

I sort of like "Lullaby of Cape Cod." You should be aware of the fact that it's ninety-three lines longer in the translation than it is in the original. In the original it's a bit more concise. And I think it's a far more lyrical work than "Big Elegy." In "Big Elegy" there is indeed a certain clarity of the spirit. It is a vertical job from the threshold. But "Cape Cod Lullaby" I was writing not as a poem with a beginning and end but more as a lyrical sequence. It was more like playing piano than singing an aria. Actually, I'd written that poem because it was the Bicentennial, you see, and I thought, well, why don't I do something? There is one image there, I think, where I use the Stars and Stripes.

DM: As with the word *stifling*, you often use repetition. Your poetry seems centrifugal. You start from a center and move outward, turning and separating different aspects of the subject. Whereas Akhmatova would be more centripetal.

Brodsky: True, there is obviously a difference of temperaments. She seldom operates in big forms. She is a poet of great economy, and she's a more classical poet. Well, I wouldn't like to be compared to her.

DM: What gives you the least confidence now in poetry? Is there any particular problem that you're trying to solve?

Brodsky: The poems are always particular when you are writing this or that one. I'm not trying to bill myself in any spectacular fashion, but I think, as somebody who has always written in meter and rhyme, I do increase the purely technical stakes. Those two aspects, especially rhyme, simply are synonymous with compounding your own problems from the threshold, from the first impulse to write, which is fairly frequently a blissful one, in my case, or the sense of guilt. But I know what I'm going to do more or less from the moment I set out. That is, I more or less have the sense of form at the moment I'm starting with some sort of content, and the form gives you a great deal of headache.

DM: Like Auden, you have a fascination with form. Do you think structure itself sometimes leads you into new content?

Brodsky: Presumably, because by and large it's very seldom that one knows at the outset where one is heading. Simply by virtue of being a citizen of a different era, you're *bound* to invest the ancient form, old form, compromised—if you will—form with a qualitatively new meaning. That creates contrast; it creates a new tension, and the result is always new. It's bound to be new. And it's terribly interesting. Apart from anything else, sometimes you write about certain things precisely for the form's sake, in many ways. That's not to say that you're trying to write a villanelle and la-di-da to check whether your facility is still there. No, it's simply because, otherwise, to write about certain things wouldn't be as appetizing a prospect. After all, you can say only so many things; you can express only so many attitudes toward the reality of this world. In fact, all the attitudes in the final analysis are computable. And forms are not. Or at least the interplay of an attitude and the form in which it is expressed in writing increases the options.

DM: Some poets now don't use rhyme and meter, they say, because they feel such form is no longer relevant to experience or experience doesn't have the continuity or structure that such form implies.

Brodsky: They're entitled to their views, but I think it's pure garbage. Art basically is an operation within a certain contract, and you have to abide by all the clauses of the contract. You write poetry, to begin with, in order to influence minds, to influence hearts, to *move* hearts, to move people. In order to do so, you have to produce something that has an appearance of inevitability and that is memorable, so that it will stick in the mind of the reader. You have to wrap it in such a fashion that the reader won't be able to avoid it, so that what you have said will have a chance of entering his subconscious and of being remembered. Meter and rhyme are basically mnemonic devices. Not to mention the fact to which Ezra Pound alerted us, I think way back in 1911 or 1915, by saying there's too much free verse around. And that was in the teens of the century.

DM: Or, as Robert Frost said, free verse is like playing tennis without a net.

Brodsky: Well, it's not tennis. And not cricket either.

DM: Are you getting together a new book of poems in English translation?

Brodsky: That's somewhere on the horizon.

DM: Will it be by various translators, as was *A Part of Speech?*

Brodsky: I would imagine so because, otherwise, the book would be very slim.

DM: As a translator yourself, you've done particularly difficult poets, John Donne, for example. Do you feel your work's been well translated into English?

Brodsky: Sometimes it has; sometimes it hasn't. On the whole, I think I have less to complain about than any of my fellow Russians, dead or alive. Or poets in other languages. My luck, my fortune, is that I've been able to sort of watch over the translations. And at times I would do them myself.

DM: Since Russian is an inflected language and phonetically very different from

English, it must bother you that the sounds, the syntax, and the quality of the original can't be conveyed.

Brodsky: Yes, but that's what makes translation intricate and interesting. Curlicue. Other people solve crossword puzzles; well, I have translations. Essentially the operation is like solving a crossword puzzle, except that the next day they don't print the answers. On the whole, though, the principles of assonance or consonance in English are not that drastically different from the Russian. A word is a word. A sound is a sound, after all.

DM: Are you translating anyone into Russian now?

Brodsky: Not for the moment, no.

DM: If you object to the next questions, please tell me.

Brodsky: Go ahead.

DM: I want to ask you about the trial.

Brodsky: That was many moons ago. Nothing interesting about it.

DM: We can read the shorthand account of it, but what was it like from your point of view? It was a mock trial. It must have seemed absurd, though it was no joke. It must have made you angry.

Brodsky: It didn't make me angry. In fact, it did not. Never. No, a joke it wasn't. It was dead serious. I can talk about that at length, but in short . . . how shall I put it? It simply was an enactment of what I knew all along. But it's nice when things are *enacted,* you know. I knew who the masters were, and I knew that I had no other choice, that one day sooner or later it was going to happen that I would be in that position. I didn't expect a worse position; I didn't expect a better position. It didn't surprise me in the least that it happened, and the only thing I was interested in was what kind of sentence I was going to get. It looked rather dreadful because there were lots of people. It looked like what I've seen of a Nuremberg trial in terms of the number of police in the room. It was absolutely studded with police and state security people.

It's funny how—looking back now with the benefit of hindsight—I didn't really pay very much attention to what was going on, because attention was exactly what the state would have liked you to display. Or feel, indeed. The state wants you to get . . . well, you don't allow yourself to get scared, and you just think about something else. You pretend it isn't happening. You simply sit there, and, as much as you can, you try to ignore it. In fact, the only time I was moved during the whole thing was when two people stood up and defended me—two witnesses—and said something nice about me. I was so unprepared to hear something positive that I was a little bit moved. But other than that, no. So I got my five years, and I walked out of the room and was taken to the prison, and that was it.

DM: You had already spent three weeks of interrogation in a hospital?

Brodsky: It was more than that. It was the mental institution. But that wasn't for the first time. It wasn't the first arrest either. It was the third, I think. I'd been twice to mental institutions, three times to prisons. All that sort of thing. And since it wasn't terribly new or terribly fresh, I wasn't shocked then.

DM: Why did you feel that this would eventually happen?

Brodsky: Because one way or another I knew that I was running my own show, that I was doing something that amounts essentially to private enterprise in what is otherwise a state-owned economy, so to speak. And I knew that one day I would be grabbed.

It's simply the different tonality, the different use of the language. In a society where everything belongs to the state, to try to speak with your own voice, et cetera, is obviously fraught with consequences. It's not so interesting. It's simply an idiotic situation, and you find yourself in the position of a victim, as a sort of martyr. Well, you find you're sort of ashamed of it. It's *embarrassing.*

DM: You said once that your months of forced labor near Archangel in 1964 and 1965 were perhaps the most normal time in your life.

Brodsky: True, almost two years of it.

DM: In fact, the people there, you said, treated you well, like a son.

Brodsky: Well, a son . . . that was a bit too much. As one of their own, yes.

DM: You mentioned at one point that they were pleased to have a poet among them.

Brodsky: What they were pleased with, if they were, was simply another pair of hands, and also because I knew a little bit of medicine and could assist them. They were highly uneducated people, and the closest medical help was about twenty-five miles away. So I was simply helping them as much as I could, and they were just nice to me, not in exchange but basically because they were normal people and had no ax to grind with me.

DM: And you continued to write and to study English?

Brodsky: Yes.

DM: And translate?

Brodsky: Well, as much as I could. I had to work in the field, et cetera, but there you get this normal life, a hired hand sort of thing. Perhaps a little bit more work sometimes, and you're not being paid. But essentially it was okay.

DM: In 1965 you were released, and you remained in Russia until 1972. You did a lot of writing during that period also. Were you interfered with by the authorities?

Brodsky: Not very much. They would interfere with publication, but with life as such, no. Several times there would be subpoenas for interrogations and this and that . . .

DM: When you first came to the United States, what surprised you most? It's been said that you drew some of your expectations from reading Robert Frost, that you felt America would be more rural than you found it.

Brodsky: Not more rural, but I thought that the people would be less vocal, less hysterical, more reserved, more prudent with their speech.

DM: Could we talk a minute about current politics?

Brodsky: Be my guest.

DM: What do you think Gorbachev's effect will be in certain areas of the world, in Afghanistan, in Poland, and on United States–Soviet relations in general? Do you think he'll make drastic changes?

Brodsky: When Gorbachev became general secretary, Derek Walcott asked me what I thought of him. Well, frankly, I said, nothing, and I hope it's mutual. Since then I haven't changed my opinion.

DM: Let's go on to two other people probably more pleasing for you to talk about. You knew Auden and Akhmatova, and they seem to have been very important to you. Could you say something about Auden and also about Akhmatova, how they struck you or how they affected you?

Brodsky: I can tell you how. They turned out to be people whom I found that I could love. Or, that is, if I have a capacity for loving, those two allowed me to exercise it, presumably to the fullest. To the extent that I think—oddly enough, not so much about Akhmatova but about Auden—sometimes that I am he. That shouldn't be reported, perhaps, because they would fire me everywhere.

Essentially, what you do love in a poet like Auden is not the verses. Obviously, you remember, you memorize, you internalize the verse, but you internalize it and internalize it and internalize it until the point comes when he occupies in you more of a place perhaps than you yourself occupy. Auden, in my mind, in my heart, occupies far greater room than anything or anybody else on the earth. As simple as that. Dead or alive or whatever. It's a tremendously strange thing, or maybe I'm freaking out, or maybe I freaked out at a certain time, or maybe I've just gone mad. I simply think about him too often. In a sense, I can go as far as to say that, if I could supply an index to my daily mental operation, I think Auden and his lines would pop up more frequently there, would occupy more pages, so to speak, than anything else. And similarly Akhmatova, though to a lesser extent, oddly enough, I must confess. Well, I shouldn't pretend.

Both of them I think gave me, whatever was given me, almost the cue or the key for the voice, for the tonality, for the posture toward reality. In a sense, I think that their poems to a certain extent—some of Akhmatova's and quite a lot of Auden's—are written by me or that I'm the owner. That is, it doesn't matter what I do in my attitude toward people, in my attitude toward what I'm writing. I know that I'm myself, that gender distinguishes me from both of them, I would say, in many ways. But I sort of live their lives. Not that I'm a postscript to either one of them. Both would rebel against that. But to myself it's more sensible or more pleasant perhaps to think that I'm a postscript to them than that I'm leading my own life. I happen to think of myself as somebody who loves Auden or loves Akhmatova more than myself. It's obviously an exaggeration, but it's an exaggeration I feel comfortable with sometimes. I know quite clearly one thing about both of them: that they were both better than I in all possible respects. And that's enough. You simply think about people who are better than you are, and you spend your life sort of—how shall I put it—thinking about everybody you bump into.

DM: In your poem "Nature Morte" is there an echo—maybe it's because of the shortness of the lines—of "September 1, 1939"?

Brodsky: No, no. That's not true. I know what makes you feel that way. It's the opening of "Nature Morte." Well, there is that. There are other poems perhaps that have strong echoes of Wystan's [Auden's], but I think at that time I was more under the influence of MacNeice than of Auden. That poem is an old one.

DM: You've stressed several times in your writing how language outlives the state. But in our precarious age the life of the state may in fact be the life of the language.

Brodsky: No, not at all. No.

DM: What I'm getting at is the nuclear threat.

Brodsky: Yes, I know.

DM: A sense of the continuity of language is so important, not to mention confidence in the future, which may seem very fragile or even nonexistent to some. Does this have an effect?

Brodsky: No, I don't think that the future's fragile or nonexistent. I think we are in very good shape. That is, I don't think nuclear disaster is to occur. The greater the proliferation of all that nonsense, the safer we are, if only because the machines will try to control one another and the sense of command, the sense of responsibility is going to be far more diffused. Today it already takes two to launch a missile. So, eventually, it will require three, four.

DM: Nobody can do it.

Brodsky: Yes, nobody can do it, and so forth. It's of course a little bit silly, but something along those lines sort of instills hope in you. But should the worst come, should the worst happen, I don't think that will automatically mean the end of language. In the first place, I think, whatever the destruction inflicted by the states upon one another, something will survive. And language obviously will survive because the funny thing about language is that it knows better than anything or anyone what it means to mutate. The language's ability to mutate is terrific. It's a bit like roaches.

DM: A last question. Absolutes are something you deal with a lot in your prose. What absolutes would you say we have to live by if our sense of good and evil is somewhat oversophisticated, perhaps, or sophisticated to the point of paralyzing us? What other types of absolutes are there, if any, or do we need them?

Brodsky: Well, there is one. It's kind of a funny thing to be asked. And it puts me immediately in a position where I am tempted to proselytize, to a certain extent. But, first of all, one shouldn't really allow oneself into that situation where one's sense of good and evil gets so, as you say, sophisticated. Basically, there is one criterion that nobody with sophistication would refuse: that you should treat your own kind the way you would like to be treated yourself. It's a tremendous idea offered to us by Christianity, in a sense. It's a terribly selfish idea, and it finally established the bond.

DM: It turned the urge toward self-preservation into a social value.

Brodsky: But of course. Frost said once: To be social is to be forgiving. And that's basically the requirement, to forgive because you would like to be forgiven yourself, not only by the Almighty but by your fellow beings. And I thought the other day, well, I looked—now it's going to be a little bit maudlin, but, then, in effect I prove my profession—out of the window, and I saw a star. Then I thought, that star over there, presumably, with some help, is the domain of the Almighty, all the stars, et cetera. Then it occurred to me that this thought about loving your neighbor as yourself traveled here from quite afar. I thought, how appropriate is the origin. That is, the stars being the origin of this idea. For a star to like its neighbor, it takes something, yes? It's kind of interesting to think about, to think it through. I don't really know ... I don't think any magazines will want this interview.

DM: Do you think they won't swallow it?

Brodsky: No, it's not that they won't swallow it. They'll probably find it too lyrical.

Odysseus to Telemachus

My dear Telemachus,
                    The Trojan War
is over now; I don't recall who won it.
The Greeks, no doubt, for only they would leave
so many dead so far from their own homeland.
But still, my homeward way has proved too long.
While we were wasting time there, old Poseidon,
it almost seems, stretched and extended space.

I don't know where I am or what this place
can be. It would appear some filthy island,
with bushes, buildings, and great grunting pigs.
A garden choked with weeds; some queen or other.
Grass and huge stones . . . Telemachus, my son!
To a wanderer the faces of all islands
resemble one another. And the mind
trips, numbering waves; eyes, sore from sea horizons,
run; and the flesh of water stuffs the ears.
I can't remember how the war came out;
even how old you are—I can't remember.

Grow up, then, my Telemachus, grow strong.
Only the gods know if we'll see each other
again. You've long since ceased to be that babe
before whom I reined in the plowing bullocks.
Had it not been for Palamedes' trick
we two would still be living in one household.
But maybe he was right; away from me
you are quite safe from all Oedipal passions,
and your dreams, my Telemachus, are blameless.

1972

Plato Elaborated

I

I should like, Fortunatus, to live in a city where a river would jut out from under a bridge like a hand from a sleeve,
     and would flow toward the gulf, spreading its fingers
like Chopin, who never shook a fist at anyone as long as he lived.

There would be an Opera House, in which a slightly overripe
tenor would duly descant Mario's arias, keep-
     ing the Tyrant amused. He'd applaud from his loge, but
I from the back rows would hiss through clenched teeth, "You creep."

That city would not lack a yacht club, would not lack
a soccer club. Noting the absence of smoke from the brick
     factory chimneys, I'd know it was Sunday,
and would lurch in a bus across town, clutching a couple of bucks.

I'd twine my voice into the common animal hoot-
ing on that field where what the head begins is finished by the foot.
     Of the myriad laws laid down by Hammurabi
the most important deal with corner kicks, and penalty kicks
                     to boot.

II

I'd want a Library there, and in its empty halls I'd browse
through books containing precisely the same number of commas as
     the dirty words in daily gutter language—
words which haven't yet broken into literary prose. Much less
                  into verse.

There'd be a large Railroad Station in that city—its façade,
damaged in war, would be much more impressive than the outside
     world. Spotting a palm tree in an airline window,
the ape that dozes within me would open its two eyes wide.

And when winter, Fortunatus, threw its coarse shroud over the
                square,
I would wander, yawning, through the Gallery, where
     every canvas, especially those of David and Ingres,
would seem as familiar as any birthmarks are.

From my window, at dusk, I would watch the horde
of bleating automobiles as they flash back and forth
     past shapely nude columns in Doric hairdos,
standing pale and unrebellious on the steps of the City Court.

III

There would be a café in that city with a quite
decent blancmange, where, if I should ask why
     we need the twentieth century when we already
have the nineteenth, my colleague would stare fixedly at his fork or
                his knife.

Surely there is a street in that city with twin rows of trees,
an entranceway flanked by a nymph's torso, and other things
             equally *recherchés;*
     and a portrait would hang in the drawing room, giving
              you an idea
of how the mistress of the house looked in her salad days.

I would hear an unruffled voice calmly treat
of things not related to dinner by candlelight;
      the flickering flames on the hearth, Fortunatus,
would splash crimson stains on a green dress. But finally the fire
          would go out.

Time, which—unlike water—flows horizontally, threading its way
from Friday to Saturday, say,
      would, in the dark of that city, smooth out every wrinkle
and then, in the end, wash its own tracks away.

IV

And there ought to be monuments there. Not only the bronze riders
      I would know by name—
men who have thrust their feet into History's stirrups to tame
      History—I would know the names of the stallions also,
considering the stamp which the latter came

to brand the inhabitants with. A cigarette glued
to my lip, walking home well past midnight, I would conjecture
      aloud—
      like some gypsy parsing an open palm, between hiccups,
reading the cracks in the asphalt—what fate the lifeline of the city
      showed.

And when they would finally arrest me for espionage,
for subversive activity, vagrancy, for *ménage*
      à trois, and the crowd, boiling around me, would bellow,
poking me with their work-roughened forefingers, "Outsider!
      We'll settle your hash!"—

then I would secretly smile, and say to myself, "See,
this is your chance to find out, in Act Three,
      how it looks from the inside—you've stared long enough
      at the outside—
so take note of every detail as you shout, *'Vive la Patrie!'*"

1977

Poems translated by George L. Kline

Linda Ty-Casper

Linda Ty-Casper was born in Manila. Her mother wrote textbooks for the public schools, and her father was operations manager for the Philippine National Railways. Married to writer-critic-professor Leonard Casper, they have two daughters. She holds law degrees from the University of the Philippines and Harvard.

Her first book, *The Peninsulars* (1963), is set in the Philippines of the 1750s. *The Three-Cornered Sun* (1979) deals with the 1896 revolution against Spain. *Ten Thousand Seeds* (1987) is set during the Philippine-American War of 1899. Her historical novel-in-progress is *Stranded Whale* about the first years of the American regime and the civil government. She plans another about World War Two.

Her contemporary novels are about martial law and the years leading to its declaration: *Dread Empire* (1980), *Hazards of Distance* (1981), *Fortress in the Plaza* (1985), *Awaiting Trespass* (1985), *Wings of Stone* (1986), and *A Small Party in a Garden* (1988). Her work-in-progress *DreamEden* is set during the 1986 revolution. She has also published a book of short stories, *The Transparent Sun* (1963).

Just six weeks before our interview, which took place in June, 1986, Ty-Casper had returned from the Philippines where the People's revolution had recently toppled the dictatorship of Ferdinand Marcos, who had ruled for twenty years.

At the end of 1990, Ty-Casper, again just back from the Philippines, gave this account of the current state of affairs there.

The present confusion in the Philippines has to do largely with the narrow difference between a former dictatorship and the present democracy. Very careful to appear legitimate, Marcos subverted the constitution "legally." Aquino, with a presumption of a mandate from the People Power revolution, ignores constitutional processes. Instead of an elected convention to write a new constitution, she appointed a commission, which framed a constitution giving her a term of six years. She fired civil service employees and postponed local elections in order to save the expense—at the cost of establishing dangerous precedents.

As during Marcos, image building takes priority over substantive reforms. As a result of the self-serving pieties of self-proclaimed heroes, the national spirit and will are sapped. The new leaders appear not so much to govern (there is a clear sense of drift, with the poor being asked to wait, as during Marcos) as to reign over poverty, human rights violations, and chaos. Establishing a revolutionary government, Aquino deferred to the Congress (made up largely of landowners like herself) the grave matter of land reform. As under Marcos, the new government has deputized vigilantes against the Communist New People's Army; fanatics and ill-trained groups actually posing as great a danger as the NPA to civil peace and rights.

During the Marcos regime, publishers were reluctant to take a chance on any manuscript the least bit critical of Marcos. Under Aquino writers are reluctant to be critical because it might be the last chance for democracy, and no one wishes to precipitate, in any way, further disintegration or to be denounced as a Marcos loyalist for expressing independent views.

A West Coast newspaper, two years ago, asked me for an article about loyalty as it concerned Filipinos in the United States. Enthusiastic about the piece, the editor asked for another a year later. "The People Are Dying! Long Live the People!" was never used, though I based it on Amnesty International and United Nations reports on the Philippines. The editor, I found out, had been appointed Philippine liaison with American media. After much effort on a friend's part, the article finally appeared in the *Manila Bulletin*—so drastically cut as to have been a waste of paper and print. I have heard that the government keeps tab on antigovernment opinions expressed abroad.

A Small Party in a Garden, which I set under Marcos's regime, can just as truthfully be set under Aquino now.

Literature is even less a priority in the Philippines today. With very limited outlets for publication, there is very little incentive to write and, especially, to experiment. Still some is being written, mostly apolitical. History, as it is commonly understood, is seen as irrelevant to literature, because writing that implicates lives deprived of justice and peace, which nurtures soul and body, can be very painful to read. Critics call my novels grim, though these works can show only a fraction of the desecration.

Hope remains in the narrow difference, one of degree, between Marcos's dictatorship and Aquino's democracy. But to keep comparing them with Marcos is to indict current leaders for being only slightly better, at most. Next to Marcos anyone would look progressive and disinterested. Years have passed since 1986: Not everything can be blamed on Marcos anymore.

David Montenegro: The note about you in your early book, *The Transparent Sun,* mentions that you were influenced in becoming a writer by your grandmother, who told you stories during the Second World War to entertain you.

Linda Ty-Casper: Well, actually, she was more direct than that. She said, "Write a story of my life." She knew that she had gone through upheavals. She had lived through the Philippine Revolution of 1896 and the Philippine-American War of 1899. She had seen part of the Sakdal Uprisings in the 1930s. And each time she had suffered; her personal life had gone through great changes. For example, her family's house had been burned two or three times; each time they would lose everything because they were not insured.

Hers wasn't any kind of continuous narration. One day she would talk about her father or about the parish priest or the revolution. For instance, I remember her father, she said—and it was her father who gave me the idea for Blas Viardo in *The Three-Cornered Sun*—was a gambler; he didn't work. He was a landowner, of course. His wife was the one who saw to the family business.

But the interesting thing is that, when my grandmother was widowed and lost everything, she trusted her brothers and never really got her share of the inheritance. The old man in the story "The Transparent Sun" is patterned after her brother and something that actually happened. He really married several times and had really cheated his brothers and sisters. For instance, he would give them the titles to work animals that were already dead.

So when she was widowed—and she had seven children, three of whom died very young—she raised her children by gambling and by peddling. But her peddling wasn't in the street. She would get mats, woven mats, and then she would go to houses of relatives and present these as gifts. She knew instinctively that they would not pay for these but would give her more than the value of the mats. That's how she raised her children. And she would also give her relatives the family's remaining statues of saints. She sometimes described them. They had hands and faces of ivory.

Her gambling was most interesting. I'm surprised I've never used it. Because people knew her father had money, she would go to a house where they were gambling, and she would say, "Oh, my allowance has not come in for the week." And the owners, of course, would advance her some money. That would be—what do you call it?—a stake for the game. Then she would play, and usually win, by *her* account (*laughs*). She was able to return the money right away and continue the game with what was really profit. She was very resourceful in that sense.

As for my paternal grandmother, I don't know too much about her. I've asked my father, but he either doesn't remember or . . . But I remember she was quiet. She looked like my father a little bit, very fine-featured and sort of dreamlike. She was widowed early and had only two children. Her name was Tarsila. *Hazards of Distance* is dedicated to her. Do the dead know they are in our thoughts?

My maternal grandmother, whose name was Gabriela, never saw the book I dedicated to her, *The Three-Cornered Sun* [1979], because she died in 1953. My paternal grandmother died during the Second World War, the Japanese occupation. She starved to death, just wandering, lost and without food.

And that's like some of the stories my grandmother Gabriela would tell me about, during the revolution, trying to get away from the fighting. One time they got into a hut where there was only a handful of *palay. Palay* is rice with the husks still intact. They had to pound that, and then they cooked it in a lot of water. But they took the water from the rice fields where there were dead animals. They fed the children first from this. You see, they had gotten separated from the servants who were carrying the food, and so they had to scrounge around for what they needed.

But when she told this story—by that time years had passed—she was very calm in her narration. For instance, she'd say, "The bodies were left in the street, and the dogs fought over them." So I think I tend to write the stories that way. And people say that's underwriting, but that's my grandmother's voice probably coming through. It's how she told me those stories that has influenced my writing.

DM: Understatement or a sense of distance?

Ty-Casper: A sense of distance, and maybe it's self-protective, too. There are some things that are too strong to remember in detail.

DM: She would state them almost as plain facts?

Ty-Casper: Yes. She was a very unusual woman. I remember that my younger sister—there were two of us—would be sitting in the playpen, and my grandmother would be taking care of her. But pretty soon my grandmother would be in the playpen, and my sister would be outside, because my grandmother didn't want to be disturbed, reading her weekly *Liwayway;* that's in the vernacular, the weekly magazine. Well, of course, there were my aunts who would take care of the babies roaming around. But my grandmother is in the playpen *(laughs).*

DM: Did her storytelling affect the way you think of writing or the role of writing?

Ty-Casper: Yes—her way of passing on something to us. She had lost everything. I remember on several occasions she would tell me, "I have no jewels left to give to you but these stories." And by that time we were living in the city. I imagine in the provinces these things were talked about as if they'd happened recently. You know, it's part of their personal history, their personal stories.

I'm sorry I wasn't paying attention really when she was telling the stories. Half my mind was somewhere else, but, occasionally, if something very striking was being narrated, I would pay full attention to her. Pay her all my attention. But now I think I should really have listened to her more, though I was too young to realize what was being told to me. I know that I thought it was funny that she would say to me, "Write my story." I never thought that I would do it. And

I haven't done it yet. But she is *in* my stories. She's in *The Peninsulars,* and she is in the short stories. Maybe her *way* of seeing, her response, is there more than I realize.

DM: In the story you mentioned, "The Transparent Sun," would she be the person who was coming to her cousin's house to ask for the pawned necklace back?

Ty-Casper: Yes.

DM: And, in a way, the necklace is the *story.* It's returned to her.

Ty-Casper: Yes. She would be Sepa or Cela. I realize now there's a pattern. I tend to use that name for an older person, that name Sepa or Cela.

We knew a farmer's wife like Sepa, who, for me, stood for an old way of living and yet an honorable way. She would come and bring whatever she had to sell. She would pass by our house first, and my grandmother would wait for her. Sometimes she would bring just three pieces of fruit or a gourd or a squash. And then they would talk, and it seemed as if it weren't selling that was happening; it was a way of visiting.

I would remember old relatives from Malabon. Malabon is a fishing town, and the people there, the older generation particularly, didn't dress up. They wore old shirts and kerchiefs—dark, usually dark. But some of these old women would be very, very rich. And I've never tired of telling how one of them had gone to an expensive store in the Philippines where the salesclerks are very snooty. She had gone in there wearing these things—slippers, kerchief on her head—and looking like a farm person or a peasant and asked for the price of a piece of jewelry. And the salesclerk just gave her a price off the top of her head, without thinking anything about it. When she said, "I'll take it," the clerk said, "Oh, that's *not* the real price." The old woman went to the manager and said, "She told me this was the price." And I think I was told she got it at that price.

It was a lesson. She wanted to teach them a lesson, you know. Very often I find older people wanting to teach lessons. They *do* something not really to impose themselves on others but to tell them what's right, that this is the right way to live, this is the right thing to say and the right way of doing something. And I don't know if it's true, but I have that impression the older ones were always trying to teach us in many different ways—outright and by example.

DM: And what about language in your family? Is English your first language?

Ty-Casper: No, it's not, but it was the language we were taught in school. At the time I was going to school we were *fined* if we spoke in Pilipino, in Tagalog. We had to speak in English. But at home we used both languages.

See, my grandmother did not go to school the same way her sisters did. Her sisters knew Spanish, and she knew a few words but never used it. She was, she said, the *ugly* one, or the one who refused to go to Manila. You'd have to go to Manila to go to the private school. She stayed home. And so, to talk with her, we used the Tagalog, which is now the bulk of the national language, Pilipino.

But in school we *had* to use English. And, you see, my mother was writing textbooks in English. Also, almost all our books at home were in English. She had a lot of . . . I think mostly Protestant ethics books. You know, good manners and right conduct.

About ten years ago I was at a conference. And I can count the number of conferences I have been to, because I don't usually go. At this conference, one of the questions was: If you are a Filipino writer, should you write in English or shouldn't you be writing in Pilipino? And at that time I *tried* to write in Pilipino, and I found I *can* write in Pilipino. But I write more slowly, and I tend to write only certain kinds of stories. I have a short story that is published in English translation. I don't know if you saw it: "Gently Unbending"?

DM: Yes.

Ty-Casper: In Pilipino it's very beautiful. It's . . . I don't know. It's not diffuse so much as . . . there's a control there, but it's a little more vague, and the stress is different, I think. What I thought was that maybe I could start writing in Pilipino, but I find I take longer, and the story turns out to be different from what I intended to write.

DM: Are there certain subjects you can deal with only in Tagalog and others that you can deal with only in English?

Ty-Casper: Probably, yes. But I tried at that conference to defend writing in English because Rizal, our national hero, wrote in Spanish, and you can ask: Is he a Philippine writer or not? I said, suppose a foreigner knowing Pilipino wrote his stories in Pilipino. Is that Philippine literature? Should we be so strict and confine ourselves? And, in fact, I wrote an article asking how strict we should be since there are various strains in our culture—languages as well as other cultural traits.

You know, now there are, I think, more people writing in Pilipino, the younger ones, and they're *very* good. I can read it, and I can appreciate it, but I hesitate to . . . Well, I've reached a certain stage in my life when I know I don't have too many writing years left. And I want to write certain things, but, if I stop now to retrain myself, I have a feeling I won't be able to write them. Whereas I think if I continue writing in English . . . Then if I find I have time I can do the translations, or maybe somebody will translate them for me.

DM: So writing in English still raises some conflicts for you?

Ty-Casper: Yes. Somebody said that the way I write English is the way a Filipino would use English. I don't know if it's true. If it is, maybe that would be the compromise, you know, as long as it's not just a cop-out. I translate from Pilipino into English.

DM: While you're writing?

Ty-Casper: That's what one reviewer said.

DM: Do you think that's true?

Ty-Casper: I don't *think* so, but I might be doing it without realizing it.

DM: Have you written other stories in Pilipino?

Ty-Casper: I've started several, but I don't know where they are. They're not sentimental, but there are more emotions in them than I like to use. I haven't really thought much about it. It's not that they're diffuse. But what is it? I can't tell.

DM: Tagalog has a tradition, has a longer history than English in the Philippines. Has that influenced you in any way?

Ty-Casper: I haven't read much Filipino literature, because at the time I was growing up it was mostly sentimental love stories that my mother thought we shouldn't read. So I haven't had that background. Maybe that's another reason why I write in English.

DM: English literature in the Philippines is not even a century old. Does that make you feel more free as a writer or as if you're writing under the weight of the whole tradition of English and American literature, rather than starting fresh as a new culture, that is, an *old* culture in a *new* language?

Ty-Casper: I don't know how to answer that, David, because I haven't read much. I don't read much. In terms of influence, there is Robert Penn Warren. You see, Len* wrote the first critical book on Penn Warren. But I haven't been reading his works. I've started some but haven't been able to finish. And I know about other American writers, but I haven't . . . but I have read some of Katherine Anne Porter's short stories. I don't think I've read *A Ship of Fools.* So I don't know what the influence on me is.

What I try to do when I write is think of characters, and, since the people I know tend to be the source of my characters, I think, in that sense, it's really a Filipino story. And yet I don't know how entirely correct that is. You see, I went to Radcliffe for a year in 1974, and I noticed after 1974 that my short stories were different. In 1976 I wrote a story called "Triptych for a Ruined Altar," which was included in the honor roll of best American short stories for that year. It struck me that it hadn't been put in with the foreign authors. Yet that story happened to my aunt in the Philippines, so I wondered if I was moving away or in what

---

*Her husband, Leonard Casper.

direction I was going. Then I said to myself, I won't write any more stories until I figure this out.

But actually I wrote other stories, some without any Filipino motifs in names. I was really writing about myself in this country. They're all published except for the most recent one. For instance, there's "Fellow Passengers," which is about a priest and is set here in our parish in Saxonville. It's my response to a very old priest who came to reside here.

But, going back to your question, I don't know what tradition I'm following. I'm probably just writing out of my own impressions, and my impressions in this country are affected by the fact that I grew up in the Philippines and continue to be very close emotionally, though not physically, to the family I have there. But I'm also almost rooted here, because, if I stop to think, probably half my life has been spent in this country.

That doesn't quite explain my recent stories. You know, it's really as if I've reached the point where I don't have to use a Filipino word or name, because these places are more or less inside me, I think. It's as if I carried it . . . I don't know . . . I should look into that. And Len says law school has influenced my writing. The case system, for example. I'm writing briefs, really, he says.

DM: It sounds as if you're in the middle of . . . a change.

Ty-Casper: That I had not noticed. But I haven't written short stories since 1984.

DM: Do you feel as if you're living, in a sense, in two worlds?

Ty-Casper: Yes. So I tend to limit the information that I get. I don't usually read newspapers or watch television, especially now when I'm trying to get into the Philippine-American War of 1899. They're distractions. And, as you can see, when you sit on this porch—or I write in the bedroom up there—all you can see is the yard and the trees, and it could be a place anywhere that you wanted it to be. And maybe having the river there gives me a sense of not being trapped. Something like that. I don't know.

On Sundays I read *all* the newspapers, but during the week I tend not to. I have a very simplified life—and maybe it's not so much by chance, but it just so happens. I go to church in the morning, and there's a very small group. The Daily Mass Group. That doesn't distract me that much. I think it's the most important part of my day. When I need to shop I will shop, but not extended shopping, except when I have to get things to send to the Philippines or I'm with a friend. Then that's a way of visiting. And in that sense it's sort of, by choice, a life given to writing, although I don't write all the time. I spend more time pulling weeds or clearing the desk so I can write. I do my own housework. That's a kind of excuse, for not writing every day, for not writing more and better. Yardwork and volunteer work.

DM: Do you think American culture has affected your point of view, either positively or negatively or both?

Ty-Casper: I'm sure it has. I tend, probably, to be more efficient when I have to be. You see, writing is only one of the things I do, but the other things don't, usually, compete with it. I've been asked why I don't practice law. I think, if I did, it would compete with writing, and I'd be afraid I'd gradually stop writing. Law practice requires as much attention as writing does; it requires a different attitude. I like the person I am now.

Writing to me is sort of like waiting. I don't work every day, but, when an idea comes, then I like to be able to catch it. Although, if someone asks me to go to lunch, I will. I now belong to two writing groups. The Workshop is informal, with unwritten bylaws. I'm comfortable with the group. Then the PEN Women, Wellesley branch. That's organized. Writers and artists. We have guest speakers and art exhibits. But I've given up long-standing commitments that either involve confrontations or become pointless. I join Nuclear Freeze meetings, prison ministry, and that kind of thing. But not with the same dedication I bring to writing, perhaps.

It's not that I cut off all connections or, in reverse, that I'll do anything not to write. What I mean is I try not to have anything pressing, so if I choose to write I can. So, you know, those parts of the day when you go with a friend or work in the garden, those can be dropped when a strong idea comes to me. They're also part of writing.

I realize now I probably have ten years left to write, and I have at least three historical books ahead of me, which will require a lot of research and enclosing myself to be able to write them. In the States there are so many distractions, so many things possible to do. Sometimes I say, "Why don't I just drive up to Rockport for the day?" Or a friend will ask, and I'll go. But I haven't done it that often. I'm more time-conscious now.

DM: Are you finishing your trilogy?

Ty-Casper: I'm on the third.

DM: The first was *The Peninsulars;* the second, *The Three-Cornered Sun;* and the third . . . ?

Ty-Casper: *Stranded Whale,* on the Philippine-American War of 1899. Len chose the title. I started it in 1974, but a lot of things have postponed the writing. One day I told Len, "I've suddenly realized it's the *title.* It's *stranded;* that's why the book's still beached."

DM: Do you already have a publisher for it?

Ty-Casper: I have a publisher in the Philippines who wants all the historical novels. It's not a written contract. The editor just said after *The Three-Cornered Sun* that she would like to publish all the historical novels. And I keep promising her *Stranded Whale* in two years ... in two years ... Meanwhile, she has published two other books, two novellas: *The Hazards of Distance* and *Fortress in the Plaza*. But I really would like to have that book out of the way.

DM: You mentioned before all the research that's necessary for doing a historical novel. How is writing a historical novel—besides the research—different from writing a work of pure fiction?

Ty-Casper: It's different in that these contemporary novellas are about things I know for facts, and I'm more confident. Whereas with historical fiction, especially with Philippine history, there aren't that many sources; I worry about certain things. For instance, when I write about people going on horseback, I want to know if the soil is damp or not. I need details that you don't find in the history books. Probably all historical fiction writers have that problem. You're in the middle of writing, and suddenly you wonder: Was there a moon when they were ... ? Or where was the sun in the sky at that time? So, where would the shadow fall?

Fortunately, I've been to most of the towns in *The Three-Cornered Sun*. And I've seen the rivers. But now and then I stop. Would this fruit be in season? What would they be wearing? At what time would this be available, this kind of fabric? Do they use this kind of fabric, or another kind? Or it depends upon the class of the people. What kind of material would they use? It's those little things that are not that crucial but important, because knowing them gives me the confidence to write, gives the story its roots.

Also, history is so intrinsically interesting that I take *more* time than I should, and I get carried away, you know. For *The Peninsulars* I have boxes and boxes of notes that never got into the book. And I used to worry that they should be in there. Then I realized if they all were, the book would be just too scattered, too diffuse and out of control. So I think I'm beginning to be able to control my research.

DM: To know when to stop the research and to start writing?

Ty-Casper: Yes. When not to get carried away. You see, when you do research, one book leads to another. I used to read practically everything I could find. And I *did* that for the Philippine-American War. Now I've forgotten a lot because it was twelve years ago when I started. But I made notes to myself, and I separated them in four boxes upstairs, plus piles of Xeroxed material I haven't read.

Finally I decided I'm not going to read the whole thing. If I have four "books," I'll read only the parts pertaining to a particular year. I'm not *supposed* to know what's to come, anyway. So that's how I'll do it now, and I'll start maybe in the fall. I'll just read 1898 first. Then 1899, and so on. That's being more efficient, I think, though sometimes perversity forces me to read everything; then it's all there floating in my head, and I can't get a handle on what happened.

I don't know if that's the way it should be done, but I'm more confident now than I was when I wrote *The Peninsulars*. I wasn't quite sure then how I was going to go about it. In fact, I wasn't planning to write another book. I began *The Peninsulars* because I'd read some historical accounts that were derogatory to the Philippines, and I wanted to answer them. In the course of my research and readings I realized, though, that nobody would be interested in a plain refutation of some accounts of what went on in the Philippines two hundred years ago. But, if I wrote a *novel* that refuted what they said without saying so, it might have a better chance. So I started *The Peninsulars* and wasn't going to write another. But, as it turned out, I have *(laughs)*.

DM: When did you begin *The Peninsulars?*

Ty-Casper: I started it in 1957. It wasn't published until 1964. I wasn't ready to give up the manuscript then, except we happened to be in the Philippines, and we met N.V.M. Gonzalez, who's a very good Philippine writer. He and Len are friends, and Len said to me, "Well, N.V.M. will bring the book to the publishers." And he did, and they accepted it. But then I said that it wasn't finished and I wanted to work on it. They said, "No, you'll *kill* it."

DM: Your trilogy spans several centuries. *The Peninsulars* opens in the mid-eighteenth century, just before the British invasion of Manila. Then *The Three-Cornered Sun* is about the Revolution of 1896. And *Stranded Whale?*

Ty-Casper: ... is the Revolution of 1898 and the Philippine-American War, which ended in 1901. *The Three-Cornered Sun* actually goes up to 1897. It and *Stranded Whale* were supposed to be one book, but it got too long, so I cut it up. In the Philippines they can't publish a really big book. They would spend so much money, and it's not cost-efficient, as they say here. But here people want longer books, bigger books. That's why I'm lucky Readers International, my publisher for *Awaiting Trespass*, accepted the manuscript. In fact, some American publishers wanted to know if I could add more, but I told my agent I couldn't because I wasn't interested in the characters anymore. And, besides, I can't write a long book. My attention span is short. Or, maybe, my patience. I want to know how it will end. I think basically I'm a short story writer.

DM: What difficulties did you find in moving from the short story to the novel?

Ty-Casper: Nothing, I think. You probably noticed that the chapters tend to be short stories. I write them as short stories because that's how I work. I have to write each chapter at one sitting. If it doesn't go, then I can't ... That's how my short stories are. And now I'm at the point where I know when I'm starting it if it will go or not. I have a feeling. And if it doesn't seem that promising, I won't start it.

DM: When you begin a story, do you start with an incident or an event or a character or an image or just a mood?

Ty-Casper: I think it's a line. Like *Awaiting Trespass*—just that sentence, as it is, came to me. I was thinking really of the way street names in the Philippines change. You're never sure what the street is going to be named. I was intrigued by the idea, and so I played with the three names of Recto. Then it went on. Somebody dead, like the street dying. A body; a wake. At that point, I didn't know what to make of it, but, you know, I have a big enough family—not the nuclear family but cousins and friends—and so, if I wanted a character, there's always somebody I could use. That's what Len said. I just let them in on the wake.

I said, "A wake, for what?" And it didn't go anywhere far until I suddenly saw a closed casket. And that did it. Once it became a closed casket, then I could go on to the contemporary scene, the politics. Then I got the three sisters. Like a chorus.

I tend to have sisters about that age in my stories—like the Monsignor's sisters in "The Wine of Beeswings." I don't know why. They come to me. Recently, somebody called me from California to say he had assigned the book to his students. He mentioned that they had noticed the woman who called about the closed casket called three times. And I didn't realize that. I'm not aware of the way I use numbers either.

You see, what I usually do is: I end a chapter, then I wait, and, if an idea comes to me, if a *line* comes to me, I'll sit down and work with it for the next chapter. The characters are doing all the work. Some are short chapters and some are longer. That's the way. And maybe I'm thinking of characters and moods. Once I remember I was vacuuming the house, and the first line of a story came to me. I stopped vacuuming, but usually I just say, "Well, it's not going to do anything," so I won't be interrupted. Especially when I'm tired.

DM: To begin *Awaiting Trespass,* you had to discover a closed casket. Then, in a way, the writing of the book was the opening of the casket.

Ty-Casper: Was opening the casket.

DM: Finding out what the meaning was?

Ty-Casper: Yes. By putting in people who would be affected by this closed casket, something like that. The meaning to them. Yes.

I write in longhand. Then I will type a draft from that longhand. As I type the first draft, I make changes, and usually I'm typing things that I'm not really aware of. When I read it again or somebody asks me, I can't explain how those words got in there in that kind of order. So it's probably writing when the story takes over, you know. It's almost as if the story is telling itself. There are some parts I can't explain or even *remember* writing. It just keeps going.

DM: Then *Awaiting Trespass* isn't based on an actual occurence?

Ty-Casper: No. A lot of things were happening in the Philippines, and people were telling me about their relatives being found dead and stabbed and ... But there wasn't any closed casket. The closed casket came by itself, unrelated, and I just connected things, you know, as if you found some loose yarn, and you started with that, and you found other yarns that matched and went on.

DM: When you've written about other periods, as in *The Peninsulars,* for example, were you conscious of writing historical fiction as a reflection of current events or current political figures?

Ty-Casper: No, I wasn't. That was my first book. I wasn't aware of what I was doing. Except I was writing a story. Probably what I did was I had a character, then events, and I let them live through the events. And, as I said, I had this research material. I even read a lot of books written around that period to get a sense of the sentence length or what people were thinking of around that time.

With a contemporary novella, I *know.* I don't have to stop and think. I'm less self-conscious. It's as if I'm writing something somebody has just told me. That's it. In that sense, it's more fun ... well, not fun, not that I don't agonize over it. Sometimes. It's just that I don't stop so often to wonder should I have done that or ... Having been able to go back to the Philippines every year, I *know* what's going on without stopping to look for it in the newspaper or a book. I can *feel* it. I'm there, too.

DM: What would you say are your themes?

Ty-Casper: I couldn't even tell you what the themes are. I think what I have are characters and situations and the meaning comes out of that. For example, I couldn't tell you what the theme of *Awaiting Trespass* is except it has to do with people living through martial law and how it has complicated their whole lives ... their physical, emotional, and mental lives, how it takes over. Is that a theme, how martial law takes over?

I've been asked about theme often. When I was younger, I would try to come up with an answer, but now I just admit I don't know. I start, as I tell you, with a line, and the characters come in, and basically I say: "Is the character likely to do this or how would this character act?" And since I'm writing in longhand, I have enough time to wait. Although sometimes the ideas come too fast for the pen to write down. Have you noticed sometimes an idea comes in a certain run of words, and if you can't write it down right away it's hard to capture again? The idea is so simple, and the words are so simple, but if you put it aside and don't write it right away, you can't go back to it. It's lost. I don't know why.

DM: You've just returned from the Philippines.

Ty-Casper: I've been back six weeks now. And I haven't written anything. I was going back to *Stranded Whale,* but then I thought I probably should write another novella—and that's it; no more after this—about the recent events in the Philippines. When I was there people would say: Write about it. And I would say: Somebody *else* should write about it because you were here. And I'm sure with the freedom of the press returning, there would be people who could write about it now, so I said, I'm not interested in . . . I mean, I would rather not. If somebody would write about it, I'd rather not.

And then, during the last two weeks, I've been thinking, why don't I write about it? But there's an ulterior motive. I know especially Marxist-style critics will say my books . . . well, they call them upper class. They're really not upper class; they're middle, middle class. But these critics will say, "Well, that's *all* she knows. She doesn't really know the life of the country."

But, *of course,* I do know the other life, except I couldn't put it in a book like *Awaiting Trespass* because it would have been a bigger book than I could handle. As one reviewer in the United States* said: It's a small book demanding to be an epic novel. And that's a fair statement, but the fair reply is that that's *what* I wanted to write.

I thought this new novella would probably be about the people who live away from the main streets, down toward the river, back in the fields. I have characters already, but I don't . . . I don't dare start writing unless a first sentence comes to *me.* I like the phrase "It so happens." Maybe I'll start with "It so happens." No idea what's coming after that. My grandmother starts that way.

But this morning I was waiting to go to church, and a line came to me: "What she saw was the light groping . . . forming shadows that made her think of angels in pain." I don't know if that would go with this book. I wrote it down anyway, and I'll see if that will work. I have to see if this character really thinks that way. I also don't want to write another Telly character. I know people like Telly, but I don't know any more about Telly. So if I can find a name and a character to go with the first line *(laughs)* . . .

DM: In *Awaiting Trespass,* you have—because of martial law, because of the closed casket—each of the characters really examining what they want in life and in what ways they are responsible for other people. Some of the characters, like Telly or Sevi or Aurelio Gil, are idealistic or sway from idealism to disillusionment, back

---

*Los Angeles Times, February 2, 1986.

and forth, and it's a constant struggle for them. What kind of idealism do you like or do you honor or do you think works?

Ty-Casper: Probably Rizal's, you know. Doing something for your country ahead of doing something for yourself. Rizal was really thinking always of others. He became an ophthalmologist because some relatives were blind and he wanted to help them. His mother's eyesight was failing. In fact, my grandmother said that one of her cousins was on the docks waiting for Rizal to be brought back to Manila, hoping that Rizal would operate on her eyes. But, of course, Rizal was brought back from Barcelona straight to jail, so she was never able to have her eyes operated on. That was 1896.

When we were growing up, we were always asked: What do you want to be? And I think at that time I never heard anyone say, "I want to make money." Mostly, I want to be like Rizal, you know . . . probably seeing yourself in terms of the country and the people. And money was not part of it. If money's part of it, it's incidental; it's a happy surprise. Maybe that's why I'm happy, you know, not making money from writing. If it comes, well and good. And I tend to think there's nothing much you can change. You can change yourself, but you can't change what's going to happen to you. You just have to *confront* it. I don't know, that's probably pessimistic.

Something to help other people, to put yourself in the service of. That's actually what my parents did. My mother could have written for private publishers, but she chose to write textbooks for public schools, and she would go around giving workshops to teachers, although it was very hard on her to travel. Traveling is difficult in the Philippines. And my father was in the Philippine Railway—it used to be called the Manila Railroad—from the time he graduated from Lapoa Institute of Technology. He went up through the ranks but retired with the same house he had when he started.

I don't know if that's idealism. Toward the end of his career he was operations manager, so he knew where the lines would be extended. And I knew one relative wanted to know where the tracks were going, because then you buy the property along the lines and you're going to make a big profit. My father never told him, nor did my father take advantage of it to buy property himself. I don't know.

And my characters tend to act that way, I think. I'm not so sure. I think there are some heels there. In fact, in the next manuscript that's going to come out in August, *Wings of Stone,* I *deliberately* chose a character who's really an awful, awful woman, based on an actual person somebody had told me about. But when I wrote the character she wasn't half as bad as the actual person, you know. She was bad enough, but I can't put in . . . I don't know . . . Maybe that's a tendency that I've absorbed. When I'm writing, almost anything can go into it, anything that happens. It's sort of like life: Everything that happens to you becomes a part of your story.

DM: So you feel like you don't censor yourself as you go along?

Ty-Casper: No, I tend not to. Basically I'm trying to tell a story and really trying to get to the end of it, to get it over with, because I feel so good after it's done, you know. Maybe that's it.

DM: What about censorship? It's clear why *Awaiting Trespass* couldn't have been published in the Philippines, because it's so critical of Marcos, and also *Dread Empire,* which was published in Hong Kong. All of your other books, though, were published in the Philippines. Did you have any censorship problems with *Fortress in the Plaza,* for example, which implicates Marcos in the Plaza Miranda bombing in 1971?

Ty-Casper: Gloria Rodriguez, who published *Fortress,* said she would take a chance. And at that time, I guess, she was fed up with the system. I told her, "I hesitate to give it to you." But she said, "I'll read it, and I'll decide." She took a chance on it, and it came out last year toward the end when to have some kind of, I guess, dissent, any kind of dissent, worked in Marcos's favor. Then he could say, "Well look, there is freedom to dissent." The thing about a dictatorship like that is you never know what they would do. Gloria was really taking a chance.

But that book was written in 1971; I started it in 1971. I tend to write something as soon as the idea comes to me. I wrote it soon after the bombing at Plaza Miranda. Then rewrote and rewrote.

DM: Wasn't that bombing used as one of the pretexts for declaring martial law?

Ty-Casper: Yes. And *Dread Empire,* which is about the beginning of martial law, was written around 1972. Actually, I was trying to see if I could write something in six weeks, because we went to a party and George Higgins, one of Len's former students, said he writes his manuscripts in six weeks. I said, why don't I try it? And I *did* finish the draft in six weeks. But then I had to *rewrite* it. It took two years to rewrite, you know (*laughs*). So I could say I wrote it in six weeks and not admit it really took longer.

DM: In the book there is that rapid journey.

Ty-Casper: Yes, in one day.

DM: Those two books, *Fortress in the Plaza* and *Dread Empire,* are both centered on the approach of martial law, but the two main characters are so different. In *Dread Empire* we have Don Paco, a cynical and corrupt landlord who's losing his grip and eventually dies. Then in *Fortress* we have Don Miguel, a young, somewhat idealistic politician, who is killed still holding to some of his beliefs. Somewhere in *Awaiting Trespass* you say of the poet Telly, she could either bring John the Baptist's head in on a platter or entertain the angels. Is the writer, then, a witness or a partisan? Does the writer take sides?

Ty-Casper: I write out of what I believe, I think. I don't know if that's taking sides. That part about the angels was, I think, added on. I had seen something about that and decided to add it. Really, in the sense that I was opposed to martial law—dictatorship—I *was* taking sides. And if I wasn't that strongly opposed, I would have written a different kind of book. I could have written books that would probably sell better. It has been suggested to me that I write romance. I could have probably written *Awaiting Trespass* differently, as a romance, except I don't know how to write a romance. And I have certain ideas that I want to put down, to pass on.

It's probably like my grandmother telling me these stories to hand down these ideas to me, these thoughts. And in my writing I'm probably doing the same thing. These thoughts are valid, and at the time of the story it was *crucial* to the life of the country that there were people who *had* these thoughts, people who didn't all go along, didn't all wait meekly, you know. It's crucial for the future to know that there were *some* people who took a chance—in fact, some who went beyond what the characters had done. But I was allowing the characters to act the way I thought they would act. They couldn't go beyond their limits at the moment.

In that sense I probably *am* taking sides by projecting my beliefs and what I think ought to be, *should* be. I don't know if a writer should do that or should be just a dispassionate witness, but I think witnessing can absorb or reflect a stand or a position, because you tend to remember what you think is crucial or important, and the rest fades.

And you're right. Writing is witnessing; the characters are witnesses. And they're witnesses *in place* of the writer, probably. And in certain books they are *braver* than the writer. It's indirect witnessing, although you really shouldn't hide behind your characters; you have to be right up there with them. You *have* to be.... I probably take sides.

DM: You wrote "The Longer Ritual" the day after you received your masters in international law at Harvard. There's a certain candor in that short story, an almost shocking honesty in the young boy who's observing the funeral of his father. How would you describe that tone?

Ty-Casper: The distancing, I suppose. War survivors do that, too. I've read a book about children who have been through war, and their narration of war is impassive. The memory is too strong to put into words intensely. If they did that, they would just fall apart. That's what the psychologists said. I don't know if that's what happens.

DM: As a woman writer, is it harder for you to be published in the Philippines or to be taken seriously by critics, whether in the Philippines or in the United States? And a second question: Are there any taboos, whether in the Philippines or in the United States, that hamper you as a woman writer?

Ty-Casper: To answer the first part of your question, no, there are many women writers in the Philippines. The difficulty for me especially is: I'm out; I'm not in the *in* circle. I don't go to the literary activities. I don't join. But that is by temperament. I'm not a joiner.

Also—I don't know if you've noticed—there are no introductions in my books. That's deliberate. Up to the time I wrote *The Peninsulars,* I noticed that all the books in the Philippines were introduced by a famous writer or a politician, General Romulo, for example. When I was asked if I wanted introductions, I said no, because it's my work. It stands or falls as *my* work. Not on the word of somebody else.

And in connection with that, at that time Len was a critic and forthright and stepped on a lot of toes. So I don't get reviewed in the Philippines. I do get reviewed now and then, but critics who are *in* don't have a *reason* to review my work. They probably don't even read it, or maybe they read it but think it not worth mentioning.

When I go to the Philippines I see my family and my friends and a writer who's a friend. Two or three times I went to the workshops, but that's all. But then I tend—and maybe that's the American influence—I tend to speak out. I mean I don't always say something; I usually just listen. But when they turn to me and say it's my turn to speak, I tend to say something which is not *tactful.* I say what I mean.

So I don't know the real reason why I don't get reviewed there. One of the writers there told me, "Well, don't feel bad. They haven't reviewed my book either, and I'm *here!*" And he's a good writer.

I hate to say it, but sometimes it's who you know and whether you're willing to do something in return. I'm *not* willing. I'll accept not being read if I have to do certain things. I think I put it in a character. I said, "A person has to know the things he will *never* allow himself to do. He might not know the things that he wants, but he should know what he will not do." Maybe that's part of it.

"The Longer Ritual" was actually . . . did I tell you? I was going on the trolley to Boston, taking it from Harvard Square, and I saw this sign that said, "Those who mourn will be comforted." That was a strange thing to have there. Usually you see cigarettes or Pepto Bismol, that kind of thing. And on the way there the first line of that story came to me. So I was *so* anxious to get over the dinner. I was meeting Len to go to a play. And I don't remember the play; I don't remember what I ate. But I remember coming back home. We had a tiny apartment. It was supposedly a three-room apartment. It was one room cut into three, and it was along the sidewalk. And I wrote the story over the ironing board. That's what I remember about writing that story.

DM: Looking back, do you see an evolution in your work? How would you describe your growth as a writer between *The Transparent Sun* and *Awaiting Trespass?*

Ty-Casper: I think I'm more confident now. At that time I was straining a bit, although trying not to. I was just looking at a line here [leafing through a copy of *The Transparent Sun,* which she has been holding throughout the interview] that I wouldn't have written now or that I would have cut out: "He would let others outrage the land." You know, that's stiff.

But these are my first stories, and at that time I was trying to decide what I should do. For a long time—I think until 1980—I wasn't sure I was a writer. I never told people I wrote because I had to explain a lot of things. And in 1980. . . . You see, my mother had come here, and then, going back, she didn't have anybody to go with her, so I accompanied her. In fact, she passed out in the plane going there. But, anyway, this was my *first* trip to the Philippines without Len and without the girls. While there I met Father Ortiz, who had married us. He was with Billy Abueva, who is a national artist. And Father Ortiz said, "This is Linda Casper, Billy Abueva." And Billy Abueva said, "Oh, she's the novelist." And that had never happened to me before, I realize, looking back. It was: This is Len's wife; this is Gretchen's mother; this is Catalina's daughter; this is Francisco's daughter. That kind of thing. And this was strange, I thought; this was different. Soon after I met another person, a very famous architect whose name I knew, and somebody introduced us. He said, "Oh, she's the writer."

Then it sort of dawned on me later on, I shouldn't really feel apologetic about being a writer. So then I wrote in my passport "writer." It used to be "housewife" (*laughs*).

Or, you know, people tend to ask you, Do you work? I used to say no. But now, when they ask, I say I write. And then *some* people say, You must make a lot of money. I answer no. Then they say, you must be very famous. No (*laughs*). But that's another thing. It's a step. I go step by step. I'm a writer now. And I think that's the reason I allowed myself to be invited to that workshop. I was a writer, so I was in that 1980 workshop.

It was a strange experience. The young writers are very good. They're really very good. And I hope they're getting more chances now.

DM: Is there anything particularly new in Philippine writing, a new style or point of view? Are the young writers more tame or more rebellious since they have spent most of their lives under Marcos?

Ty-Casper: You see, these stories were not published; these could not be published. There are very few outlets in the Philippines. And so these were stories written and read in workshops. What I noticed, though, was that the craft was very good. The rebelliousness was controlled. But that's only to be expected, because they *hoped* to be published. But they were daring in the choice of subject matter, as long as it wasn't political. For example, they would write about incest, which I never think of writing about because I'm timid. I think maybe I haven't reached the point where I could write about it.

The young writers' craft is very good, and they write both in English and Pilipino. Taglish, it's called, Tagalog and English, and you switch back and forth.
DM: Readers International is publishing *Wings of Stone* in the fall?
Ty-Casper: It's supposed to come out in the fall. It will be my *first* manuscript that had not been rejected. Yes, *all* of them have been rejected so many times. But that one went directly to Readers International.
DM: Would you tell me a little about the book?
Ty-Casper: I started it in 1984, because there was the election for the Batasan Interim Assembly, and I was in the Philippines at the time. The question was whether to boy-cott or not. People were agonizing over it. Well, I didn't think I was going to write about this until, again, a line came to me, and it was about a person, a Filipino in this country who goes home for the first time in thirteen years because he has acquired papers. And he has acquired his papers illegally, you know. So, at that time I wasn't sure what he was going to do. Then I said, Why don't you put what happened that year or the year before into that book? And I did. Also I didn't want to write about priests any more. I had too many priests in *Awaiting Trespass*.

So I started the book in 1984, but it didn't go anywhere. Then late that year I got a grant to go to the Djerassi Foundation in California, so I put *Wings of Stone* aside and—probably the tenth time—started working on *Stranded Whale* again. But *Wings* was on my mind. It kept coming back to me.

Then I went to the Philippines again in 1985. I have a friend there who's paraplegic. At that time she was running out of antibiotics, and another friend said, "Let's go to this priest." Well, he's not a priest; he ordained himself. We didn't take it seriously, but, since she was really desperate, we went to this very old church, and he blessed her, blessed us, you know. It looked as it if were raining. The aspergillum was all over the place.

Somehow that priest, without my knowing it then, would be the focus of the book, would move the story forward. It's just that whatever happens . . . Maybe I'm open to what the book needs. Maybe that's why, when I'm stumped, I can even just pick up a newspaper and there is the word I've been looking for, or a friend can call to tell me about something, and I'm writing, and I put the conversation in the story. In this case, I met this priest, and I put some things together. Everything can be absorbed . . . It's like a stone gathering moss.

But that really doesn't tell you about the story. It's about a person who has been in this country too long, and so, when he goes back to the Philippines, he can't really defend himself from the people who try to use him. And he can't see the horror of what's happening. He's suffering from jet lag and culture lag and emotion lag. He's trying to reestablish contact with his father, who doesn't talk much anyway. And besides, in order to get his papers, the man has gotten married in the United States. It's a fake marriage, so he knows the green card is not valid—that kind of thing.

Then the girl I told you about earlier, who I thought would be an awful, awful person, at the end asks him to marry her. And, of course, he can't, first because he can't absorb what she has said, and second because he's married legally though not in fact. Then, when the priest is killed, he can't react. He has been so long away from the country that he's not part of the scene anymore.

That's what the story's about. I don't know if that's the theme. It's a kind of emotional distance that he's trying to bridge. He *wants* to. He wants to feel. He wants to be back; he wants to know if he *should* be back. He tells his father: "Tell me something. How did you love me into life?" This is in silence, because his father isn't talking. "How did you love me into life? Anything, anything, even something that deforms. *Tell* me something!"

And then he finds out that he's not really his father's child. A woman had given birth in a clinic and the next morning was gone. He thought the abandoned child the servants talked about was his brother. Well, at the end his father finally is talking, saying something like: "We loved you as if you were our own child." And then he realized the truth.

So why was he going back to the United States? His pain is relieved by the fact that his father is talking to him as a son. Maybe that is enough *claim,* the father claiming him as his son. I don't know, maybe that's what he came back for.

Then they go to the slums so that the father can build a clinic there. His father has retired but feels that he *should* do something for the people. When they go there, the priest is killed by people in the pay of the government; the slum dwellers are forcibly taken out of the place. The priest has told the squatters, "Don't give your *cedulas,* your registration cards, to this man because he will vote *for* you. You can't surrender this, you know. You shouldn't allow the government to tell you how to vote." And so the men kill the priest, and they toss him into a bonfire. And the son stands there and doesn't know how to react.

The editors said they wanted me to take out the last line of the book, and I said no because the last line *means* everything. The clarity of fiction is not the same as that of an essay. It could be vague and in the vagueness be precise. The last line is: "And the fire went on and on, until the sun looked hanged above it." If they didn't want to publish it that way, it's okay, but I wanted that line in. I don't know if that's being strong-willed or stubborn. So that's the book.

DM: Just a few more questions. In *Dread Empire* you begin with silence, the silence of the radio, indicating martial law has been declared. And all through the book silence is an important . . . it's something that happens very significantly. What do you think the power of silence is, whether in a political or a private sense, as something the writer has to deal with, to fight against?

Ty-Casper: Until you asked, I hadn't realized it, but you're right, the radios are silent, and it's as if the people are trapped in a desert. No news coming from the city and they have to. . . . It's like the Desert Fathers, when they went deeper and deeper until they were all by themselves. They had to test themselves and rely on God. I think they went there in order to be dependent on their God, to *not* be able to live without Him, without His help.

But, since I had not thought of that or even noticed that, I don't know. I might have been thinking unconsciously of *imposed* silence. At that time in 1972 people were *really* not talking. For instance, I have a cousin across the way who talks a lot—he's a lawyer—but at that time he wouldn't even talk to me. When I said, "What do you think of the situation?" he said, "Well, you can see it as well as I can." You know, that kind of thing.

Maybe that's it. People were really afraid to talk then. We didn't know whom to trust. Toward the end, before Marcos fled, people began to take chances because it began to be clear that there was a widespread opposition, and therefore you could talk. Still, people would say you'd better be careful. When I called my parents, they didn't want to talk about martial law. They would not talk about it on the phone. And my father kept saying, "Don't write *anything*, don't mention Marcos in your letters." When I wrote a couple of articles against martial law, he said, "Don't send them."

There's the silence of the father in *Wings of Stone;* and of the slum dwellers.

DM: Did the declaration of martial law in 1972 move politics more to the center of your writing?

Ty-Casper: Probably. Before it was background. In historical fiction the politics becomes the background. It's sort of part of the atmosphere. But, since you ask the question, since *Dread Empire* and *Fortress* and *Awaiting* and *Wings of Stone,* it has probably become more like a character too, you know, something to contend with. You can't ignore it because it's there; it's to be faced. Out in front.

You're right, it has, but not by design or by any kind of deliberate act. It's because that's what the characters are confronting. Politics had *invaded* their lives, their private lives. And, you know, at one of the workshops I was saying, "You should be writing about martial law." And they said, "Well, how could we write about it? Definitely we won't be published." And I said, "You don't have to write about martial law as the machinery or the government administration. You could write about what martial law *forces* people to become, the choices they have to make because of martial law, because that's also writing about martial law—its effect on peoples' lives."

Probably that's what I was doing. I'm not so much writing about the amendments and the power struggle on the national level but how this has sifted down and affected people. Some have been forced to make a stand.

DM: When you were in the Philippines six weeks ago, what was your sense of what was happening, what *is* happening, there?

Ty-Casper: I arrived there April 4, which was almost two months after the elections and little more than a month after Camp Crame. The people were still euphoric about the quiet revolution, the nonviolent, peaceful revolution, but there was already a kind of dissatisfaction coming in because of certain things the government had done, for instance, laying off civil service employees. And there was a sense of groping that seemed unnecessary, mistakes that didn't have to be made. Like appointing delegates to the constitutional convention. The harping on Marcos deflects the attention from the critical problems.

But what I noticed generally was the patience people had. The prices were still the same, and some people had been laid off. Unemployed, some were facing paying for tuition and books when school started in June. There was a kind of disappointment and yet a feeling that anything is better than Marcos. There was a hopefulness that maybe, given a little more time, things would work out.

Still, there were some things . . . and that's the reason I thought that I should write a novella. For example, while I was there, there was a strike in the next town, near where my father lives. Some of the scabs were killed. And they were killed violently then left on top of this public vehicle in the sun all day. The police were afraid to intercede. The troops were not called out. And that . . . I couldn't sleep after that. I kept seeing—I didn't see it in the newspaper—I kept thinking of it. I mean here is this revolution at Camp Crame when the people did great things, when God was on our side and we had the prayers, the nuns on our side. But what happens when disorder, injustice, still have a place, when the politicians are still politicians, thinking of themselves instead of the country? And, yet, anything is better than Marcos. That is both a relief and a curse.

From *Awaiting Trespass*

On Azcarraga, which is now Recto but was Iris at the turn of the century when the gray house was built, wreaths start arriving before the body of Don Severino Gil. They are lined up along the sidewalk on wooden stands, until those who sent them—identified by bright ribbons across each offering—come to pay their last respects. Their flowers are then carried up the dark wide stairs and placed before the temporary altar where the casket is to lie.

In order to accord the same courtesy to everyone, the wreaths are moved down the long hall after the visitors leave. On the stone porch, the *azotea* at the back—from which the spires of San Sebastian can be seen through the shiny leaves of the *caimito,* the tree of Paradise—stand the already dying wreaths of the very first to come.

The three surviving sisters of Don Severino arrive in time for a second breakfast. They learned of their brother's death only late the night before, but already they are dressed in full mourning: the same black clothes that for years they have been wearing to wakes—heavy *sayas* with large hidden pockets; *baros* as stiff as armor down the front; and over these, triangular *panuelos* held in place by jeweled pins. Appropriate to those born in the last century, the fashion is as rigid as the garments of saints inside old churches. The skirts are sad and heavy, but just right for January in Manila when the city is cool and *mantons,* for the elderly, are necessary.

The sisters greet, not each other, but the visitors who have lingered in the chance that their coming would not have to be repeated, or wasted on the servants of the house. After a round of kissing and rubbing of cheeks, in quick succession three orders are given to set the table in the long hall that divides the house like a highway.

Then, critically, the sisters and the visitors look at one another, trying to assess how the past is to be resumed for the duration of the wake. All of them appear to be the class of people who are safe from mourning.

With earrings as heavy as pendants pulling their ears, a strange impulse comes upon the sisters to sing. Their voices rise. But like a fixed solitude, a dark star, the death of their brother is remembered. Their hands reach for handkerchiefs deep in secret pockets. Their voices fall and they look properly bereaved again.

"Perhaps he called to us." After some silence the oldest sister speaks, only loud enough to make others wonder what she could have heard. Maria Esperanza is certain it is her name. She and Severino had secrets together. It was even her best friend whom her brother finally married. And it was she more than the others who understood that infidelities become a man; she never chided Severino. Feeling young somehow, her thick hair barely streaked with white, fully stretched and excuding sweet odors to tempt the sun, Maria Esperanza lifts her neck clear of the *panuelo* into which is woven a design of dark lilies. Yet as soon as someone else speaks, she feels old again.

"At eleven last night, I happened to look at the time. Perhaps that's when he died." Maria Paz, second eldest, is impressed with this possibility. She starts to cry, then looks about for the clock that she hears ticking. All the others in that house have stopped telling time and are as useless as the chandelier wrapped in gauze, a nest of sorts above them. "I don't understand it. I never look at clocks. But last night, as if Severino himself made me look. Who else could it have been?"

Assurance does not come from the others who want it for themselves, though they are not certain any more that such communications occur across the distance of time and other possible divides.

"I look at the clock every time I pass one, Paz. At every one I pass," Maria Esperanza exaggerates. After the other two are silenced by this fact, she proceeds to elaborate upon the lie. "The governor general, a tall man with whiskers like a cat, used to throw his hat at that clock the minute he cleared the last step."

She faces the one beside the stairs, a large standing clock inlaid with mother of pearl and various contrivances to indicate the phases of the moon and the tides. She is not certain it was the governor general; it only pleases her to identify him so. She would have just as easily said admiral, except that Montojo lost the battle of Manila Bay to Dewey in 1898. She does not recall the battle, of course. It was part only of the memory of her father who had stood on the seawall while the Americans and Spaniards exchanged shot and shell. So confident was he in his telling that sometimes people got the impression that it was Dewey who steamed out of the harbor that morning in May, scared and scarred by the cannons on the walls of Manila, by those at the arsenal in Cavite and, most grievously, by the long guns on the battleship *Castilla,* which stood on its concrete bottom in the Bay of Canacao.

Fact and memory have become one for Maria Esperanza, and wish as well, and dreams. "I look at every clock I see; how can you say Severino called to you just because you happened to look at the time? Besides, we do not know when he died."

Or where he died, or why, Maria Caridad thinks, waiting for her two sisters to declare everything so it can be known, and thereafter fixed in the mind. Habits of deference have been born into her, are as old as her bones. Being the youngest, she is satisfied with what her sisters remember, what they know.

Maria Esperanza feels cross because Maria Paz is giving herself such importance, taking precedence for herself. She is, however, distracted from this transgression by the servants, who have set the table and are pulling out chairs for them. Obediently, she sits down, her dark clothes spilling about the chair. Her feet barely touch the floor. Under her heavy *saya* they are as soft and plump as her hands.

They begin looking about to see who is sitting next to whom. Across the table, their voices weave over cups of thick chocolate, which they stir with lightly held spoons, allowing the drink to cool a bit before tasting to see what spices have been churned into it. Memories come upon them in waves, join their thoughts so that they complete one anothers' remarks and anticipate laughter soon enough to withhold it.

By the time the hard ball of Dutch cheese is sliced paper thin—its odor promptly mixing with the scent of flowers and the smell of mothballs rising from their mourning clothes—death is forgotten. Everyone begins to recall things about each other, instead of about Don Severino Gil.

Past occasions freshen sharply like a storm forming in the sea without warning: new slights answer old ones, a turning away when a reply is expected, the passing of dishes out of turn. With some relief the sisters watch their grandchildren feasting at their own table on small biscuits, shrimp chips, pastries and cola. The girls have tiny black ribbons pinned to their dresses. The boys have narrow black armbands at which they pull and twist.

"Bring them over," Maria Esperanza orders, expecting her own grandchildren to be without comparison.

The children crowd the big table. There is much kissing and pinching of cheeks, as each child is presented and recognized. Their poses and light conceits remind the visitors of the parents. Faint resemblances spark excited comments. "I can tell that is Paul's daughter by the way she pouts," one of the visitors pulls a little girl to her; while another one declares, "Virgilio used to hold his head just like this one; and that one has his father's ears. You can't mistake it."

Some of the children are great-grandchildren, removed by three generations from immediate concerns; and the sisters cannot always tell if the correct identifications are being made, so they smile and assume it is their own who are being most admired. Names have ceased to mean anything to them.

Finally the pleasure of recalling themselves in the children fades. Servants carry the young ones back to their table as if they were dolls unable to walk on their own legs.

Anxious to start dividing the responsibilities for the wake, the sisters hurry the visitors' departure slyly by telling them, "Come every day. The full nine days of prayers will be observed after the funeral. Bring everyone." Then in the order of precedence they have followed all their lives, they accompany the visitors to the stairs.

"I'll take charge of feeding the guests," Maria Esperanza says before the visitors reach the lower door to the street. She intends to be overheard in her generosity. Large diamond solitaires bind her fingers as she stands imposed upon her sisters, as large as a major saint on a main altar.

"We can alternate," Maria Caridad suggests sharing the burden. Her rings are *sinámpalocs* or *rositas,* small stones masquerading as a solitaire.

"Nonsense!" Maria Esperanza steadies herself on the bannister. "It is I who have the cooks. I serve better *pancit molo* than they do in Iloilo. And my stuffed *morcón* should be served to the Holy Father when he comes in February." She proceeds to describe the meals that come from the harvest of her farms with the pride of one who has been assigned to attend to the Pope and his entourage.

"What can I do?" Maria Caridad asks. In order not to be saddled beyond her means, she has always avoided taking the entire responsibility for anything.

In any family, there is someone close to poverty in the genteel sense. Widowed early, with no inclination to commerce, Maria Caridad has to be included in her sisters' ventures in order to help augment the income from her short row of apartments. Over the years, however, she has learned to accept the disparities by considering some compensations. Of the sisters, she has the most children and grandchildren in the States. They send her checks inside birthday cards, and on holy days, boxes of delicacies which, on account of prohibitive prices, grow stale in the local groceries. These she shares with her sisters, out of simple generosity and also out of pride: that she is in her children's thoughts.

"I'll take care of the Masses," Maria Paz says.

"Let me share expenses," Maria Caridad is quick to offer, having computed that the casket alone will be several times the cost of any number of first class Masses.

"Since she's the one who's always in church, let Caridad take care of the Masses and you, Paz, pay for the casket and whatever else remains," Maria Esperanza decides. "But, Caridad, not just some churches. All the churches in Manila. The Cathedral and pro-Cathedral especially. The Archbishop's chapel. And don't forget the churches in the provinces of both Mamá and Papá. Include his wife's. And where young Severino was assigned. Every hour on the hour until he is buried, have a Mass said for the repose of our brother's soul, Caridad." She escalates her demands to discover the limits of Caridad's devotion. "Sung masses with *rupekes*, the full complement of sacristans . . ."

Caridad looks down the long stairs at the end of which, on the sidewalk, sunlight plays like waves on the shore. The metal of passing cars throws the sun's reflection up the treads, against the lower walls. The light startles her into remembering. "It is the thirteenth of January. Tuesday. Sorrowful mysteries. Is it not Mamá's birthday?"

How could they have forgotten? The three fall silent, thinking separately of the festivities they used to have on that day. Long after their mother died, they spent days preparing her favorite food, until they stopped altogether because the children could not always come and the food spoiled, waiting.

"Now, every time it's Mamá's birthday, we will remember Severino's wake," Maria Paz declares.

"Everyone is dead," Maria Caridad complains because she is upset that there is no one else to consult.

The sisters stand quietly, thinking of the two brothers who had preceded Severino, and their youngest sister Maria Fe who died, leaving a daughter who refused to be taken in by any of them, who insisted on living by herself as if she had no relatives, who stubbornly called herself Telly, instead of Stella, their mother's name.

"If Severino had remarried, his wife would be worrying instead of us," Maria Esperanza says, though she rejected the possibility from the start. "Everything is out of place in his house. Look. Look."

Though Severino Gil had several live-in arrangements, each lasting years, in succession and occasionally simultaneously, these were informal affairs that supplied family gossip without requiring acknowledgment, so he could claim—like their father Doctor Severino Gil who was among those exiled by the Spaniards to Fernando Po in Africa for signing a petition to Alfonso XII, and by the Americans to Guam for refusing to take the oath—that he had given his name and honor to only one woman.

"How much there is in land and furnishings heaven only knows," Maria Esperanza sighs. "We'll have to pay for everything ourselves until Attorney Sandoval finds out, and he will fill his pockets first."

Maria Paz recalls the thousand peso bills secreted in Severino's belt. "Didn't he like to say he might have to pay for his life? I can't think of many emergencies requiring that much."

"It will not help us now. It's already in somebody's pocket," Maria Esperanza pushes a hand into her own pocket, keeps it there.

"Whose?" The other two wait to see what she will bring out in her hand. Their curiosity is divided by the gesture.

"Whoever held him when he died. Whoever was with him. He could have died in the street, you know." Maria Esperanza does not believe so. Someone with whom he was living—he never lived with those women in this house—called just the past Christmas to invite her. It could not have been with Severino's consent. Such indelicacy! But times were unreasonable. People disappeared, died mysteriously and unannounced. "Didn't it happen to Amang's grandson? They waited for him at supper until the food got cold, and where was the boy found several days afterwards?"

The other two could not follow the sequence of cause and reason but they knew the answer: unclaimed in a small funeral parlor on the way to Tagaytay. By coincidence, neighbors had stopped to rest.... The boy had been a student activist. Such a waste.

"No time for regrets," Maria Esperanza mobilizes her sisters. "We must look around to see what will not have to be brought over from our houses. The curtains! All thin and faded. The drapes will not do for the wake. Does anyone know what happened to the good chairs or where the silver is hidden?"

They despaired of finding anything. When they were still carried about in arms, during the Revolution against Spain and the War with the Americans, their mother had their silver buried before they took to the hills. On their return, everything was gone. Which servant took them, going back secretly to unearth the pieces, was never discovered.

"Some things are never explained," Maria Esperanza speaks for the sisters. "The moment one stops grieving, someone dies." She is thinking of the only pieces saved, those they had brought along, which she still has, heavy spoons made of pure silver that bend in the hand.

"I can't recall when I was last in this house. After his wife died, Severino stopped giving receptions." Maria Paz walks along the windows facing the street, her heavy skirt pulling at the drapes. The large pattern of meadows are like sunlight being shred into shadows as the drapes fall back into place.

"How can people hold receptions in hotels these days?" Maria Esperanza has discovered a silver platter in one of the drawers. She is holding it to the light. It is one continuous tarnish. "How can fine educated people use spoons some stranger has placed in his mouth?" She directs her sisters to the other tables, to other drawers for the missing parts of the set, while she answers herself, "No one remembers any more what is right and what is wrong. People talk only of what is liberal or not. Pro and con. God is not pro or con. God is what is right. The Pope will be much disappointed in us. There cannot be many good Roman Catholics in the whole country, he will think, since it is in such sad state."

"Have you donated to the basilica for the Infant Jesus?" Maria Paz asks, curious as to the amount. "The First Lady's project?"

Maria Esperanza evades the question. Her son, the Dominican, had warned her, "Mamá. How can you think of giving her any amount? She will build the Santo Nino large enough to be a giant. A Goliath! Save the money for better things, Mamá. Go to Rome one more time. Think of the refugees from Vietnam." Jaime's ideas shock her. A skeptic priest! But is Severino's son, also a priest, any better?

"I will have drapes made," Maria Paz says. "What material do you suggest?"

"Damask," right away Maria Esperanza answers. "Use my seamstress. She can have them ready in one day. Buy red and yellow damask, so in case the Pope passes by he will see his colors at the windows of Severino's house and will bless it."

She looks down into the street where the old houses have become boarding rooms. She can remember when they visited with families up and down the street, not one of those houses being the type that used cotton drapes. Cotton was only for apartments; for houses of third class material, hollow blocks. She disapproves of the way the groundfloors of the residences have been converted into bookstores, all manner of shops, including restaurants. The holes gouged out by rains make her think of graves and she is about to step back into the room when she sees a long black car coming. She is as stunned as if the sun had arrived in a coffin.

Maria Paz and Maria Caridad see the hearse, too. They look at one another and away, rearrange the ends of their *panuelos* around the large pins holding them over their chests. At the sound of commotion downstairs, they begin to make way for one another, end up standing at the top of the stairs bunched together like children hiding in the open.

The hearse stops at the lower door. It blocks the rising reflections of the sun so that for a moment, all is darkness at the foot of the stairs.

Old again and frightened, their shoulders pulled close to their bodies, the three move back suddenly when the stands of electric bulbs are carried upstairs. As in a church procession, they hold their breaths until the entire assemblage passes. This time it is the casket instead of the statue of the patron saint that is brought up last. It is carried with much struggling by thin men, three to a side so that it appears to be rising through a solemn surface, breaking into the light. The polished wood catches the light from the chandelier, forces it to rest upon the surface like recurved horns.

"Where is it to be placed?" the sisters ask one another the question asked of them by the men whose hands, they notice, are too coarse to carry someone who always wore a boutonnière and light Panama, and wingtipped shoes immaculately white.

"Where?" The men wait for the answer, something close to panic in their eyes, for the wood, impervious to water, has the weight of the tree from which it was cut.

Maria Esperanza points toward the altar, her voice having swallowed the words she meant to say in order to put the men in their place. In her skirt of many folds, she looks as if she is hiding small children close to her body.

Maria Paz faces an opposite corner. Her voice trembles, as hesitant as the sunlight rising to the dark portraits on the walls. "We had Saturnino there, and Elias, too."

Maria Esperanza recovers her voice. Her body becomes firm again, able to halt arguments. "Here exactly was where we had them placed." She stamps a foot. "As well as Mamá and Papá. Everyone." Then she looks up at the chandelier still wrapped in gauze, stands even more decisively underneath, fixing the place.

"I thought..." Maria Caridad starts to say, then decides to remain quiet, speaking the names of their other dead softly, as though in response to prayers being said in the hall. The crucifix on her breast has lost a hand but she does not know it. The gold of the corpus has softened into the wood, an old body melting. "I suppose..." she gives up attempting to remind her sisters that their brothers were waked in their own houses.

All past eighty, the difference in the sisters' ages can no longer be guessed from the wrinkles and the sagging flesh. It remains only in the habit of deferring to the next older.

The casket is slowly lowered from the shoulders of the men who then stand much taller. Relieved of the weight, they attend to the other tasks of adjusting the metal stands so the tiers of light will cast no shadow on the casket. Wreaths are brought forward until the altar almost disappears beneath the flowers, whose scents hang in the air like colored bits of sound. Only the black crucifix can be seen, thrust outward like a thorn.

In the midst of these preparations the sisters kneel close together at the *prie-dieu*. Crossing themselves, they pull out rosaries of many-colored crystal beads. They bless themselves again with the crucifix at the end of the beads then, directing their prayers for their brother, raise their eyes to the coffin and notice that it is closed.

"You forgot to open it." Maria Esperanza leans toward the men, hunching the stiff *panuelo* on her back. "Open it."

The men look at one another. It is some time before one of them comes over to whisper from a distance, "It is ordered to be closed, *Senora*. We were ordered...."

"Impossible," Maria Esperanza says firmly. "How can that be?" It annoys her to be called *Senora* instead of *Dona*.

Maria Paz and Maria Caridad stand up with her but they do not know what to do, so they kneel down again, closer together.

"If they will not open it, we'll have it opened," Maria Esperanza assures her sisters that she will have her way. "We'll see."

Resuming their prayers, the sisters watch the men fussing with the flowers before plugging in the stands of light. The bulbs throb like the pale abdomen of fireflies; swollen buds.

The three sisters blink at the lights, which hold together the long hall. Meanwhile, the men walk out quietly, leaving not even footprints on the smooth polish of the floor.

Outside the house, crowds flow on both sidewalks. Students and shoppers pause in front of the stores, licking ice cream cones or cracking watermelon seeds, dropping shells and wrappers to scatter up and down Recto. The sound they make rises into the house where the sisters are hurrying with their prayers, impatient to distribute grief to those who are coming to pay their last respects.

Seamus Heaney

Seamus Heaney was born in 1939 in Northern Ireland, and grew up on a farm in Derry. He began teaching at Queen's University in Belfast. From 1970 to 1971, he taught in California, then returned to Northern Ireland, where the violent conflict between Catholics and Protestants was worsening. In 1972 he resigned his job at Queen's University and moved to Wicklow to become a free-lance writer, then settled with his family in the Republic of Ireland. He is married and has three sons. Currently, he divides his time between Ireland and the United States, where he teaches at Harvard University.

He is the author of many collections of poetry, including *Death of a Naturalist* (1966), *Door into the Dark* (1969), *Wintering Out* (1972), *North* (1975), *Field Work* (1979), *Poems: 1965–1975* (1980), *Station Island* (1984), *The Haw Lantern* (1987), and, most recently, *Selected Poems: 1966–1987* published by Farrar, Straus, and Giroux in 1990. His translation of the ancient Irish tale *Buile Suibhne* was published in *Sweeney Astray* (1984). His collections of essays include *Preoccupations: Selected Prose 1968–1978* (1980), *The Place of Writing* (the Ellman Lectures, 1989), and *The Governance of the Tongue* (1989).

This interview took place in May, 1987, at Adams House at Harvard.

David Montenegro: What do you see as the danger of romanticizing the situation of the poet with his back against the wall?

Seamus Heaney: Well, I think there are two dangers. There are dangers in it for the poet himself or herself. For example, when an Irish poet comes to be interviewed outside of Ireland, there is a certain exoticism implicit. Leaving aside the recent twenty years of trouble in the north of Ireland, there is that whole Celtic, bardic voice-of-the-people, ancient, tribal wisdom cliché hanging over the Irish poet. And of course it's a cliché because it's based on some kind of truth. But every poet I know from Ireland is in some way wary of that mantle.

The second wariness one has, I suppose, is that in talking about things that are true and real within a society that is in the news and then having it written down in an interview, then having it quoted in subsequent articles; in all of that one makes a firmed-up, cut-and-dried entity, a kind of swiftly negotiable academic currency out of something that is, on the whole, subtler, you know.

I suppose your question arises from my being from Northern Ireland or from my occasional pieces about Russian or East European poetry. I personally am enormously grateful for the translations of the poets of the Eastern bloc—especially Poland—in the last thirty or forty years, and then the Russians of the 1910s and 1920s. My gratitude *is* partly political in this way—that the Irish situation, which I've just mentioned, is different from the specifically English situation. English poetry of the last five hundred years, say, with few exceptions, has arisen out of a cultural-political milieu that has settled itself. History stopped in England in a way. After the Wars of the Roses it was secured. There was the turbulence of the seventeenth century, the civil war, but England couldn't change itself. There was an attempt to change it into a commonwealth and a republic, but it fell back into its previous mode.

Now for those five hundred years, on the whole, English poetry has been re-assuring English society that the world is a trustworthy place and that the human spirit can dwell in amity in the world. There are great, demented exceptions like Mr. Blake (*laughs*). Or there's Wordsworth, who says that we are "inmates of this active universe." Okay, he'll go that far; there's an active universe out there, but still he says *inmate* and makes us domestic within it. On the whole, though, if you think of Pope or even Milton, as political poets, they're saying it's okay. Take Milton. In his politics there's a turbulence, but there isn't a *metaphysical* turbulence really: We know where we are. We're on earth, and heaven's up there, and it's secure.

Moving on right up to Auden—a great, interesting English poet, specifically English—there is a tremendous sense of dislocation and anxiety in his early work. But there's a corresponding desire to cherish a home. It may be a home in language or a home in a polluted or industrialized landscape, but there is "at-homeness." All of that English poetry, which is the canonical poetry that I learned—that all of us learned—belongs to a history that isn't devastated. And it belongs also to a history that gradually and constantly enforces a Protestant, humanist, secular culture.

Now the culture I grew up in was Catholic, folk, rural, Irish. History, in that dispensation, had not been secured yet. It was still awaiting its conclusion when Ireland would be united. That's caricaturing it, but that cartoonish notion of a destination that will arrive at some time in the future—perhaps not in our time—that was the shape of the historical understanding common in the subculture that I grew up in.

The subculture of Catholicism never is reflected in the high art of England, with a few freakish exceptions like Hopkins and Hopkins and Hopkins (*laughs*). You might say, after Shakespeare, the unconscious of the English language loses its Catholicism. You get to Pope, and he is trying to be a Catholic, but, in fact, culturally and linguistically, he's Protestant.

Of course, I thought nothing about this at the time. I did my practical criticism and ignored all the contexts. Then in my thirties and forties I became aware, if you like, of poems not just as cherishable and delightful linguistic events, but as symptoms and conduits of history, culture, and all that. Among the Polish poets, I think one can see that they *don't* expect the world to be trustworthy— don't expect the spirit to dwell in domestic comfort. They don't expect that history will help them out. They do look forward to a day when maybe something will happen, but they know it is a dream they are looking forward to. On the whole there's a kind of hard-bitten, patient *un*pathetic awareness of the pathetic in the world (*laughs*). That much is also very much the outsiderish, laconic, marginal, untrusting nature of the Irish mind.

DM: Poland has been dominated for a long period of time much like Ireland. For the last forty years, however, the domination has been an ideological one, and, in a sense, the enemy is very clear. It is the state. In Ireland the situation is so much more complicated. The contentions are neighborhood contentions. How does this affect the writer?

Heaney: Well, Ireland is small. There are four and a half million people in it. It is a place, as Louis MacNiece said in "Autumn Journal," where a man might feel he could see the end of a particular action. It's a place where people tend to feel— without necessarily a lot of evidence but because of its scale—that the problems could be solved if only *x* and *y*. You feel that if the right, dominant, moral personality—the right leader or four or five of them—came along, they could clean things up (*laughs*). And in some way I think that that sense of manageability, which we know to be illusory, gives the writers a certain confidence.

Yeats and Joyce, let's take them. There they are: both of them, in different ways, highly political animals; both of them arrogating to themselves the right— Joyce says it—to forge in the smithy of his soul the uncreated conscience of his race. Yeats says in his "Autobiographies" that, at the death of Parnell, Ireland was soft wax waiting for an imprint. And he says—I forget the exact words—"with a deliberateness that still surprises me"—he says that he set about to imprint it. Nobody would admit nowadays to wanting to do that kind of thing because it smacks of all kinds of... Well, the arrogation is an unallowable arrogance.

But, in fact, if you take a poet like Thomas Kinsella, you have an enterprise that is highly critical and highly *public* in its implications. Its procedure is private and elliptical, but its intention on the whole is directed toward the society. Take a different poet like John Montague. A poem like "The Rough Field" is an attempt to make a public statement. Even if you take a poet as elusive and evasive of public commitment as Paul Muldoon, that evasion and elusiveness *is*, in fact, a statement of position. It also, in an intimate way, is political. People like that position, you know.

So, in Ireland, the size of the place gives that, as I say, illusion of possibility, both in political terms and in literary terms. Again, as MacNiece says, you feel you can see the end of an action. Precisely because the tradition is there—precisely because it is ratified in old Irish terms with the poet as the praisemaker for the chief and the poet as the envisager of our future history, the poet as keeper of memory—precisely because of that traditional, slightly inflationary position, I think most contemporary poets are wary of arrogating the role to themselves. And yet it remains there in the common mind. When I say *mind*, I don't mean it in any fancy way; I just mean people—whether in the academy in the United States or in the pubs in Ireland—think of the Irish poet as having some definite public status.

DM: Would Derek Mahon be another poet who, in a sense, stepped back?

Heaney: Mahon certainly deliberately stepped back. He's very much in that sense a Joycean figure or, shall we say, a Daedalus figure. I've said this about Derek before, that I see him as a kind of Stephen Dedalus of the north, withdrawing from the nets of solidarity and spokesmanship for his group. And the minute I say his group—northern Protestant Unionists—I understand exactly why Derek withdraws. Not to do so would *coarsen* and *reduce* the scope not only of the poetic endeavor but the human possibility. So Derek's cosmopolitanism, to give it a glib name, his refusals of local representation, are not just refusals; they are embraces of larger possibilities, as he sees it, for the spirit in the world.

On the other hand, it is possible for Derek's poems to be read politically. My friend Seamus Deane has done this very persuasively. And Mahon is not unaware himself of the political predestination almost of which he suffers because he has written poems whose idiom and elements are fastidiously nonpartisan and nonlocal but whose implications and applications are exact *and* local. They can be read downward toward the narrow center of Ulster; they can be read outward toward the circumference of our imagining how things are in the whole world. But they are *exactly* aware of the shape of things, you know. I think of a poem like "Rage for Order" or "The Last of the Fire Kings" or even "Nostalgias," which goes:

The chair squeaks in a high wind,
Rain falls from its branches,
The kettle yearns for the
Mountain, the soap for the sea.

In a tiny stone church
On the desolate headland
A lost tribe is singing abide with me.

While this is a jeu d'esprit and a kind of latecomerly, Frenchified, postmodern
joke, it is a also a vision of the lost tribe, a vision of Unionism's ending. It's a
kind of laconic elegy for an order that is passing.*
DM: It seems there is a sort of teetering, even between the absurdity of the images
and the plain statement at the end. It's hard to tell where his loyalty lies.
Heaney: Well, of course. This is the point. I mean it's wonderful. Derek has so
much love, and—to continue the metaphor of the kettle for the mountain—there's
a bedrock of attitude and language and native resource in Derek which is entirely
faithful. He's Joycean in that way. Joyce is so full, on one level, of disdain, and,
on another level, so completely in charge of what he disdains that it would be a
simplification to call him somebody who is anti what produced him. And the same
with Derek. To say he is a man who is unfaithful to his origin, that's a kind of
stupid remark. He is someone who would refine and verify, I suppose.

I have written a little bit about this in a thing that was published in the
Agni Review a while back. Derek is fundamentally a lyric poet, and therefore it is
the transports and completions finally of lyric art at its widest reach that give him
his justification. And one of the functions of that lyric art is, I think, to resolve
symbolically the very tensions that we're talking about, to hold, for a moment, a
point where skepticism and faith, where the line between them, is obliterated in
the act of utterance. So I think the concerns that underlie his poems are political,
yet his execution as an artist shuns the political as an executive mode of writing.
DM: Does the political as a mode of writing, then, inevitably distort experience
and language by oversimplification?
Heaney: Well, I think that that oversimplification and distortion aren't necessarily
the worst things that can happen. I mean, given a certain context, I think that
anger, excess, intensity, obsession, rage, these things are perfectly good as an
inspiration. I'd like to think that there's no rule except the vision of reality. As
Yeats says, art is a vision of reality. If your vision is such that you see the world
not in terms of beauty and truth but in terms of reality and justice, as Yeats put
it in a beautiful phrase, then surely there's nothing to stop you, in terms of that
vision, from uttering things that are political.

It's hard to think of successful partisan poems, but let us cite, say, *Howl* [by

---

*Heaney discussed this poem again in the Ellmann Lectures, *The Place of Writing*, in 1988, published
in 1989 by Scholars Press, Atlanta, Georgia.

Allen Ginsberg], as a poem that is antiestablishment. Now, of course, it's writing that's one-sided. It's distorting, and so on and so forth. But it's an *event* in language and an event in history, and somehow it is sponsored by a tradition of—bad writing (*laughs*). It is not the mot juste school of composition, I guess one could say. It's at the point where the avant-garde and populism, almost, coincide.

At a different end of the scale, the patrician Lowell seems to me to have written poems of lasting, deliberate, political value. They may not be partisan, but they are not without their divisiveness—poems like "For the Union Dead" and "Near the Ocean," for example.

I remember, though, Seamus Deane and myself discussing this and Deane making a distinction between what he called poetry of crisis and public poetry. And I think that the poetry of crisis—that is to say, the *immediate* response couched in the given terms of the topical question—that is very risky business. And this is clearly true of the unmeditated and unmediated poster poem, the throwaway poem, of the use of verse as a vehicle for controversy or a message. A lot depends, as ever, on talent, for God's sake, but the poet just surrenders a certain . . . Well, in these cases, the poet breaks the protocol of his or her art, I think.

DM: Of the imagination?

Heaney: I guess. But I'm very wary of citing the protocols of the imagination. I don't know what they are. But public poetry is possible, I mean a kind of meditated, a mediated utterance that is consonant with the poet's sensibility and that also takes in and mediates the world, the outside world, the world of public reality. Yeats's poem "Easter 1916" presents itself as a poem of crisis, but it's actually a public poem, I think. It dwells in the domain of the moment dramatically, but it already inspects the moment historically, you know. It is not a poem innocently and impulsively arising as a reaction to a stimulus. It's not simply that. There is a long, secluded incubation period between stimulus and response, and it artfully imitates spontaneous response. But it positions itself and it positions its speaker in regard to the future, in regard to the past, in regard to the moment. And, as Malcolm Brown has pointed out in his book *The Politics of Irish Literature,* although this is a poem about a great moment of Irish independence, about a great moment of Irish self-declaration by a poet who is seen as Ireland's national poet, it also contains the unexpected line and, in a sense, the unacceptable line: "England may keep faith." So it's a complicated piece of work.

DM: Then there is the last line: "A terrible beauty is born." You mentioned rage as being one source of utterance and, in a sense, a legitimate one. What about one step further? What about—and Seamus Deane questions this actually in his essay on Derek Mahon—what about violence as a source of utterance and intensity?

Heaney: The intrusion of violence is one thing. But the entering of the realm of violence through imagery, hallucinatory experience, theme and diction, the reach for all kinds of blood and guts and Grand Guignol in, shall we say, an inflated way, I think is deplorable. I think a lot of so-called violence in poetry comes from some kind of very simpleminded envy of... or some notion that the *pallid* is not the true domain of human experience, that the real thing is the nightmarish awful. I mean, always when violence is abroad in poetry—the violent content, the blood-and-guts imagery—I ask myself: What is the necessity for this? Where is it coming from? Is it coming from the airwaves? Is it coming from the age? Is it coming from rent-an-image? Is it coming from, you know, the usual sewage of the age, which flows past us all? Or is it coming from an individual necessity and an individual cesspool? If it's coming from an individual cesspool, fair enough, you know. But what is just picked up in the street...

In other words, I think there's a lot of gratuitous violent imagery in a lot of American poetry written by people living perfectly comfortable middle-class lives, and I think that's stupid. I mean, I can understand that it is for kicks, and I don't inflate it into some visionary poetry of the age thing. I think that post-Holocaust discourse, the awareness of the deplorable that all of us live with, that whole intellectual coming-to-terms that has been done in the last forty to fifty years, has given a permission, oddly enough, for the awful image. And because it has been codified now and patented and everybody can talk about it, the word *Holocaust* itself inspires no fear in a lot of people. I find that sort of scaresome, but it's understandable. So there's a sort of writing that pretends to cope with these enormities that are mind-stunning, and it copes with them at a level of innocence and at a level of glibness that is often considered violent, dramatic, and awesome. In fact, there's an element of spectator sport about it all.

We tend to think of the true witness figure as being specifically middle European and Soviet, but actually the first witness who impacted himself upon me was the poet Wilfred Owen. Owen wonderfully presents this challenge to subsequent readers and subsequent writers: What is the difference between action and aesthetics? Can you enter a position when not living it, you know? Owen presents the ultimate challenge—that is, if you're going to protest against the war, know what you're protesting against, earn your credentials, live with the soldiers, live with the polis, live with the group that you are politically responsible to. I have written about this in another context, how I often felt, twenty years ago, when I was teaching at Queens University in Belfast—I was teaching Owen's poetry and nitpicking about the overwriting, you know, discussing the lushness and the over-explicitness of certain things—I often felt that this man had perhaps earned his overwriting at an enormous price. So Owen, I think, stands within the English imagination and the English-speaking poetical culture as a reminder that things just aren't as simple as I suggested they were earlier on in the English situation.

I just don't know why I'm hesitating to say violence is a...legitimate subject...I think that the greatest poetry gazes upon it as a factor in human experience, recognizes it as deplorable, but then somehow must outface the deplorable or at least gaze levelly at the deplorable and put it in its place, place it in the scheme. Yeats does that. There are those who say that he relishes it too much. There are certain poems that do seem to do that. But, overall, Yeats is the greater poet—as far as I can see—for taking it into account. He is a great *political* poet.

DM: Your poem "Strange Fruit" ends:

> Murdered, forgotten, nameless, terrible
> Beheaded girl, outstaring axe
> And beatification, outstaring
> What had begun to feel like reverence.

Is one meaning here that to be reverent of what actually happened to this person is in itself a crime, in a sense?

Heaney: Yes, well, I suppose what that poem got to eventually—and it was a sudden addition—was the awareness that one was making a literary emotion out of the atrocious. And that *has* to be done too, you know, if literature is to measure up to it. And yet, at the same time, we've got to beware of what we're doing.

All one wants, I suppose, is that, as far as possible, poems that arise from the bed of concern with these matters keep the sprightliness of poems, that their origin is innocent, you know, rather than calculated, that inspiration is there—to put it at its broadest—that the poems are not like social services *applied* to the situation, that they are unpredictable. Think of Wilfred Owen's protest. With Owen this was won at a high price. Taking the position he did was a new thing to do and a daring thing to do and a hard thing to do. And it sprang unexpectedly and in an unlooked for way out of individual experience. It was a swerve. It so happens that the swerve has now become a motorway full of cars that can drive on without that gamble, at great ease. But in order to go there first there was a price to be paid, and there was an originality called for. So I think that the imagination, to be engaged, has to reenact this each time. Political situations are repeated and repeated and repeated, but the artistic event has to happen anew each time, even though the political context is essentially the same.

DM: Imagination has to absorb the political event almost?

Heaney: Well, I think there are different situations. I mean, take the Vietnam

War—unabsorbable, almost, by the imagination. Maybe somewhat manageable at a political discussion level. Well, maybe it's not unabsorbable, but let's look at the difference between, say, the Vietnam War and the Ulster situation. Now this is comparing a large international war with a small endemic one. But the small, endemic one is precisely my point. Everything in the consciousness of a child and then a young man or woman and then a mature man or woman brought up in Ulster over the last fifty years, everything in that consciousness is aware of certain things: the intuited conditions of division, the subtleties and silences that surround the clamor and obviousness of division. At a local level the Ulster sensibility and the Ulster language are completely impregnated, and almost everything can be made to serve a political purpose or made to have a political meaning. So, to write *out* of that is to write *about* it. It is necessarily to be involved in something much deeper, much more all-embracing, much more *given* than it is for someone to come along and write about a critical move of American foreign policy which lands the nation in a tight corner in Asia. Okay, the results of this tactical and, in historical terms, momentary engagement may be desperate and deplorable and hurtful, but they aren't embedded in the American mind. The American imagination isn't polluted with the thing. People haven't experienced it deeply enough or long enough. It may be that a novel can deal with the Vietnam War or an individual poem can deal with it at a glancing level, but I think that in some awful way the problem is too accidental for poetry.

DM: Robert Bly, of course, dealt with the war in his poetry at the time. What do you think of the way he approached it, artistically?

Heaney: Well, I heard Robert Bly and Gary Snyder give a big reading in San Francisco at the time. I was very much excited at being in the Bay Area for a year from 1970 to 1971. I found the reading exhilarating, but the glamour of such occasions was part of their value. The readings were communal; they were rallies, you know, as well as readings. I think that Bly's procedure was the right one, to try to find dream levels in dealing with this subject. You remember his long poem "The Tooth Mother Naked at Last" with its long riffs about the bombers taking off and so on.

The problem is that Bly's rhetoric was, I think, stretched beyond its limits. The problem with a poem like "The Tooth Mother Naked at Last" is that it conjures images of dreams and the unconscious, and yet it is an enormously conscious piece of rhetoric. It deplores, if you like, the willfulness, maleness, and destructiveness of the "imperial American war effort." And yet, by the very determined and polemical and willful single-focus of its own rhetorical intentions, it is somehow a literary equivalent of maleness, willfulness, and so on. Now this is certainly not to impugn Bly's effort. It's just to reveal what he himself must know, that once you get into *intention* like that, once the civic and the moral intelligence gets a grip, then poetry as he would love it and understand it is imperiled. One can then see the deliberation and the push of the poetry, that it is a form of *action*. And I think that is the problem. The problem with poetry that would forward a cause, even if it's a good cause, is that it becomes a form of action. Now, God knows, I'm not saying that poetry is not an action. Poetry *is* an action, but its action is not necessarily to forward other actions (*laughs*).

I think that Bly, during all that period, was a man of great *pedagogical* purpose. He's always been an enormous animator. And that has been part of his contribution and still is. His readings are classes, and, like a good teacher, he has several ways to get something across—sort of aids to learning, you know. His means have changed, and the theme of the classes has changed over the years. I would say his action as a lyric poet is one thing, and his contribution to the discourse about poetry is another. And then there's a third element: his contribution as an educator on campuses, which is different. And that kind of a pedagogical action necessarily simplifies things.

DM: At the end of "Station Island" you have the ghost of Joyce say, "keep at a tangent." Is this point of view reflected, for example, in your use of Sweeney as a persona or, earlier, of the bog people? Are these tools for keeping a certain distance?

Heaney: None of these things was approached as a tool; none of them was written with any view to Joyce's fictional advice. I myself strongly believe in what the Polish poet Anna Swir calls a psychosomatic condition. That's her definition of inspiration; a psychosomatic condition gives certain poems or certain themes, she says, a *biological* right to life.

So, as to the discovery and entry into a poem, a subject, a theme, an image source: as far as I'm concerned, if that discovery and entry is foreseen, foreplanned, and executed with a predatory intent, it doesn't work. It must be come upon like the other in life, like the friend or partner—like whatever truly wakens your interest. There's a great deal of accident involved. But what distinguishes the writer, I suppose, is that the writer knows which accident to suddenly become involved with, you know.

Take the Sweeney thing, for example. In 1972 I had moved—I would now say this was an accident—to Wicklow. I had resigned my job. I had time. I needed a project. I knew that the Sweeney poem hadn't been translated as a whole. I was living among the trees suddenly, too. Various things. Great excitement, animation, a sense of possibility. Then, very quickly, over the first six weeks I thought to myself I could make this poem into this, that, and the other. I was, at that time, a free-lance writer. I could make it a radio play; I could make it a children's book.

Then I asked myself, what right have I to it? Well, Sweeney was a poet of the North, too. So it came all of a sudden . . . the whole river of delight and possibility opening.

DM: You said that, when you moved to Wicklow, you were living among the trees. You have a story in your essay "Mossbawn" about climbing inside a hollow tree, a boundary tree, and you describe a sensation of becoming part of it. In fact, you say you're in the *throat* of the tree. This tree appears again in one of the Sweeney poems.

Heaney: That's right.

DM: You open that essay with the word *omphalos* and write about sources and origins of your work—the well, stream, bog, burial ground, lake. How do you see this now?

Heaney: Well, obviously, I think the first life of my work has been related to the first place and my feeling for where I grew up. There are poems set there in *The Death of the Naturalist,* and, in a way, the bog poems relate to that place, too. The bog poems are complicated by Jutland bog burials, archaeology, and so on. But the primal mosslife of the spirit in those poems relates to the prereflective animal inhalations that I had savored in bogland (*laughs*). So, I would say that a lot of the work is somehow in grateful relation to a life of sensation and prereflective being in County Derry. And the language of the early books was most gratifying to me when it opened some channel to that life.

On the other hand, I have to say that, once your language verifies all those things—well, bog, *omphalos,* spring, river, wood, burial mound—that's still not enough. All of them have probably become textual counters by now. I happen to be somebody for whom they were actually sensational realities. And I wrote in innocence of all this textuality danger. But one could not fail to notice that the images were cherished because they fulfilled certain expectations, and they slid neatly into certain formulae of the anthropological, methodological, academic mind.

So one has a desire then to escape from all that. It's the perversity of consciousness itself. And I think, if you lose that perversity, you're just going to be afloat on your own myth (*laughs*). And that finally renders you comatose, you know. So, while I do not want to be untrue to the verity of my experience, on the other hand, I do not want to be true to the reader's expectations.

In other words, lyric poetry is an *extremely* complex and difficult thing to bring off. It's not a product. If you take it as a product, you could do it every day: You get a theme, you get a skill, and you sail on. But if you think of it as an action, an event, something that attempts, something that achieves *half* adequately the truth of perception or the truth of a whole state of mind, then it's pretty difficult.

DM: You're very much a poet of the ear rather than of the eye. Sound—how does it trigger the imagination? Or what is the power of sound?

Heaney: Well, that's a large question. I think that poetry is a curious mixture of consciousness and unconsciousness, both in the writing and the reading of it. I have a few old, usual, familiar citations and corroborations that match my feelings as a reader and a writer: Frost's essay "The Figure a Poem Makes," Eliot's notion of the auditory imagination. And these imply that individual utterance, individual rhythmic postures, accidental accoustic events link into, if you like, an evolutionary chain of human *ear*-knowledge. I believe that. I can't explain it. So cadence and vowel music and the uncanny appeal of certain rhythmic combinations, these mean a lot to me.

I began possibly too much in thrall—well, probably not too much—to Hopkins and Keats and to a poetry of very deliberate, rich texture. And I love that sort of thing, but I think the older you get the more interested you are in purer, clearer, finer effects. The less interested you are in triumphing by excess *(laughs)*. So now what I would love to do is to write a poetry of enormous plainness, something possessing that mysterious clarity and line which you get in, say, some of Blake's "Auguries of Innocence." Take a couplet like:

> The wild deer wandering here and there
> Do keep the human soul from care.

You know, it's not a stylistic lesson that you have here; it's a very different kind of line from another Blake line like:

> The harlot's cry from street to street
> Shall weave old England's winding sheet.

There's drama in that, and there's a coloratura that is more like poetry one can write *(laughs)*. But "The wild deer wandering here and there / Do keep the human soul from care" is *clear* as water, and it can't be explained, and it's utterly accessible and utterly convincing. It's visionary, religious, simple. And I think, just to take that as an example, the older you get, the older *I* get, that is the kind of thing I love in other work and that, you know, you would love to achieve for yourself. But what you would like to do and what you can do are two different things.

Twenty years ago, starting to write, I suppose,

> Thou mastering me
> God! giver of breath and bread;

World's strand, sway of the sea...
Thou hast bound bones and veins in me, fastened me flesh...

...that kind of Hopkinsian thing gave me great joy. God, you know, "*hewing continents*" and with "*trickling increment*" veining violets...That gave me enormous delight. There's such relish in the particular, in the "inscape," as Hopkins said, in the phonetic deliciousness. And I do not discount that. I think that's a sine qua non. One's palate, I suppose, still enjoys the lush, but it yearns for something thinner, and purer and purer. Take Eliot's sound in "Little Gidding," the Dante section:

Let me disclose the gifts reserved for age...
First, the cold friction of expiring sense...

It's sibilant and rustling. And then there's: "rats' feet over broken glass in our dry cellar."

I suppose the phonetic pleasures are never to be detached from the vision or action they are part of. Much hefty, good executive writing sometimes is just inert because it's *writing* rather than *action*. I mean, you shouldn't lay it on, you know (*laughs*). It just has to come up rather than be laid on. And I think that's part of my problem with Lowell, that he lays it on a lot of the time. I love it when it's coming up. He's a writer, of course, who keeps a very fine balance between having it come up and having it laid on. In *Life Studies* it comes up and is laid on in equal measure. I think in the *Notebooks* and in *History*—the blank sonnets—it's laid on, it's hammered down, it's sledgehammered in. So you resist that. I personally feel it rising up in *Day by Day*, which some people have condemned as an exhausted kind of book. But it's precisely that feathery and open-weave, unforcing aspect of things that I like very much in that book. I think there *is* tired writing in it, but there is a kind of *good* writing which is the equivalent of tiredness.
DM: It's clear but not exhausted?
Heaney: That's right.
DM: In looking at form, what would you say your evolution has been from, for example, "The Forge," in your second book, to a more recent poem like "First Flight," which is so fluid?
Heaney: I think in *Wintering Out* there was a moment of formal evolution and discovery. But I don't have any ideology of forms. I have sonnets in *Field Work*. I have sonnets in my new book, *The Haw Lantern*—eight sonnets.

I also have in *The Haw Lantern* poems that I think are clearer and plainer and have a voice that is...more talky. I hope I don't mean just loose-mouthed but more like *speech*. In other words, there are two musics. One is a formal music. I've got poems in that book in rhymed quatrains, very dainty *abab* rhymed quatrains, one an elegy for a niece, one a sort of ballad. I've got a poem I wrote in 1972 in rhymed octosyllabic couplets.

I think what I'm grateful for is that at last I'm more relaxed. And in this particular book, and this is a *political* position, I've just taken enormous pleasure in the writing, which is what I would like to do more and more, just to—as Mr. Joyce said in *Station Island*—write for the pleasure of it. I mean, we all know that is the true thing to do, but I happen to have gone through a period of sullenness against it. Now I write in any form that presents itself as a source of pleasure and possibility and isn't just an exercise.

There seems to be a lot of political talk about "form." I think many people use the term to mean writing in stanzas with rhyme. But there's a lot of writing in stanzas with rhyme that has no sense of stanza form or no *living* rhyme principle. I don't think that's a development or a rebuke to open form; I just think it's a complete innocence. I think it's very difficult for an ear that has not somehow been ministered to by the musics of formal verse to achieve a formal completion itself. And it's just a matter of educational fact that thousands of young poets have never *heard* a sonnet. The sonnet form or the quatrain form or the couplet form hasn't bathed their ears, you know. I, just by an accident of education at a moment of time, got a hell of a lot of that packed into me. I learned it by heart. And that is true of a lot of people just coming out of the educational system in Britain and Ireland. So that's kind of a cultural *given,* but I'm certainly not, therefore, saying that American poets cannot have a sense of traditional form. This is patently untrue. Frost! Wilbur! Hecht! Dickinson!

There is an anxiety, an orthodoxy, that you have to master traditional form in order to be a master of your craft. There is something in that, but perhaps you can't master all crafts. Take D. H. Lawrence's poems. Lawrence just couldn't rhyme with any security. But when he takes the governor of rhyme off, you know, loosens the belt and the belly of the poem hangs out, then it's fine (*laughs*). You can see that he's at his ease, whereas it's unimaginable that Frost would write a verse like that.

James Merrill's a very interesting case of a poet whose relationship to traditional forms seems to me to have always been sportive and hedonistic. The *merriment* of a performance is always implicit in Merrill's use of form. He's a kind of Byronic, show-off writer. There's a kind of covenant with the reader that he's not going to bore you, and he's not going to be Sturm und Drang, and there will be no heavy breathing in the poem, you know. Rhyme and all those things are like trapeze wires where the artist is going to show how it can be done: I'll do a few turns for you. So there is that lightness.

DM: Just a few more questions. In your first four books, even in the titles you gave them, it seems almost as if you're working your way to a pole, to ninety degrees north: *Death of a Naturalist, Door into the Dark, Wintering Out,* and *North.* And then, in *Field Work,* there's a certain sense of relief. The work begins to open out.

Heaney: Yes, that's right.

DM: You're in the country, and ordinary daylight is more dominant, as opposed to that, say, in *Wintering Out,* which is a sort of arctic light. You were speaking before about a need for plainness in language. Is this related to a changed sense of ordinary life?

Heaney: Yes, well, I think so. I would agree with your perception of the thing there. I would *like* to agree with it. And I think that this recent book, *The Haw Lantern,* allows the writer in me to take more pleasure. It tries out a few things but also goes back to certain things. I gave myself permission to write a couple more childhood poems.

On the other hand, the motif that recurs in this book is one of emptiness. The tree in it is an *imagined* tree, a tree that has been cut down, leaving an empty space. And I think it's a kind of middle-aged book in that way.

I have a little poem in it called "The Disappearing Island," which is based upon a moment in the voyages of Saint Brendan—Saint Brendan and his monks pulled up on a whale, and in the morning the whale swims away. I did this lightly for Tim Severin, who wrote a book about Saint Brendan. But, though I did it lightly, at the same time I was thinking of it as a kind of allegory for Ireland itself. And yet it was written out of the *pleasure* of writing, not out of the heaviness of writing a poem about Ireland (*laughs*). So, in *The Haw Lantern,* there's that kind of appearance, disappearance; fullness, emptiness. There's a more venturesome and less somber, less uptight tone to it. The book comes out in four weeks. My editor sent me one copy, but I gave it to Bernard and Jane McCabe who are the dedicatees.

Actually, speaking of all this, *Station Island* ends with this kind of *dry* font where there's a deer with its nose stuck into it, cut into stone "at the font of exhaustion," it says. But then the McCabes and I went to a place called Gregory Minster, an Anglo-Saxon church in this little vale in Yorkshire with a very old setting, a valley and trees at the end of the churchyard and a river. I heard this river all the time, running at the bottom of the churchyard. So I went down and looked and discovered it was a *dry* riverbed. It was the trees, the wind in the trees, that gave me the sense of the river, you know. The world is irrigated by the imagination.

From "Singing School"

1. The Ministry of Fear

For Seamus Deane

Well, as Kavanagh said, we have lived
In important places. The lonely scarp
Of St. Columb's College, where I billeted
For six years, overlooked your Bogside.
I gazed into new worlds: the inflamed throat
Of Brandywell, its floodlit dogtrack,
The throttle of the hare. In the first week
I was so homesick I couldn't even eat
The biscuits left to sweeten my exile.
I threw them over the fence one night
In September 1951
When the lights of houses in the Lecky Road
Were amber in the fog. It was an act
Of stealth.
        Then Belfast, and then Berkeley.
Here's two on's are sophisticated,
Dabbling in verses till they have become
A life: from bulky envelopes arriving
In vacation time to slim volumes
Despatched "with the author's compliments."
Those poems in longhand, ripped from the wire spine
Of your exercise book, bewildered me—
Vowels and ideas bandied free
As the seed-pods blowing off our sycamores.
I tried to write about the sycamores
And innovated a South Derry rhyme
With *hushed* and *lulled* full chimes for *pushed* and *pulled.*
Those hobnailed boots from beyond the mountain
Were walking, by God, all over the fine

Lawns of elocution.Have our accents
Changed? "Catholics, in general, don't speak
As well as students from the Protestant schools."
Remember that stuff? Inferiority
Complexes, stuff that dreams were made on.
"What's your name, Heaney?"

"Heaney, Father."

"Fair

Enough."

    On my first day, the leather strap
Went epileptic in the Big Study,
Its echoes plashing over our bowed heads,
But I still wrote home that a boarder's life
Was not so bad, shying as usual.

On long vacations, then, I came to life
In the kissing seat of an Austin Sixteen
Parked at a gable, the engine running,
My fingers tight as ivy on her shoulders,
A light left burning for her in the kitchen.
And heading back for home, the summer's
Freedom dwindling night by night, the air
All moonlight and a scent of hay, policemen
Swung their crimson flashlamps, crowding round
The car like black cattle, snuffing and pointing
The muzzle of a sten-gun in my eye:
"What's your name, driver?"

"Seamus ... "

Seamus?

They once read my letters at a roadblock
And shone their torches on your hieroglyphics,
"Svelte dictions" in a very florid hand.

Ulster was British, but with no rights on
The English lyric: all around us, though
We hadn't named it, the ministry of fear.

2. A Constable Calls

His bicycle stood at the window-sill,
The rubber cowl of a mud-splasher

Skirting the front mudguard,
Its fat black handlegrips

Heating in sunlight, the "spud"
Of the dynamo gleaming and cocked back,
The pedal treads hanging relieved
Of the boot of the law.

His cap was upside down
On the floor, next his chair.
The line of its pressure ran like a bevel
In his slightly sweating hair.

He had unstrapped
The heavy ledger, and my father
Was making tillage returns
In acres, roods, and perches.

Arithmetic and fear.
I sat staring at the polished holster
With its buttoned flap, the braid cord
Looped into the revolver butt.

"Any other root crops?
Mangolds? Marrowstems? Anything like that?"
"No." But was there not a line
Of turnips where the seed ran out

In the potato field? I assumed
Small guilts and sat
Imagining the black hole in the barracks.
He stood up, shifted the baton-case

Further round on his belt,
Closed the domesday book,
Fitted his cap back with two hands,
And looked at me as he said goodbye.

A shadow bobbed in the window.
He was snapping the carrier spring
Over the ledger. His boot pushed off
And the bicycle ticked, ticked, ticked.

Stanislaw Baranczak

Stanislaw Baranczak was born in Poland in 1946. From 1969 to 1977 he taught as an assistant professor at Adam Mickiewicz University in Poznan. In 1977 he was fired from his teaching position, ostensibly for publishing his books in the West without official permission. Since 1976 his name had appeared on the censor's blacklist. He had also long been active in Polish human rights organizations and had been a cofounder of KOR (Committee for the Defense of Workers). He also had founded the first underground literary journal *Zapis*. In 1980 he was reinstated in his former teaching position, at the demand of Solidarity. In March, 1981, Polish authorities finally issued an exit visa, and he arrived in the United States with his wife, son, and daughter, to accept a teaching position at Harvard University, offered to him three years earlier.

Baranczak has published many books of poetry, criticism, and translation. His book of selected poems in English translation, *The Weight of the Body,* was published in 1990 by TriQuarterly Books/Northwestern University and was the winner of the Terrence Des Pres Prize for poetry. He is also author of an important study of the poetry of Zbigniew Herbert, *A Fugitive from Utopia,* published by Harvard University Press in 1987. His most recent book in English is *Breathing under Water and Other East European Essays,* published in 1990.

This interview took place in November, 1985, in his office at Harvard. In November, 1990, Baranczak speculated on how the year-old democracy and the lifting of censorship in Poland would affect Polish literature.

Something truly unexpected has happened in Poland with these changes in the political situation. I do think that, in time, the sudden shift toward democracy will repair some of what happened to the society because of political oppression and violence. But what will remain unchanged for some time, I'm afraid, will be the pressure exerted on people by collective norms of behavior— so long imposed, it's hard now to shake them. Censorship, for example, though gone, will continue to leave its mark by way of the strategies people have developed in order to survive it, and which have become stubbornly ingrained. Having experienced censorship or something like martial law, you can't so easily forget what they can do.

Another problem is that, now, in a way, people are facing a more complicated reality. During the years of martial law the oppositions around you were, in a sense, clearer, more black-and-white. This led to a tendency in literature to reinvoke the national myth of Poland as repeated victim in a vicious cycle of catastrophic events and the related tendency to idealize the victim. These tendencies, in turn, didn't leave much room for coming to terms with the possibility that the victim may not be completely innocent, the many acts of heroic resistance notwithstanding. As with censorship, the victim is in some ways tainted by oppression.

It may be that poetry that reflects the new and complicated pluralism that exists now in everyday life will most clearly capture the reality of today's Poland and speak to people's needs. For some writers the new freedom may encourage a need to become even more political in their work; for others this freedom may in fact lead in the opposite direction, toward a need to relieve literature of the necessity for direct involvement at a time when such involvement can now take place in real life.

David Montenegro: In Poland poetry matters. Traditionally, it's had a political role. In the West we view this with some degree of envy and perhaps also with suspicion, since common wisdom has it that poetry should be separate from politics. Your own poetry is often political. Do you feel any such conflict?

Stanislaw Baranczak: The thing that makes these discussions slightly oversimplified, in my opinion, is that by "political" people tend to mean something very limited, you know, representing a certain party line, for instance. But the circumstances of poets in countries like Poland are such that actually any poem that defends the individual's right to live and think independently is a political statement. I mean the pressures of collectivity and some superimposed norms are so strong that virtually every avenue of resistance is closed. Even writing on, say, flowers or love can be—doesn't necessarily have to be, but it can be—a political gesture, if it's written in the spirit of defending your right to be independent. Just pure description, if it describes the world faithfully, is a kind of political act.

I'd like to quote my own example here, by which I don't mean to be presumptuous, but I perhaps went quite far in one direction—of being faithful to reality. Say you write a sequence of poems, as I did, on the housing problem—it sounds terrible: poems on the housing problem—poems about moving to an apartment in a typical housing project, which is the fate of anyone in Poland if he waits long enough. In fact, it takes fifteen, twenty years to get your own apartment, not even your own but a cooperative apartment in a housing project. But you are very happy about moving and so on. Then you move, and you are terribly disappointed, of course, because the apartment is just horrible. And that feeling of disappointment is some inevitable shadow of existence, so to speak. It's not merely an economic or social problem but also a metaphysical problem of thwarted expectations. Also, there's the problem of your personal space and your place in life, et cetera. So there are many poetic possibilities in this situation.

Now, if you write a poem on this subject, you can write it just as pure poetry, but, if you are faithful in the description of those apartments, it becomes political poetry, because it appeals to certain collective feelings. It refers to certain things that bind people together, in a sense. And you can try to be as politically innocent as possible, but in countries such as Poland, if you write about reality, you have to be politically involved sooner or later.

DM: And in the United States?

Baranczak: I think, in countries such as the United States, it's simply that writing and politics can be quite easily separated from each other. Your personal problems may have, to be sure, nothing in common with the problems of society. In other words, you can build your private world to which nothing public has any access. And you can move to, I don't know, Arizona to live in the desert, and nobody will trouble you, except the IRS perhaps. Even the police will leave you alone if you are a peaceful, law-abiding citizen.

But in Poland, you can't escape. You *must* be involved, at least—I have to stop generalizing—at least at certain political moments, in certain political phases. There are situations in which nobody can stand aside, in which even the most passive observer has to be involved. Even a gesture of rejection—escape or hiding in a cave or whatever—is a political gesture anyway. It's at least considered as such. So there's no escape from such things.

But poets must make an artistic use of them. I mean the poet must be political and personal at the same time. You can't escape those problems and necessities, but you must try to express them in a personal way so that you don't represent any collectivity in the sense that you don't represent any superimposed set of values. You express your own point of view, but at the same time you are not an eremite, someone who'd artificially live on the margin of society. But, by defending your personal rights and your personal independence, you are in a way defending also every individual's rights and independence.

And that's what makes poetry so important in Poland. People instinctively—even if they are not very well educated or not very acquainted with poetry—people instinctively seek more personal responses to the situation. They seek some ways of expressing the situation which would allow them to understand it, or at least to obtain some translation of it into the language of feelings, of reflection, et cetera.

DM: Will you describe what you mean by "the situation"?

Baranczak: For the man in the street, so to speak, in countries such as Poland, the reality in which he lives appears as something incredibly absurd, as something devoid of any logic, of any common sense. In other words, you can behave in a rational way, but the world behaves irrationally around you. And you don't have any key to that reality. For example, you can be a law-abiding citizen and just walk down the street and be attacked by the police for no reason whatsoever. That creates in people not only a sense of fear, which is quite obvious, but also a need for a clue to the understanding of that world. It cannot be rationalized because the world *is* absurd as it is. But you have a need for certain ways of making your existence in that world justified. The way of making such a justification is the very attempt to understand this reality.

DM: And poetry can be a part of this attempt.

Baranczak: Yes. This attempt can be spurred by reading poetry, by trying to grasp from poetry some clues to your own existence. Which doesn't mean in turn that poetry is just a substitute for, I don't know, philosophy or social science or whatever. It's rather that people look to poetry in order to find some specific ways, which only poetry can provide, of accommodating themselves to that reality—only poetry precisely because of its personal point of view, its proneness to the concrete, its potential for revealing a certain ambiguity, for revealing the coexistence of opposites within reality, which is what poetry does best.

DM: Is there, then, a conflict between poetry as powerful language and the language of power—newspeak, for example?

Baranczak: That's a very good formulation, yes. It touches upon the problem of language itself, which is another matter, a very important one. People in Poland read poetry not only because of their need for some explanation of the world but also because of their need for an authentic language, one not distorted by propaganda, not worn-out by constant repetition of the same slogans, et cetera. So, in other words, they are not satisfied with—they *hate*, in fact—both the official language of propaganda, of newspapers, and they hate their own language, the language of everyday life, because it's contaminated by the attitudes that are expressed in the official media. In other words, even if the language of the street counters the official language, in a sense, by, I don't know, creating some jokes or allusions, it's not free, it's not independent. It's still dependent on this official language and lives only because of it. And people yearn for some language that would be free and authentic, that would express the individual's world and attitudes.

DM: And how did your generation react to this problem of language?

Baranczak: What Polish poetry went through in the last twenty years—it probably started in the late 1960s—was that it went from opposing the official language to abandoning that language altogether. I think the novelty of my generation, its discovery—and I somehow contributed to that, perhaps—was that for the first time we noticed the presence and the ominous danger of that language. And we tried to counter it by creating poems that are simply variations, ironic and satirical variations of certain of its set phrases and worn-out concepts. By ridiculing it, we tried to become independent.

But we were still very much dependent, and that's what [Zbigniew] Herbert criticizes in his poem to Ryszard Krynicki. Herbert says he was aware from the very beginning that to deal with the language of newspapers is to become dependent on them. So, why bother, why touch this garbage at all? But we had to go through that stage. We had to do so because we had to be faithful to reality, to the reality of Poland, and a very important element of that reality was precisely this oppression of language.

DM: When you look back now, how to you assess your generation's reaction?

Baranczak: Even if I'm slightly distanced from that stage right now, I still consider it necessary. I think it was very important. It gave Polish poetry a certain momentum in the late 1960s, early 1970s, a momentum that was necessary in order for us to detach ourselves completely from official language and to become individuals with many different, poetic idioms. And this has been achieved at least partly by the more original members of that generation such as Adam Zagajewski and Ryszard Krynicki. These people have been very independent and self-reliant since at least the early 1970s. So they went through that stage very quickly.

I perhaps stayed a little longer because I was always interested in some linguistic experimentation and continued in that vein until the late 1970s. Even in *Triptych of Concrete, Weariness and Snow,* completed in 1980, there was a *small* number, but a number, of poems experimenting with language. But in that particular volume I think I had already overcome the limitations of such linguistic poetry, and the center of gravity, so to speak, was on the reality itself, not on the language.

DM: We have been talking indirectly about the problem of censorship. Ironically, it seems censorship can give language a potency that freedom of speech destroys. Is that true?

Baranczak: I wonder if it's true. I've heard that opinion very often, particularly here in the States, and I think what is a certain instigating power of censorship is rather overstated in such opinions. After some time of writing under conditions of censorship, you experience a certain atrophy, so to speak. The popular image of censorship is that a writer thinks freely about everything but simply cannot publish certain thoughts. But the truth is that, if censorship is a continuous feature of a writer's existence, you simply *cease* to think about certain problems. You know there's no way of publishing such thoughts, so why bother? And in this way the whole field of social history, certain tendencies in philosophy, certain approaches in poetry, et cetera, are completely eliminated, not only from public existence but also from people's thoughts.

On the other hand, it's true that the necessity of bypassing the censor can give rise to some new means of expression, some more intricate, more allegorical ways of putting certain problems into words. Censorship, it can be argued, enriches poetry in a sense, but it also diminishes poetry's power. The problem of which approach is most effective in poetry is very complicated. Sometimes indirect approaches, even though they seem quite in accordance with the spirit of poetry, sound somewhat false.

There are certain problems about which you can speak only directly, fundamental matters deserving an unequivocal stance. For instance, if you write on the death of someone who was beaten to death by the police—as certain poets of today's Poland have to do from time to time, because such things happen constantly—you cannot be evasive. If you write about it, you have to state your position. Either you are against it or for it. And there's no other way. There's no in-between, partly for, partly against. And because censorship is absolute on such occasions, certain poets react by creating complicated or flowery ways of expressing the truth, but this can hardly be considered an achievement of their poetry.

But in order to be as fair as possible in my assessment of this problem, it's also true that certain phenomena in, let's say, Polish literature wouldn't exist if not for censorship. For example, during the Stalinist period, when the establishment was absolutely dominant and, moreover, people feared for their lives, it was common knowledge that certain Catholic writers, who were unable to become social realists because this was against their most profound beliefs, chose to write historical novels. And some wrote them very skillfully. Some were even able to express truths that varied from the contemporary point of view. So these writers were by no means an insignificant, literary phenomenon during Stalinist times.

But was this phenomenon to literature's advantage? It could be argued that these writers created a certain lack of proportion in novelistic themes and approaches. They *had* to do so; there was no other way for them. They wanted to write, but they couldn't write about contemporary subjects. Still, the objective result was that a certain branch of the novel was heavily overrepresented, while there was nothing to balance it. And, again, I'm not accusing those writers. I'm simply stating the fact that this created a very abnormal situation. And, in general, the result of censorship's existence is always some kind of abnormality.

I think anything is better than censorship, even total freedom in which—as it's very true, and I have every right to say, here in America—in which there's a certain void, in which nothing really matters, in which the words, circulating quite freely, don't mean anything, by the same token, because everything can be said, and there's no hierarchy of things more or less important. But even such a state of affairs is better than the existence of any censorship. And I'm personally very disturbed by certain attempts here in American life to impose censorship. You know what I mean, all those school committees and so on. I don't consider myself an American liberal, you know, although my political stance is completely impossible to define in American terms. But here I'm sticking with the liberals because, in my view, even the least presence of censorship is always a threat. It spreads like a disease. If you introduce it, there's no way to stop it. If you have censorship, you can't do anything about it. So anything's better. Even some kind of anarchic freedom, in terms of freedom of expression, is better than any restriction.

DM: Herbert's generation was born when Poland was independent. Yours, born just after the war, had no chance to experience political independence in your own country. How do you think this affected your generation?

Baranczak: Herbert, as an example of his generation, was shaped much before the war. He was a very young man to be sure, but still, his family, his background, the place where he lived, and so on, all shaped him considerably. He was already a well-formed personality when he was entering the postwar reality.

But, in our case, we were born in People's Poland. We were educated in Communist schools. And I think actually everybody from my generation with no exception whatsoever was at least partly contaminated by the official ideology, by the spirit of conformity.

Some of us parted company with that spirit very early in our lives, people such as Adam Michnik—not a poet, to be sure, but an excellent political writer and also literary critic who is in prison right now for the...I don't know, for the umpteenth time in his life. He is a brilliant example of someone who was intelligent and independent enough to get rid of those limitations very early in his life. As a high school student, he was already in trouble with the police, with the political authorities, et cetera. He was always very independent minded.

But some people simply took more time to get rid of that stuff, people who were—I don't want to say less independent—but who were influenced by various circumstances: the fact that they lived in a provincial town, for instance, or were born into a Communist family. Or just the reverse: If someone was born into a very traditional, Catholic family, sometimes that person rebelled against such a background by becoming a true-blue Communist in his early youth. And so such things could happen.

I think the crucial point for my generation was 1968 when there was the famous student protest, and after that it was actually impossible not to notice what was going on around you. On the surface it was a political event; it was a protest against censorship, et cetera, but, in fact, it was a moment when a certain generation was coming of age. Graduating from college, we were entering adult life. And at this moment your eyes have to open. Suddenly, you have to realize you are living in an abnormal world in which nothing functions properly, in which there's a great deal of injustice and absurdity and so on. Some people, of course, understood it much earlier. That's why this general movement was possible. They prepared it somehow by their personal influence, by their independent thinking. I have in mind again Adam Michnik.

For many others, though, it was in 1968 that they opened their eyes, so to speak, because the absurdities were most visible at this point. Take, for instance, the presence of continual lying in public life. Everybody knew about it more or less theoretically before, but in 1968 you had to encounter it quite personally. For instance, you were in a student demonstration that was very peaceful, and the very next day you could read in the newspaper that some hooligans broke windows and beat policemen and so on. You knew from your experience that this wasn't true, that this was a vicious lie. After experiences like this, you simply *had* to take a more independent stance, and you had to think on your own.

And this also concerns literature, of course. First, you had to describe that reality; then you had to—or simultaneously—you had to try to understand it somehow by trying to find the system that stands behind and supports it. And, by system, I mean not only a political system per se but a certain system of values, biases, attitudes, et cetera, which made such a society possible. And by trying to interpret this society, we were pushed toward some other problems, from religious to moral.

DM: Though literature played a role in sparking the student protest—Adam Mickiewicz's anticzarist play was forced off the boards by the authorities—the generation of 1968 takes its name more from a political event than a literary one.
Baranczak: Yes, that's right. Well, it's not the only moment in Polish history that a literary movement starts with a political event. Throughout the nineteenth century, as a matter of fact, every major uprising against the czarist oppressors was actually a signal for the initiation of some literary movement. The insurrection of 1830–31 started the period of the so-called Great Romanticists, for example. Now, the very next insurrection in 1863 ended the influence of romanticism, and a completely contrary current began.

So these were events that shook the very foundations of people's attitudes to the world. I mean it was not only a political event, but it was also a proof that something was wrong with things in general. For example, the failure of the insurrection was generally considered an act of some high injustice, some divine injustice, as a matter of fact. So such a failure also started investigations of a more religious and metaphysical nature, and so on. What I'm saying is that a political event is often only the most visible form of an underlying process—of a process, let's say, of growing doubt in certain illusions of the Age of Enlightenment, for instance. And many political events can be interpreted in this way, including the events of 1968.

DM: You've lived in the United States for five years now. How has this affected your poetry?

Baranczak: Well, it has affected it to a great extent. To begin with, I had a long period when I wasn't able to write anything, not because of America and the American experience but, rather, because of a certain traumatic effect the events in Poland had on me. I simply wasn't able to put it into words. Martial law was such a total disaster, I simply had to cope with it psychologically for some time. Then I wrote a long poem, but it wasn't mainly on martial law. It was, rather, on the distorted ways in which this event was perceived.

DM: Was this poem *The Restoration of Order*?

Baranczak: Yes. It was translated very well by Richard Lourie and published in *Dissent* in the winter of 1984.

In this poem a certain American perspective is perhaps slightly visible. Even though it's about Poland, it's also about the Western reaction to Polish events. In certain parts there's a reconstruction of the tones people used when reporting about Poland here in the media. This is not the entirety of the poem, but, still, there is a sort of mixed perspective.

But, after writing that poem, I had another period of total exhaustion, as a matter of fact. I was also busy with many other things, traveling across the States to give some guest talks about the Polish situation and also working here at the university, which is sometimes exhausting.

But during the past two years I've returned to writing poetry again, and I think there's something very new in what I'm writing now. That's not only my opinion, but also some of my readers tell me that they find my recent poems very different. I now tend to write—I don't know if it will last long—but I tend to write poems that are more narrative perhaps, situational, anecdotal, not merely based on some play on words, as was very often the case before.

DM: Can you give me an example?

Baranczak: Yes, but I can only describe this poem because it hasn't been translated yet. Quite recently, after Hurricane Gloria, I wrote a poem that was about the storm but also about something else. The situation of the poem is this: After the hurricane, on a certain street in a certain town in New England, some neighbors gather to discuss what's happened. These are people from various parts of the world. They are immigrants. One has lived through the Nazi genocide. Another is a Cambodian who has recently arrived. And there are others. But for all these people—and this is the underlying tone of the poem—the hurricane was actually something very pleasantly disappointing, because they had expected a disaster like those they had experienced in the past. But this one was quite nice, you know. The storm was reported on TV. Everything was predictable. There were some forecasts that proved true. All the destruction will be very easily repaired. The insurance agent will come very early in the morning, and so on. The whole mood is of some kind of picnic during which the neighbors simply exchange information about what happened. And the poem ends on that note, that everybody's quite satisfied, and this is nothing to be compared with what they've lived through.

I'm very boring, I realize, because I'm telling a poem in my own English, but I want to give you an example here of a poem in which two perspectives again are combined. And I don't mean to say in the poem that I've lived through anything like the Holocaust or the Cambodian genocide. These people, these neighbors, are simply representatives of what's going on in other parts of the world. A poem showing their presence here in this country reveals certain problems much better than could be done, for instance, in a poem *on* Cambodia or the Holocaust. I don't know if I make myself clear.

DM: It sounds as if the threat of the hurricane opened up in each of these people some reservoir of fear . . .

Baranczak: Yes, yes. But I think I tried to express it very discreetly, of course. The underlying tone of the poem is of some inner devastation of those people. I mean the important point here is that they would be too optimistic if they used their American situation only to reflect on how happy they are, as if they had nothing in common in their pasts. On the contrary, they have much in common because each of them is somehow devastated. . . . I mean inwardly devastated, so to speak. For each of them the necessity of forgetting about the past was something that impoverished them. And all these people are not only your nice neighbors but also quite horrible examples of what history can do to a human being.

I don't have to add that the poem is, of course, purely fictional, because I don't have such neighbors. I don't happen to have that. But it's a quite possible situation, on the other hand. A Jewish woman, a young Cambodian immigrant, and the third person, then, is a Lithuanian who went through imprisonment in Siberian camps.

DM: Will you be making a collection of your poems in English translation sometime soon?

Baranczak: I've been trying to do so since 1982. Or 1983. But I'm still not finished because, on the one hand, there are new poems that I constantly write and which I hope to have translated and added to this collection. On the other hand, I'm increasingly critical of some of the existing translations of earlier poems that I initially included. Now I'm hesitant about these translations. In fact, I've been trying to work with certain American poets and translators in order to get a sense—because my English is very limited—a sense of the naturalness and faithfulness of these translations. Well, the issue of faithfulness is not as important as the issue of their unrestricted existence in the element of the English language, so to speak. The problem is that they should sound like English poems in order to be good at all and in order to exist in this language.

And that's very hard to achieve. Though the translators were usually very careful and hardworking and so on, in the case of some of the poems, at least from my earlier period, I have the feeling right now that it was probably a mistake even to try to translate them at all. They owe too much to certain linguistic mechanisms that exist only in the Polish language. You can try to make a copy, you can try to find some analogy, but it's never quite the same. But poems in which there's some event or story or human portrayal are perhaps more translatable.

So I'm still working on this collection. In general, some sixty of my poems have been translated into English, but I'm satisfied with only about thirty of them. Maybe some new translations will emerge, and that will make some forty or fifty poems.

DM: Do your new poems present any new problems for the translator?

Baranczak: Yes. With increasing frequency I write in rhymed verse—a fact strange even to myself. But somehow I feel I have to. The point is, you know, that in Polish poetry there was such an abundance of avant-garde verse systems in the twentieth century that it simply became boring at a certain point. And from, I don't know, probably the early 1970s there's been some unexpressed need in Polish poetry, a need one could feel almost physically for some return to—I don't want to say regularity because this is not the point; it may be irregular in a sense—but to some point of inner organization of the poem. I mean there was too much carelessness, too much complete anarchy in handling the verse. And now there's a very apparent tiredness, particularly with the [Tadeusz] Rozewicz kind of verse— you know, such verse that consists mostly of very simple, brief phrases just put together.

DM: A poetry of reduction?

Baranczak: Yes, and one that simply offers not enough possibilities, in my view. I mean some natural possibilities of poetry are completely lost and eliminated in this type of writing, although historically it was very necessary to introduce effects like those used by Rozewicz. But after some time all his imitators made it completely boring.

I was opposed to the model of Rozewicz from the very beginning in my own work. I always tried to do some more interesting things with the verse. Even in my first volume, I wrote a number of sonnets, of all things. They were the sort of sonnets that treated—how shall I put it?—treated very controversially ... I mean the structure of the sonnet was needed only to break it, as a matter of fact. But still I'm one of these poets probably who needs a certain rigid structure if only to resist it, to play against it, to make some variations on it, and so on. And it can be a completely circumvented structure, of course.

I'm always reminded of the example of Marianne Moore, who uses syllabic verse with very intricate stanza patterns needed only in order to make it more difficult for the poet. The reader doesn't really notice them because there's no reflection of them in the sound of the poem. The whole issue is purely numeric. Right? The number of syllables has to be such and such. This type of structuring, as I said, is necessary only so that the poet can create some resistance to be overcome. And it makes not only writing more interesting but also the poems themselves because there's some greater degree of complication, of inner tension, of ambiguity, which is revealed by playing with some formal issues. For me, stanza pattern first of all then rhyme create such possibilities.

I should mention that Polish rhyme has a lot more possibilities than English rhyme because of certain purely linguistic problems. First, there's the fact that Polish rhyme is, as a rule, paroxytonic, that is, the stress is on the penultimate syllable. And as such there is a greater variety of rhymes. Also the inexact rhyme is much more acceptable than in English poetry. I'm too technical right now, but the point is that some technical resistance is necessary. And, of course, it makes translating such poetry more difficult because, as a rule, English translators skip rhyme altogether, and the poem is somehow deprived of something important.

DM: Has translation in any way added something to the poems?

Baranczak: Certain new meanings can appear. I don't have any examples on hand, but there are some instances in which I felt that the very translation of my poem into English has significantly enlarged its meaning. The poem's simply put in another context, and not only in the context of a certain tradition that is different from my own but also in the context of another language that has its own rights and its own semantic possibilities.

DM: I feel very lucky to have had the chance to read your superb book on Zbigniew Herbert's poetry. In *A Fugitive from Utopia,* you stress that Herbert is often labeled and oversimplified: Herbert as classicist, for example, Herbert as praiser of the past, praiser of the West, and so on. Was one of your goals to give a more balanced picture?

Baranczak: My aim in the book is simply to render justice to the whole bulk of his poetry as a consistent structure, a structure in which everything has its place, as it does, because he's truly a great poet and knows what he's doing. To give you one example: Many critics who write about him tend to focus on political or social points, Herbert as poet-moralist, for example, and they usually mention very briefly, as if on the margin of their analysis, that he also writes poems about objects such as a stool or a wooden die or a pebble, et cetera. They quite visibly have trouble locating those poems in the bulk of his work. They don't see the interrelation between these object poems and some other historical or moralistic poems of his. My purpose was simply to find a link between the various aspects of his poetry. I tried to put things in a consistent perspective. And I hope I succeeded in doing so.

DM: Your book also examines Herbert's recent poetry from *Report from the Besieged City.* Among the new poems, is there a change in tone or content or point of view?

Baranczak: I don't think there is a very significant change. Probably not. In particular, he continues to use the persona of Mr. Cogito and in almost exactly the way he did in the previous volume, written more than ten years ago. I think what makes his new poetry sound fresh is perhaps the fact that he is able to deal with the most recent problems of Poland in a very unexpected way.

I say unexpected because what prevails in Polish poetry today is a contrast between two attitudes. One is a kind of postromantic or neoromantic tendency to put things in historical perspective, to see the present ordeal of Poland as only one link in a long chain of persecution spreading throughout centuries and repeating itself time and again. By the way, such a vision is closely linked to the notion of catastrophism as a cyclical course of history. This poetry is utterly traditional, especially in the context of the Polish romantic tradition. But there are many contemporary poets, some of them really prominent, who simply rejected all their experimentation with form and subject and so on and jumped with both legs, so to speak, into that neoromantic reservoir of motives, of subjects, of approaches. So that's one extreme.

The other, as I've mentioned, is a poetry of very scrupulous observation of modern reality. It's an opposite extreme because, while the neoromantic is focused on trying to grasp what's repetitive, what's stayed the same in Polish history, the extreme of observation is focused on trying to understand what's new in our present situation, what's unexpected, what's abnormal, atypical, et cetera. So all the illogicalities and abnormalities of the present situation are brought to light in such poetry. I personally value this kind much more. And it is represented by various excellent poets, I think.

But what Herbert does is something that cannot be imitated. Anyone who would try to write in the same vein would produce just mindless repetition. What he does is to combine the two perspectives to show a certain continuity of struggle, resistance, continuity of catastrophes, and so on but from a very modern point of view and one not of a social group, not of a nation, by any means, but rather of an individual, that is, of Mr. Cogito, who is simply in the middle of all that. His work is very consistent because he never gives up his constant method of confronting the past with the present, the Western tradition with the local Polish reality, et cetera.

So, in his new book, he is doing precisely the same as he always did, but never before has his poetry been so contemporary, so focused on what's going on in our times. And I think only in that is there something new. I hope he continues his present methods.

DM: In "The Envoy of Mr. Cogito" from his previous book and in the title poem from *Report from the Besieged City* there is a similarity in tone. But the first poem is more imperative: "Be faithful. Go."

Baranczak: Yes. But what's interesting about "The Envoy of Mr. Cogito" is that most readers don't really appreciate how ambiguous a poem it is. It seems very imperative, as you said. It seems even somewhat didactic in its general tone. It's an instruction: "Be faithful. Go." But before these final words there are a lot of indications that the speaker is not so self-confident as he seems. Put more precisely, it isn't the problem of self-confidence but, rather, the problem of his continual awareness of the fact that all his imperatives can be countered by the possibility of defeat. And even the *certainty* of defeat. So he's honest in that. I mean he admits— and there are places in the text which can be pinpointed—he always admits, while encouraging people, that he must also warn them not to count on anything, not to expect to be trimphant in any way. You will be defeated, you will die on the garbage heap. The executioner will come to your funeral . . . He constantly warns his audience. He doesn't offer the promised land to anybody, so to speak. He points out that the effort to behave decently in life won't be rewarded. The only reward is the defeat. But still it is necessary to behave decently because only that makes us human.

DM: The last line of "Report from the Besieged City" is:

and only our dreams have not been humiliated.

Baranczak: Humiliated, yes.

DM: Why is this line not sentimental?

Baranczak: The whole bulk of his poetry makes the meaning much richer than it seems to be. It's by no means sentimental. It's rather a tragic consciousness that only your inner world cannot be conquered by oppressors. Only what's hidden inside you is the domain of your freedom.

DM: One last question. It's a broad question, and maybe, after all, it's irrelevant. What good does poetry do? Or why write poetry when it doesn't seem to have much effect on what happens?

Baranczak: In my view, it only seems so. And, in fact, regardless of any social structure or political system or any cultural position, poetry has always existed and will always exist. The very continuity of poetry's existence is something significant. It tells us something. There are two points to be made here. There is the need on the part of readers, a need for poetry, and this need can sometimes diminish and sometimes almost completely disappear. In fact, there are certain periods in certain cultures when there's been no visible interest in poetry. Poets can feel completely abandoned at such times. But another matter is the need of the poets themselves to write. And this is something completely indestructible, so to speak. I think this need will exist as long as humanity exists.

Also, I don't believe as some people do that a poet who writes for no audience whatsoever is by the same token ridiculous or unnecessary or somebody who can be left on the margin. I would say that even a poet without an audience is to be appreciated. (Of course, there is another matter of the artistic quality of any writing, but we can't go so far into detail.) And the audience's requirements and demands and expectations can change. The point is, you know, to be true to the spirit of poetry.

But what's the spirit of poetry? you may ask. Why does poetry exist at all? To begin again. The usual circumstances of life make you immune to certain feelings. You behave in the course of your life more and more automatically. You are shaped by circumstances. You are a slave to certain learned reactions that are imposed on you by collective customs, by culture, by ideology, by certain patterns of behavior, and so on. What arts in general do and what poetry does in the very specific sense of a certain treatment of language—a very important part of our lives—is to deautomatize you, to make you react in a more authentic way to the world, to life, to reality. It allows you to find a language that is free from any external distortions, the distortions of ritual ways of using language.

Again, I'm not sure if I make myself clear here. But somebody who neither writes nor reads poetry is a very unhappy creature, in my view. And it doesn't have to be avant-garde, you know. It can be even very popular poetry, a song or children's verse. But the presence of some poetry in human life is absolutely necessary.

And, if the poetry is good, it has the same effect as the most avant-garde poetry. Namely, it deautomatizes you. It takes away all those layers of ritual, custom, whatever is socially acceptable, whatever is normal and by the same token boring and conventional and stifling to your individuality. Poetry helps reveal that individuality.

And the miraculous thing about poetry is that, by revealing your individuality, it binds you together with other people. By making you individual, it makes you social at the same time. The reverse paradox is that all these automatized ways of behavior in society make you feel isolated, as a matter of fact, because you can't have a true contact with other people. You are more and more enclosed within your shell, so to speak. You can't find appropriate words to express your emotions, to understand other people's emotions, et cetera. And poetry, again by making you utterly individual, helps restore those possibilities of communication within you and helps to restore some common language—but in a much more profound sense than the language of everyday life—a common language that is at the same time spontaneous, true, and authentic.

Some Day, Years from Now

"Some day, years from now, History will prove us to be right."
But History will prove nothing, will plead nothing, will confess
nothing, History will never say another word, History
lies under five feet of sand or dirt,
the blood underneath History's skin, thickened into bruises,
slowly moves downwards, in accordance with the law of gravity,
History's eyes are empty, and over its knocked-out teeth
there is no movement in its forever-set,
forever-silenced, forever-eighteen-year-old lips.

A Second Nature

After a couple of days, the eye gets used
to the squirrel, a gray one, not red as it should be,
to the cars, each of them five feet too long,
to the clear air, against which glistens the wet paint
of billboards, puffy clouds, and fire-escape ladders.

After a couple of weeks, the hand gets used
to the different shape of the digits one and seven,
not to mention skipping diacritical marks in your signature.

After a couple of months, even the tongue knows
how to curl in your mouth the only way that produces a correct *the*.
Another couple of months and, while tying your shoelace in the
    street,
you realize that you're actually doing it just to tie your shoelace,
and not in order to routinely check
if you're not followed.

After a couple of years, you have a dream:
you're standing at the kitchen sink in the forest cottage near Sierakow,
where you once spent a vacation, a high-school graduate unhappily
    in love;
your left hand holds a kettle, your right one reaches for the faucet
    knob.
The dream, as if having hit a wall, suddenly stops dead,
focusing with painful intensity on a detail that's uncertain:
was that knob made of porcelain, or brass?
Still dreaming, you know with a dazzling clarity that everything
    depends on this.
As you wake up, you know with equal clarity you'll never be able
    to make sure.

After Gloria Was Gone

After several hours' showing off, the hurricane figured out
that it makes no sense to perform on three channels at once
as a whistling background for interviews with a local mayor
from another disaster area, disrupted by dog-food commercials,
and, at the same time, to put on a live show in our street.
So much work for nothing? Behind our windowpane, crossed aslant
with tape, we waited for the wind to get disheartened,
to go on strike, to leave for the north, toward New Hampshire.
The door opens to the smell of ozone, wet leaves, and safe adventure.
We stop by the knocked-down maple tree that snapped the electric
    line
while falling across the street in front of Mrs. Aaron's house.
Tapping her cane and still looking not that old,
almost like the time when, because she was blond,
the nuns were willing to hide her, Mrs. Aaron walks around and

calculates
the repair costs. On the nearby sidewalk, Mr. Vitulaitis
examines the tree trunk thoughtfully, volunteers his help
and electric saw for tomorrow, those years of practice in the taiga
will come in handy, he jokes. Crushing sticks that lie on the asphalt,
here comes the pickup truck of the new neighbor, what's his name,
is it Nhu or Ngu, who brakes close to the tree and gets out,
surely without recalling the moment when, on the twenty-ninth day,
their overcrowded boat was found by the Norwegian freighter.
In something like a picnic mood, we all share comments and jokes
about the disaster. After all, it wasn't so fierce
as the forecasts had warned, no big deal, no big scars;
the harm it did to us is a reparable one, and tomorrow,
first thing in the morning, there'll be another expert visit
from the electrician, the sunrise, the insurance inspector.
It's time to go back home, remove the crosses
of tape from our windows, though we can't do the same
to our pasts or futures which have been crossed out
so many times. "The so-called pranks of nature,"
Mrs. Aaron sums up disdainfully, and she adds
that whoever is interested may inspect the devastation—
as far as she's concerned, she's going in to make some coffee.

Poems translated by the author.

Yehuda Amichai

Yehuda Amichai, born in Germany in 1924, emigrated with his parents to Israel in 1936. At the age of eighteen, he joined the British army and served during World War Two. He served with the Palmach during Israel's War of Independence in 1948 and with the Israeli army through the war of 1973. He began writing poetry in 1949. He is married and has three children. He has made his living as a teacher in Israel and has recently been a visiting professor at New York University.

He has published ten books of poetry, among them *Songs of Jerusalem and Myself* (1973), *Amen* (1977), *Time* (1978), *Great Tranquility: Questions and Answers* (1980), and *Love Poems* (1981). He has also published two novels—including *Not of This Time, Not of This Place* (1963)—three children's books, one book of short stories, *The World Is a Room and Other Stories* (1985), and one book of plays. His work has been translated into twenty languages. *The Selected Poems of Yehuda Amichai* was published in 1986.

This interview took place on a Sunday morning in November, 1986, in a Greenwich Village delicatessen, which became more crowded and noisy as the conversation went on.

David Montenegro: You left Germany for Palestine with your parents in 1936 when you were eleven. During World War Two, you joined the British army, then you served in the Palmach and have been in many wars in Israel. When did you begin to write poetry?

Yehuda Amichai: Well, I started writing poetry toward the end of 1949, after the War of Independence. Before that I didn't write poetry.

DM: You didn't write at all?

Amichai: No.

DM: What brought you to write poetry?

Amichai: I loved to *read* poetry, and it helped me. I really admired a lot of poets in all languages I could read. But after some time I had this need for a kind of do-it-yourself poem, as if I wouldn't completely trust others to write the real poem for me, for my needs.

DM: Poetry helped you—in what way?

Amichai: Poetry helped me to speak things clearly and to make my life more livable.

DM: Did you feel any conflict between poetry and your experience in the army?

Amichai: No, because that's exactly what I think about poetry. It's not about "nice" things. Poetry has always been as much or more about sadness than happiness, more about death and disasters, and so on.

Actually, poetry is a kind of—should I say—a by-product, but in the highest sense of the word. It's a certain way of documentation—not a willful documentation like a journal or letters to someone that you really write, as Rilke did, you know, keeping in mind constantly that this letter would be published—but documentation for my own private needs. I hated to write journals, and I'm not a great letter writer, so I think poetry's a kind of concentrated letter for lazy people—or a journal where you really can concentrate on a few sentences and that's enough.

DM: Almost like cues?

Amichai: Yes, cues or even codes—codes, I think. Or sometimes, I would say, even like private jokes where only one or two persons in a room understand exactly what is meant and the others understand something but don't know the raison d'être of it.

DM: Would you be writing in code in any way?

Amichai: No, hey, like in political dictatorships when there are certain codes? No. I don't hide away things.

There is no censorship in Israel. Anyone can write about what he wants, including antigovernment writing by both Jews and Arabs. And I want to mention that most Arabs (except those in Egypt) are still openly at war with us. Regarding this, it seems amazing how openly everyone can express himself.

DM: You said poetry is a by-product but in the highest sense of the word. Why highest?

Amichai: I don't know, it might even be lower but more concentrated than life. It's *heavier,* you see, speaking in physical terms.

DM: So it takes on weight, particularly from the harsher times in life?

Amichai: Yes, exactly.

DM: You had some harsh experiences early in your life. More than many poets.

Amichai: No, why do you think so?

DM: The wars?

Amichai: Ah, the wars. But there are the war poets, the great British war poets like Sassoon and Owen and Rosenberg and others.

DM: Or among the Germans, like Trakl.

Amichai: Trakl, yes, but . . . okay, some were killed.

DM: German was your first language?

Amichai: Yes, but I actually grew up bilingual because I went to a Jewish kindergarten, and then in the first few years of grade school I had classes in both Hebrew and German.

DM: So you were fluent in Hebrew by the time you reached Palestine?

Amichai: Yes.

DM: Did you lose touch with German over the years?

Amichai: Oh, yes. There was no one around me except my parents and a few others who could speak the language, so I quickly ... And there was, of course, a personal ... the other reason *not* to use German.

DM: So you had mixed feelings about German?

Amichai: No, not the language. I could separate them. I read a lot of German up to this present day, and I think I can even write it without mistakes.

DM: So, it doesn't carry any taint for you?

Amichai: No. Only a passive one ... as a reader. I read and I enjoy whatever I can enjoy.

DM: Was Rilke influential for you?

Amichai: Oh, yes he was—at the beginning and still up to this present day, I think. But you know how you sometimes like a poet early in your life, and then you get totally disgusted with him and fed up when the time comes. Nowadays there are things in his work that really still hold for me, especially his "Duino Elegies" and his later "Sonnets to Orpheus."

DM: You've lived in Israel fifty years. You must have seen Hebrew change as it has been revived as a spoken language.

Amichai: Not so much, no. Hebrew at the time I came was already a spoken language. There were only half a million people living in small communities, but still it was a language spoken at school and in the streets by everyone. And it has changed, I think, no more than English or German has in fifty years. It just had to take in a lot of words, conceptions from technology and whatnot.

DM: Because of its long religious tradition, does the language feel heavy to you when you use it in a secular way?

Amichai: No. For me it's natural. I grew up in a very religious household. I had to pray every day and go to synagogue. So the prayers, the language of prayer itself, became a kind of natural language for me. Also, I'm *not* religious anymore, but still it's very natural for me. So I use it. I don't try, like sometimes poets do, to "enrich" poetry by getting more *cultural* material or more *ethnic* material into it. It comes very naturally.

DM: Do you think Hebrew has any special strength for describing modern life?

Amichai: No. I *totally* reject all notions that some languages are better for poetry and some not. It's not true. You can write bad poems in Hebrew and good poems in Hungarian.

Also, there are those who say that Israel is a special place for a poet to live.

You can write the *worst* poetry in Jerusalem, although the city seems so rich. Sometimes American poets come to Israel, and suddenly it's so "easy" there to write a poem with the old and the new. But it's the worst poetry that sometimes very good poets from abroad write, because they just put in a few words like the *Wailing Wall* and the *muezzin* and the *war* and *God* and *David* and *Jesus* and so on, and then the *olive tree* and whatnot. And then they are all in bad business.

It's like if I would go to Rome and write a poem about—ah, Via Appia Antica, this "great" place, you know. Here's where all the legions marched. . . . It's so easy. Because it's lying all around.

DM: But there's no sense of a kind of double exposure in using Hebrew?

Amichai: There *is,* perhaps, more than in any other language, but I don't know whether it's good or bad. It depends on the use. Because if you make use of it too much it just becomes bad poetry.

DM: And the language of the Bible; do you feel it is something you've had to struggle against or, on the other hand, something you've been able to use?

Amichai: No, I use it by incorporating it, sometimes in ironical ways and sometimes in admiring ways. I gain mastery over it. It's just that I *use* it. I don't reject it.

DM: You've mentioned recently that real things are very important in your poetry. Would you say more about this?

Amichai: Well, it's actually a need to put something very personal into the poetry— not that you do it deliberately. Everything can be concentrated in, say, a stocking. Or a pair of shoes can become the very center of the whole love affair. And you don't need the whole love affair. You don't need to videotape the whole love affair between two young people which went on for two months, but sometimes it can be concentrated in just a pair of shoes or a book with torn pages or a broken glass or something like this.

I think that out of every experience I've had there always emerge such things, which can be even sentences, phrases I've heard other people saying, or people who have been so-called witnesses or innocent bystanders of something that happened to me and who sometimes become more important than the experience itself because they carry the whole witness, the whole image, in them without knowing it and without ever *wanting* to do so.

It's like in a court a good judge sometimes says a witness who's very much involved and knows a lot is not as good as someone who was just an innocent bystander and remembers only a few little things for himself which might be much more important because he wasn't involved in what happened.

DM: So he caught the crucial . . .

Amichai: No, not crucial, but a few clues that a clever lawyer or judge can put together and . . .

DM: Make a case?

Amichai: Make a case, yes. Or *uncase* a case.

DM: Do you mind reading translations of your poems in public?

Amichai: Well, reading the poems in public not in my language is much easier for me because it's not so personal.

DM: Speaking of real things, in one of your earlier poems, "Autobiography, 1952," you use a shipyard to describe the size of your father's worry then a train's headlight to describe his face disappearing into the distance. At the end of the poem you return to your room and a woman who is "filled with time." So the comparisons move from the metallic to the human.

Amichai: I never thought of that. From means of transportation to means of genetics, yes (*laughs*).

But, you know, I really don't ... That was one of my earlier poems, and I'm sure I must be totally unaware ... The point is to use real things, at least as metaphors, especially if the experience itself is very emotional or very brainy. Because you can't describe a feeling.

I even have a certain—well, I wouldn't say a theory; that's too much—a notion that people are much more articulate than usual when they describe pain. If you go to a doctor and listen to people who are sometimes very unlearned and don't know how to express themselves clearly, when it comes to pain, they try very hard. And they sometimes can really describe where it pains and if it's a *burning* pain or a *pressing* pain or whatnot. But about well-being we don't say, "Oh, I have a good feeling in my arm." We say, "I have a headache." We don't say, "I have a good feeling in my head."

And, actually, that's the one thing that is in the Hebrew. In the Hebrew language you have an expression if you want to say to a doctor that your knee hurts or your arm hurts. You don't say that your arm hurts. You say, "I *feel* my arm."

DM: You become aware of it.

Amichai: You become aware of it, and that means it hurts. Because you don't become aware of your body unless it hurts. And so, actually, what we *should* do is use the exactitude of describing pain in order to describe happiness, to describe beautiful things.

DM: To reverse the knack for describing pain?

Amichai: Kind of *cheat* it, yes (*laughs*).

DM: So precision is important in your poems?

Amichai: I'm crazy about exactitude. There's nothing more terrible to me than poetry that is all just very beautiful sentences or emotional ones or long, tedious tracts of half-abstract philosophy.

DM: Rhetoric?

Amichai: No, rhetoric can be filled with things. For instance, I think the "Four Quartets" of Eliot until this present day are still to me one of the greatest pieces in literature. It's rhetoric, and it's a sermon. It's like a minister preaching. And, again, I think every poem is kind of a little sermon that we give the audience of believers or, in most cases, we ourselves. But Eliot uses also a lot of real things.

DM: In a way it's amazing those poems work because they use so many abstractions.

Amichai: Yes, abstractions, and the philosophy is very shallow; it's not a very deep, new thing. That's actually how it should be. Poetry should never be a kind of new way in thinking. It should be very old ways in thinking but newly told. That's the difference between a philosopher and a poet.

DM: Would that mean that the poet has to have the thoughts already in the blood?

Amichai: Yes, exactly. That's why Sartre never could become a good poet.

DM: Metaphor and simile—what work do they do? What do they satisfy?

Amichai: Well, I think, first of all, they're a way out of loneliness. If you use even a very worn-out metaphor or simile—for instance, you are beautiful like a rose— you are not alone. The rose becomes an equal, and it's like stretching a hand out.

By the way, here in America you use one word that I really don't like, *outreach,* which is a terrible word. It's an American, half-poetic intellectualism. I'm really a great admirer of American culture, but sometimes it uses words in a very funny way. Another is *share.* Would you *share* this poem with me? You know, I'm getting gooseflesh all over! It's like saying President Reagan has an outreach to Iran. He's sharing his arms with Khomeini.

So I think metaphor is a reaching out. We are groping for words. We say, "Ah, I'm looking for words. I can't express myself." So we need something, again something *real.* Because if I want to say "He's such a cruel man," I might say, "His heart is stone," which is also an overused expression, but you are *groping* for words. You want to keep your head above water, so words become a kind of, I would say, *solid* thing, which you can hold onto in order to make yourself understood. I personally believe that the invention, so to speak, of the metaphor is the greatest human invention, greater than the wheel or the computer.

DM: It allows people to think, to bridge . . .

Amichai: To bridge. It's also the very source of science, scientific thought. A great inventor has to be a poet, in a way, because he can't see just one way of doing things. He immediately builds bridges to other ways.

Incidentally, I've met quite a lot of very good artists—most in the visual arts—who are very good artists but not very intelligent. But I've never met a *good* poet who is stupid. I've met poets who are crazy but never one who is stupid, never, or dull.

So making metaphor is a certain way of thinking which incorporates emotion into intellect. It's actually the ideal, basic, human condition. I still think the poet—not *a* poet, because a poet is nothing, but *the* poet—actually is the quintessence of human culture.

DM: How do you know when a metaphor doesn't work, when it doesn't ring true to you?

Amichai: Well, I find out only after some days. It takes days. But in most cases I know exactly. It's almost the same process as falling in love. Sometimes love also may turn out to be false and happened because you were in a certain mood and so forth. But in most cases it's a little like falling in love with something, of one thing with another.

DM: Somewhere in your novel *Not of This Time, Not of This Place* you describe Joel's thoughts as moving up and down like an elevator between floors while something is going on on each floor. In your poetry you cover many levels at the same time.

Amichai: Yes, but every good poem is like that. Even if it seems it's not, it is. But the poem shouldn't immediately look that way. On the surface it should be very smooth and very easily understood. But, if someone wants to look again, he suddenly may find out there are stops in between and the doors open.

DM: There's a poem by Uri Greenberg "We Were Not Likened to Dogs among the Gentiles" which seems striking because in it simile breaks down. Actually, the poetry comes to a halt.

Amichai: Well, he's referring to the Holocaust. How to say this very simply? I must say that's the limit of human experience. The moment something real happens to you, whether good or bad, you don't *need* poetry. Either you don't need it, or it doesn't help you.

You would think, for example, someone who has written about war would find that poetry helps him when he's out there. And it *doesn't*. When you are out there nothing helps you, no words, nothing. Just a few words like *mother* or *God* or whatever you use.

I think such thinking about poetry is a big romantic mistake. There was this Hungarian Jewish poet Miklós Radnóti, who was considered to be one of the promising younger poets of the 1930s. Then the Germans sent him on this famous death march. But his wife or friends around him saw him scribbling things on little pieces of paper and putting them in the pocket of this heavy oilskin raincoat. Eventually, he died on that march of typhoid fever or exhaustion. They buried him in a mass grave. Then a few months later someone came back to open the grave because they thought maybe the things he had written would be good. Well, the body was already decayed but the oilskin had preserved the paper.

Finally the poems were published. You would think they would be the strongest poems. But it's so disappointing. The story is very moving, but the poems turned out to be just a few more Holocaust poems, which actually are my big disappointment.

Listen, if someone would write a love poem while lying in bed with a woman, well, it should be actually the greatest, but it's not. It's the worst. Poetry only comes after such things. It's not the real thing. In *real* situations you either don't need it or, as I said, it doesn't help you at all—in a way like so many other things in life.

It's movies and fiction that have made people think of the war poet sitting in trenches with shells falling, and he's writing his great poem. I don't believe it. And if anyone does write then, they probably write just journal-like notes or lines that are actually unimportant, which become like a mantra. If you just say, "Oh, God, help me! Oh, God, help me!" it has nothing to do with prayer.

Poetry starts only after the climax. It's one of the first signs that you have *overcome* something.

DM: You often use a very cool, logical tone in your poetry. At the same time your poetry's often about the illogical—for example, "God Has Pity on Kindergarten Children" or "The Diameter of the Bomb."

Amichai: That's exactly my image of the world. Everything looks very logical, but the logical order of things breaks down—not only every now and then, almost every day.

DM: The later poem, "The Diameter of the Bomb," is even tighter than the earlier one, even more logical. You move by measurements. Yet the conclusion is even more bleak: There is no God at all. How has your poetry changed over the years?

Amichai: It's very hard to say. Of course, it has changed just as *I* have changed since I was twenty. But I'm still the same person. I look like I used to look, though I'm older. Probably a biologist would say that most of my cells have changed since, but still I'm the same now. So it's not for me to judge. I really can't say. The only thing I can say is that I wrote more when I was younger.

DM: Another more recent poem, "Inside the Apple," seems different in some ways from your others.

Amichai: That's from my latest book.

DM: The images are particularly sharp and startling: "Lips are red the way . . ."

Amichai: " . . . a burnt field / is black," yes.

DM: Then you surprise again by saying "It's all true."

Amichai: Well, burnt fields are . . . Again, it comes out of something real. In summer in Jerusalem, like in California, hot desert winds come, and you have a lot of burnt fields. And this becomes so much a part of the language that you *need* it almost. And it's true, because fire's true and summer is true and the redness is true. So a burnt field is actually a negative thing, whereas red lips are a very beautiful thing. They are both real and both needed and both part of our experience.

DM: In nature the burning of a forest or a field even enriches it.

Amichai: Listen, there are some people who say that among human beings wars and epidemics are needed to decrease the number of people in the world.

DM: In *Not of This Time, Not of This Place* Joel is pursued by memory and pursues it. Why is memory so important, particularly historical memory?

Amichai: I don't know why, but it's important. It's part of my life, everyone's life. And again it's a natural thing. Body cells, as we know, have genetic memory. So, in a way, it's the same with us. The DNA remembers how I should look and how everything should function in me because I got it genetically from my father. History's a built-in memory that is part of reality.

And, like DNA, it can't just sit back; it has to go on. You know, what I so much admire here in America is the way they sometimes build high-rises in New York amidst Fifth Avenue, and traffic goes on. I think if they built one building like that in Jerusalem, half the city would be closed off. So you build, and everything has to go on. Or you tear down, and everything has to go on. I think that's what should be done.

DM: Do you think you will write another novel?

Amichai: No, that's one thing I'm . . . *almost* sure of.

DM: How about short stories? What place do they take among your tools as a writer?

Amichai: I started out as a poet. Basically, I write poetry. But then I wrote some short stories, and after short stories I wrote this novel. By the way, the translation done in 1969 or 1970 was a very cut-down version, because the original was twice the size. So I think my publisher's now considering the possibility of retranslating it fully.

DM: In *The World Is a Room* the narrator of all the stories seems to be the same person.

Amichai: Those stories are a kind of extended, well, I wouldn't say extended poetry, but in a way they show the background of poetry. Or, if this person had been a poet, these things would have made him write poetry.

DM: How autobiographical is the long poem "Travels of the Last Benjamin of Tudela"?

Amichai: Very much so.

DM: You move from . . .

Amichai: Yes, but it's not a story from the beginning to the end.

DM: Like your novel, it's musical—with several voices going at the same time.

Amichai: Yes, exactly. And it's one of the things I wrote in two or three weeks. It's also my longest poem.

DM: In what year was it written?

Amichai: I can tell you exactly: 1967.

DM: Was there anything in particular that brought that poem about?

Amichai: No, I think it was a great excitement that was in Jerusalem at that time. And it was also a great break in my personal life. And sometimes it happens that things happening *outside* collide with . . . not collide, but go together, with things happening *inside.*

DM: Was the public reference to the Six Day War? Were the public and private upheavals related?

Amichai: The Six Day War coincided with a personal crisis and a breakthrough in my personal life, in my writing, and a relief after the threatening weeks before the war started.

DM: Going back a little bit, the Palmach had no more than two thousand people. Could you say something about it?

Amichai: Well, it was just a crack unit of the Haganah underground. It was like a kind of . . . Actually, all of the Israeli army was a kind of guerrilla force, because the others had the guns and the tanks and the airplanes. The Palmach was like the marines almost, just doing the most dangerous things.

DM: You had no equipment?

Amichai: Exactly. And there were all kind of small battles in which smaller groups did quite daring things. That was actually the idea.

DM: Quite fierce battles?

Amichai: Oh, yes.

DM: Yad Mordekhai?

Amichai: Yes. Yad Mordekhai, Ashdod, and others.

DM: In one of your poems you mention the watertower at Yad Mordekhai. Isn't that tower still there?

Amichai: Yes, it's still there. It's kept as a landmark now.

DM: How did your sense of the word *heroism* change over the years?

Amichai: Well, it never was a big word for me, because when I took part in all these things I was never that heroic. When you are young you are just . . . you do things, and you want to do them brilliantly, and you want to show off. You know, it's typical of young people. You're not so much aware, on the one side, of the danger of it—otherwise you wouldn't do it—or of what it means to the coming generations. It's just a kind of bravado of young people.

DM: What about during peacetime? How do you see the poet's relationship to ordinary living?

Amichai: I believe poets start so low that our high is to do things that so-called normal people do, like having children and working for your life and doing things like every carpenter or doctor or anyone else. So, actually, my high is to live a normal (*laughs*)... an ordinary life. That's why I enjoy things, children and more, because to me they are high.

DM: That brings to mind John Cheever, who at one time had an office where he'd go to write from nine to five, just as if he were working in a bank. In a way, it seems he needed to make himself feel legitimate, since he was so aware of his neighbors commuting to New York every day to work.

Amichai: Yes, it's a kind of undercover—I don't know—a kind of camouflage.

DM: A mask of normalcy?

Amichai: But no. *Mask* of normalcy, that's another thing. On the contrary, I want to be like... to enjoy things like normal people. For instance, children. A lot of creative people think that children are bad for creative work. I think they may take a lot of time and energy, but they are good. And I like to work with them. So, to me, it's the highest to be like other people and to enjoy it. Most people living a normal life want to get more excitement, but to me the meat, the very excitement of things...

DM: It's like oxygen?

Amichai: Yes, exactly—oxygen.

DM: Among your early poems is a sonnet sequence. Would you talk about form for a moment?

Amichai: Well, the Hebrew in the Bible does not use forms like the sonnet. It uses a different kind of form. In fact, you have two very distinguished professors now writing about it. One is Professor James Kugel of Harvard, and the other is Professor Robert Alter of Berkeley. They have proven the richness of poetry in the Bible.

Then in the Middle Ages in Muslim Spain we had the quatrain, which is something like the sonnet because it's a very concentrated form. It was written in both Arabic and Hebrew, and the Hebrew poets wrote a lot of these existential little four-liners.

As for sonnets, in fact the first to be written in a language other than Italian was written in Hebrew by Immanuel Haromi, a Hebrew poet living in Italy who was, I think, a friend of Petrarch. So there is a history of such forms being used in Hebrew.

DM: How about Bialik and Tchernikovsky? How much have they influenced you?

Amichai: Less, much less than, say, the poets of Muslim Spain. First of all, there were our high school maturity programs, which examined us on some of their poems (*laughs*). That's why I'm so sorry that now *my* poetry is used in these programs.

DM: They wear it out?

Amichai: Yes, and people really sometimes may like it, but, because you have to write a paper and get marked on it, it becomes a funny thing. My eldest son, when he was in the eleventh grade, had to write a paper on my work. It seems ridiculous (*laughs*).

DM: How about other influences, from the next generation—Alterman and Schlonsky and Goldberg?

Amichai: Well, no, I don't think . . . I think at my beginning Leah Goldberg was . . . Actually, I liked her more than the others.

DM: And what about more recent people like Gilboa or Zach or Avidan or Dan Pagis?

Amichai: I like them. But these are my contemporaries, most of them, and doing more or less similar things.

DM: I particularly like Gilboa.

Amichai: Yes. He died two years ago. So did Pagis. Pagis died last summer.

DM: Pagis was younger?

Amichai: He was in his fifties. Cancer. Well, it's very sad. He was sharp and sarcastic, but very strong.

DM: Avidan's a very different kind of poet.

Amichai: I like Zach, but I don't like Avidan. Avidan is too wordy. He's talk, talk, talk. Actually, he does the opposite, I would think, of what one should do in poetry.

DM: Zach is more spare.

Amichai: Yes, much more condensed. And *ironic*.

DM: Biting.

Amichai: Yes.

DM: There's his line: "It's the salt in me that talks."

Amichai: Yes. It's enjoyable as a piece of biting salt, but maybe sometimes it's not easy to take. But it's concise.

DM: It seems he doesn't vary his tone much. He has one thing . . .

Amichai: Yes, his one ironic thing, which in Hebrew works even better than in English translation.

DM: Was he trying to break away from the earlier, more, well, almost propagandistic poetry of Schlonsky and Alterman?

Amichai: Alterman. Well, all of my generation was in the 1950s.

DM: Trying to bring in more of your own, your personal voice?

Amichai: Yes, exactly, exactly. But, of course, the previous generation like Schlonsky and Alterman was mostly influenced by the Russians. They were also socialists or left-wing people and were influenced by the rhetoric of Blok, Mayakovsky, and others.

DM: In Israel there's been a constant state of siege. Do you think the tension there increases the awareness of the senses?

Amichai: Oh, sure, sure. It still does. Especially for me, because I grew up with that situation, and the kinds of danger change. It used to be Arab dangers, then in World War Two it was the danger of the Germans, and so on. Of course this intensifies everything, yes.

DM: It's almost a feverish awareness?

Amichai: Exactly.

DM: What do you see as the poet's relationship to politics? Do you think the poet should avoid taking an explicitly political stance?

Amichai: Poets, at least in Israel, cannot allow themselves the luxury of being apolitical.

DM: How has the Arab-Israeli conflict affected you as a writer? As a person? Also, you mentioned the guerrilla tactics of the Palmach. Same as the Palestinians? How does this make you feel?

Amichai: The Arab-Israeli conflict has affected me indeed. Being a soldier and also feeling the constant threat to my very existence by Arab aggression.

The Palmach guerrilla tactics were necessary because we were only a few, poorly armed against a modern well-equipped Egyptian army (in my case). The Palestinian forces are more a conglomerate of various terrorist groups, both supported by the extreme right and the extreme left. They made it their task to kill mainly civilians in the street, buses, schools, and even outside hospitals. The Palmach fought against *armies* who invaded the country.

DM: In your poem "Jerusalem, 1967," you say:

> I think of children growing up half in the ethics of their fathers
> and half in the science of war.

How do you view the relationship between idealism and militarism in present-day Israel?

Amichai: I am part of those who demand territorial compromises on the West Bank. I don't think that Israel is a militarist country. Arab countries—most of their governments are military governments—are *in a state of war* with Israel (except Egypt). So it would be like calling England in World War Two a military country.

I also have not forgotten that the conflict started with Arabs rejecting any compromise and trying to force it with military powers. This rejection included the representations of the Palestinians, whose leader at that time was the grand mufti of Jerusalem, famous also for his open collaboration with the Nazis in occupying Yugoslavia during World War Two, and still I say there should be a compromise but one that must secure Israel's very existence.

DM: Earlier you mentioned that you're not religious anymore. Does that still bring up conflicts for you?

Amichai: No, no, no, no, no. Actually, I'm going on with the discussion I had with my father (*laughs*). We loved each other very much, but we had this problem— big problem—so we go on . . . I go on discussing it with him. The liturgy has one famous phrase: "*Al venu malkanu,*" which means "Our Father, our King." It is a bit metaphoric, because, if you say "our father, our king," in a prayer to God, it also means: our father, our God—godfather. If God is a father, then father is God. The metaphors are equal. So my father is actually my private god.

When I was a child, like every child, I thought my father was really a god, and when I rebelled against him he still was God. But then I found out, of course, he was a human being. I think it's the same with God.

So I'm not *practicing.* Only because being religious is totally meaningless. To believe in some greater power . . . everyone believes in it. But we don't believe that we can understand everything. Nothing is purposeless. There must be some reason for everything, which we don't understand. Either you become a rabbi or a scientist or whatever to find out that reason. But practicing religion is a totally different thing.

DM: So your father is still whispering in your ear?

Amichai: In a way, not whispering. Sometimes really he's *twisting* my ear (*laughs*).

DM: Your poetry is very sensuous and sensual on the outside and very stark on the inside. To put it another way, you seem to balance between Ecclesiastes and the Song of Songs, swaying more toward the Song of Songs.

Amichai: Yes, right. That's actually almost an image to describe being between hedonism and existential despair. I always move between these two states, yes.

DM: But you also wrap the Song of Songs like a piece of fruit around the knife, reversing your image in "Inside the Apple." Your poems are palatable. They're easy to swallow but hard to digest.

Amichai: Yes. Well, some poets or critics think that the poem should not be understood easily. You know how there's this big discussion. It's always going on. And I don't deny it. But a poem should be what it *is.* Whether it's understood easily or not, it's either a good poem or a lousy poem. So this argument's actually totally meaningless.

God forbid that I compare myself to the Bible or Shakespeare, but they can be understood by very primitive people and can also be a source for a lot of very intellectual, very psychoanalytical speculation or whatnot. So really I think that every piece of art should first of all have an appeal to many people, and some people hopefully can see suddenly that what seemed so simple is not so simple.

But this discussion is going on and on, and sometimes one type of work is in and one is out. But you should do what you do. That's the best thing—never to ask what's in or what's out.

DM: What are you working on now?

Amichai: Well, actually, now I'm working on a children's book. I've already done two, so it's my third. A kind of good-night book. I have two sons and a little daughter. I wrote a children's book for each one of my eldest kids—the two boys. So now the little one is, of course, saying "Hey, what about *me?*" So for the first time in my life I sat down and just started writing.

The Diameter of the Bomb

The diameter of the bomb was thirty centimeters
and the diameter of its effective range about seven meters,
with four dead and eleven wounded.
And around these, in a larger circle
of pain and time, two hospitals are scattered
and one graveyard. But the young woman
who was buried in the city she came from,
at a distance of more than a hundred kilometers,
enlarges the circle considerably,
and the solitary man mourning her death
at the distant shores of a country far across the sea
includes the entire world in the circle.
And I won't even mention the crying of orphans
that reaches up to the throne of God and
beyond, making
a circle with no end and no God.

From "Seven Laments for the War-Dead"

I
Mr. Beringer, whose son
fell at the Canal that strangers dug
so ships could cross the desert,
crosses my path at Jaffa Gate.

He has grown very thin, has lost
the weight of his son.
That's why he floats so lightly in the alleys
and gets caught in my heart like little twigs
that drift away.

3
The Tomb of the Unknown Soldier
across there. On the enemy's side. A good landmark
for gunners of the future.

Or the war monument in London
at Hyde Park Corner, decorated
like a magnificent cake: yet another soldier
lifting head and rifle,
another cannon, another eagle, another
stone angel.

And the whipped cream of a huge marble flag
poured over it all
with an expert hand.

But the candied, much-too-red cherries
were already gobbled up
by the glutton of hearts. Amen.

4
I came upon an old zoology textbook,
Brehm, Volume II, *Birds:*
in sweet phrases, an account of the life of the starling,
swallow, and thrush. Full of mistakes in an antiquated
Gothic typeface, but full of love, too. "Our feathered
friends." "Migrate from us to the warmer climes."
Nest, speckled egg, soft plumage, nightingale,
stork. "The harbingers of spring." The robin,
red-breasted.

Year of publication: 1913, Germany,
on the eve of the war that was to be
the eve of all my wars.

My good friend who died in my arms, in
his blood,
on the sands of Ashdod. 1948, June.

Oh my friend,
red-breasted.

Inside the Apple

You visit me inside the apple.
Together we can hear the knife
paring around and around us, carefully,
so the peel won't tear.

You speak to me. I trust your voice
because it has lumps of hard pain in it
the way real honey
has lumps of wax from the honeycomb.

I touch your lips with my fingers:
that too is a prophetic gesture.
And your lips are red, the way a burnt field
is black.
It's all true.

You visit me inside the apple
and you'll stay with me inside the apple
until the knife finishes its work.

Poems translated by Chana Bloch.

Epilogue

No series of this kind could possibly include all of the contemporary writers who have forcefully and eloquently addressed the subject of writing and politics in their lives and work. Similarly, it would be impossible to balance all sides of the issues discussed herein. Because of conflicting opinions about censorship in Israel, I particularly regret not having been able to include a Palestinian writer. The following brief and in no way complete list of international writers on the subject of writing and politics may provide some points of departure for further reading: Chinua Achebe, Marjorie Agosin, Paula Gunn Allen, Margaret Atwood, James Baldwin, Breyten Breytenbach, Michelle Cliff, Terrence Des Pres, Ariel Dorfman, Athol Fugard, Allen Ginsberg, Nadine Gordimer, Judy Grahn, Susan Griffin, Emile Habiby, Vaclav Havel, Zbigniew Herbert, Maxine Hong Kingston, Ursula Le Guin, Denise Levertov, Audre Lorde, Derek Mahon, Adam Michnic, Czeslaw Milosz, Toni Morrison, Shiva Naipaul, Alicia Ostriker, Marge Piercy, Irina Ratushinskaya, Edward Said, Jimmy Santiago Baca, Anton Shammas, Leslie Marmon Silko, Josef Skvorecky, Marta Traba, Adam Zagajewski, among others.

The following are some related essay collections: James Baldwin, *The Price of the Ticket;* Vaclav Havel, *Living in Truth;* Zbigniew Herbert, *Barbarian in the Garden;* Audre Lorde, *Sister Outsider;* Czeslaw Milosz, *The Witness of Poetry;* and Alicia Ostriker, *Stealing the Language: The Emergence of Women's Poetry in America.*